THE INDIAN YEARBOOK OF LAW AND INTERDISCIPLINARY STUDIES

This yearbook focuses on law and its interdisciplinarity in India. It brings together scholars of law, economics, and policy to foster multidisciplinary thinking and analysis across subject areas. The contributors to this volume embody an interdisciplinary spirit through their academic experience and aim to bring to the fore unique suggestions for a better understanding of the law.

The volume explores various key issues that are central to state policy demanded by a functioning democracy, in terms of democratic quality, aspirations, and sustainability. It discusses global and social issues, such as foreign interference in domestic elections, feminism, and climate change and looks at other subjects such as economics, religion, history, and literature from the perspective of law.

A unique contribution to the study of law in India, this book will be an essential read for scholars and researchers of law, jurisprudence, political science, economics, public policy, sociology, social anthropology, the Indian Constitution, and South Asia studies.

Ranita Nagar is Professor of Economics and Head of Center for Law and Economics, Gujarat National Law University, Gandhinagar, India.

Hiteshkumar Thakkar is Assistant Professor of Economics at Gujarat National Law University, Gandhinagar, India. He holds a PhD degree in Economics & Law. His areas of research interest are macroeconomics, and law & economics. He has edited numerous books and has published several papers in indexed journals.

THE INDIAN YEARBOOK OF LAW AND INTERDISCIPLINARY STUDIES

Pluralistic Discourse

Edited by Ranita Nagar and Hiteshkumar Thakkar

Routledge
Taylor & Francis Group
LONDON AND NEW YORK

Designed cover image: @ Getty Images

First published 2023
by Routledge
4 Park Square, Milton Park, Abingdon, Oxon OX14 4RN

and by Routledge
605 Third Avenue, New York, NY 10158

Routledge is an imprint of the Taylor & Francis Group, an informa business

British Library Cataloguing-in-Publication Data
A catalogue record for this book is available from the British Library

ISBN: 978-0-367-67853-1 (hbk)
ISBN: 978-0-367-71382-9 (pbk)
ISBN: 978-1-003-15056-5 (ebk)

DOI: 10.4324/9781003150565

Typeset in Bembo
by codeMantra

CONTENTS

List of figures *ix*
List of tables *xi*
List of contributors *xiii*
Acknowledgements *xvii*

Introduction to the Yearbook 1

1 Anthropogenic Harms and Market Fundamentalisms: Solar Geoengineering: All Perils, and No Promises? 11
Upendra Baxi
1.1 Introduction: The Anthropocene as a Shorthand for Notion of Anthropogenic Harm *11*
1.2 Geoengineering Techniques: Promise and Perils *13*
1.3 Non-Use of Solar Engineering Technology? *15*
1.4 Conclusion *17*

2 Outside Influence on Democratic Elections 26
Saul Levmore
2.1 Introduction *26*
2.2 Democracy and Externalities *27*
2.3 Money in Politics *33*
2.4 Conclusion *35*

3 Jammu & Kashmir's Constitutional Status: Constitutional Bargain and 'Erosion' of Article 370 39
Zaid Deva
3.1 Introduction 39
3.2 Sheikh, Nehru, and Bargain Theory 40
3.3 Set Theory and the Two Legal Orders 45
3.4 Conclusion 52

4 Violence in Public and Private Spaces: A Behavioural Economic Analysis of Women-Specific Legislation in India 58
Rasananda Panda and Aneri Patel
4.1 Introduction 58
4.2 Theorizing Violence 60
4.3 Analysing Women-Specific Legislations 64
4.4 Violence in Public and Private Spheres: A Comparative Analysis 68
4.5 Conclusion 69

5 The Stick and Carrot Approach towards Environmental Fiscal Reform in India
Stephanus van Zyl 74
5.1 Introduction 74
5.2 Environmental Tax Penalties 75
5.3 Environmental Tax Incentives 82
5.4 Conclusion 87

6 Is There a Case for Basic Income Support in India? Assessment Based on Verifiable Criteria 98
Ram Singh
6.1 Introduction 98
6.2 Using Verifiable Criteria to Get a Sense of the Poor Households 100
6.3 Identification Based on Verifiable Criteria 103
6.4 Why Direct Income Support? 107
6.5 The Trade-offs and the Way Forward 109
Acknowledgements 110

7 'To Censor or Not to Censor' – Is It a Legal or Social Conundrum? 113
Joshua Aston and Cecilia Anthony Das
7.1 Obscenity versus *Freedom of Speech and Expression?* 114
7.2 Indian Cinema and Obscenity 117
7.3 Hicklin's Test 119

7.4 *Legal Aspects of Obscenity in India, the Censorship, and Media Law* 120
7.5 *Provisions of the Indian Constitution for Censorship* 122
7.6 *Conclusion* 125

8 The Governance of Property: The Gift Economy and the Sikh Gurdwaras Act, 1925 128
Jaivir Singh and Anmol Waraich
8.1 *Introduction* 128
8.2 *Gurdwaras – A Brief History* 129
8.3 *Seva* 131
8.4 *The Gift Economy* 132
8.5 *The Sikh Gurdwaras Act, 1925* 133
8.6 *Conclusion* 139

9 Using Contemporary Literature and Popular Culture to Study Law: The Possibilities Inherent in Fantasy Fiction and Harry Potter 143
Shouvik Kumar Guha

10 The Necessity of Teaching History to Law Students 156
V.S. Elizabeth
10.1 *Introduction* 156
10.2 *The Purpose of Legal Education* 158
10.3 *Relevance of Studying History* 161
10.4 *A Brief Overview of the Research and Teaching of Legal History Outside India till the 1980s* 163
10.5 *The Teaching of History at NLSIU* 166
10.6 *Conclusion* 169

11 Women and Empowerment: Pay Disparity in Organised and Unorganised Sectors 172
Hiteshkumar Thakkar and Anant Agarwal
11.1 *Introduction* 172
11.2 *Literature Review and Forming the Research Questions* 173
11.3 *Law and Economics of Gender Pay Gap and Disparity between Unorganised and Organised Sectors* 176
11.4 *Analysis and Conclusion* 182

Index 189

FIGURES

3.1 Illustration of the intersection of the two sets, I and J&K, during the colonial rule 46
3.2 Illustration of the disappearance of the grey area implying the end of paramountcy and those informal and formal arrangements that kept J&K under the control of the British 46
3.3 Illustration of how the India–J&K shared constitutional space comes into being in the aftermath of the execution of the IoA. Here the grey area represents the same shared constitutional space 47
3.4 Illustration of the increase in the quantum of accession as a result of the enactment of the 1954 order and the state constitution of 1957 48
3.5 Illustration of the difference between the P1 and P2. Even though both form part of the shared constitutional space, certain features of P2 demand this distinction from P1 49
3.6 Illustration of the burgeoning of the shared constitutional space and the squeezing out of the J&K's own constitutional identity 50
3.7 Illustration of how the J&K legal order was incorporated in the Indian one 51
3.8 Illustration of the establishment of the NBZ 51
3.9 Illustration of the end of J&K's legal order and the formal occupation of the legal space by the Indian legal order 52
6.1 Average income-consumption expenditure according to decile classes (based on NAFIS 2016–2017) 101
6.2 Monthly income and consumption expenditure of agricultural households by size of land possessed (Ha) (based on SAS Report, 2013) 102

6.3 The impossible trinity of Quasi-Basic Income 110
11.1 Gender wage gap: India 1999–2012. Data from the NSS; analysis by the author 177
11.2 Graphical representation of MC, MB, and contractual completeness 178
11.3 Equity–efficiency trade-off 184

TABLES

6.1 Average monthly income and consumption expenditure per household by decile class of monthly per capita expenditure (MPCE) (in rupees). NAFIS, 2016–2017 102
6.2 Estimated number of poor and landless rural households 106
11.1 Gender Wage Gap: India 1999–2012 177
11.2 Average real daily wage (in Rupees). Rate for formal and informal workers by sector and gender 183
11.3 Average real daily wage (in Rupees). Rate for formal and informal workers by occupation 183

CONTRIBUTORS

Anant Agarwal is an undergraduate student at the Gujarat National Law University, Gandhinagar. He has presented his research at the Yale Law School, Stanford University, and IIM Bangalore, and was nominated as an academically meritorious student for the Herbert Smith Freehills-University of Oxford Lecture Programme. His interests lie in law, finance, and macroeconomics.

Joshua Aston is Associate Dean (Law) and a member of the Executive in the School of Business and Law, Edith Cowan University, Western Australia. He is a member of various academic committees and bodies at the university as well as other universities and institutes where he actively participates and advises on various academic and legal issues.

Upendra Baxi is one of India's foremost legal scholars. He is former Vice Chancellor of the University of Delhi and currently serves as an Emeritus Professor at the University of Warwick, U.K. He has written and published widely on the topics of law, development, and politics and was awarded the Padma Shri by the Government of India in 2011 for his contribution to legal academia and society.

Cecilia Anthony Das is a Lecturer in the School of Business and Law, Edith Cowan University, Western Australia. She was a corporate lawyer working for various organisations of shapes, sizes, and statuses before joining ECU. As a corporate lawyer, she worked with both public and private companies in Malaysia with extensive experience in Initial Public Offer (IPO) exercises in various jurisdictions, contract drafting, negotiations, legal due diligence and mergers, and acquisitions.

Zaid Deva is a lawyer and is currently working as an Academic Fellow at National Law University, Delhi. He completed BA, LLB (Hons.), from Gujarat National Law University and then went on to pursue an LLM from the SOAS University of Law as a Felix scholar.

V.S. Elizabeth is Vice Chancellor of the Tamil Nadu National Law University and Professor of History at the National Law School of India University (on lien now) where she taught history and feminist legal theory. Her areas of research interest are the early medieval period in South India and violence against women.

Shouvik Kumar Guha is currently working as Assistant Professor of Law (Senior Scale) at the West Bengal National University of Juridical Sciences. He is also the Founding Director of the Centre for Law, Literature and Popular Culture, Joint Founding Director of the Centre for Financial and Regulatory Governance Studies, Joint Founding Director of the Centre for Competition Laws, Associate Director of the Centre for Aviation and Space Laws, and Assistant Director of the Centre for Law and Technology at NUJS. In 2019, a course designed and taught by him, exploring the interface between law and fantasy fiction literature, has received international acclaim and global media coverage for being the first of its kind in the world.

Saul Levmore is the William B. Graham Distinguished Service Professor of Law and former Dean of the University of Chicago Law School. He is former President of the American Law and Economics Association and is a visiting professor at Yale, Harvard, Michigan, and Northwestern Universities.

Rasananda Panda has been Professor of Economics at MICA since 2011. Prior to this, he has seen life in academics as a Lecturer at Som-Lalit Institute of Management Studies (SLIMS), Gujarat University (1997–2002), and Associate Professor at the School of Petroleum Management, Pandit Deendayal Petroleum University (PDPU), Gandhinagar (2007–2011). In between while serving at PDPU, he was Chief Economist (on contract) at Gujarat State Petroleum Corporation, a Government of Gujarat undertaking from 2009 to 2010. His current areas of interest are industry analysis, behavioural economics, political economy of policy making, econometric modelling, and studying the dynamics of business and economic environment of India along with other emerging markets.

Aneri Patel is a graduate student pursuing her Masters of Quantitative Economics from the University of California, Los Angeles, with an expected graduation in June, 2022. Following this, Aneri will be joining The Brattle Group, an Economic Consulting firm, as a Research Analyst in their Boston office. In 2019, she completed her under-graduation from Christ University, Bangalore with a Bachelors in Economics, Psychology and Sociology. Aneri is interested in using quantitative, economic and financial tools to address business, development and policy questions and propose adequate solutions.

Jaivir Singh is a Professor at the Centre for the Study of Law and Governance, Jawaharlal Nehru University. His research work aims at an interdisciplinary exploration of law and the economy, and he has published on diverse topics that include the Indian Constitution, regulation, labour law, competition law, corporate law, and international investment treaties.

Ram Singh is Professor of Economics at the Delhi School of Economics. He holds a PhD in Economics from Jawaharlal Nehru University and Post Doctorate from Harvard University. He is a recipient of the Fulbright Fellowship and has widely published in areas of public economics, and law and economics.

Hiteshkumar Thakkar is Assistant Professor of Economics at Gujarat National Law University, Gandhinagar, India. He holds a PhD degree in Economics and Law. His areas of research interest are macroeconomics, and law and economics. He has edited numerous books and has published several papers in indexed journals.

Stephanus van Zyl is a Professor in the Department of Mercantile Law at the University of Pretoria, where he teaches tax law. He is a research fellow at the African Tax Institute and a visiting professor at the Gujarat National Law University. He serves on the Value-Added Tax Technical Committee for the African Tax Administration Forum.

Anmol Waraich is a PhD scholar at the Centre for the Study of Law and Governance, Jawaharlal Nehru University. She has done her MPhil at Jawaharlal Nehru University and MSc in Financial Economics at Gokhale Institute, Pune. Her research areas include the intersection of law and policy, agricultural debt relief laws, and the role of institutions in the economy.

ACKNOWLEDGEMENTS

The idea of creating something new, marching across unexplored horizons, and dreaming of a discipline that is still nascent in the Indian context is daunting. However, this yearbook that you, the reader, are holding in your hand is a representation of the success of this idea. This idea emerged in our minds in a world that looked far different from the one we are in today – a world where COVID-19 was lurking around the corner but had not yet consumed our entire lives. Executing this idea in the midst of a global pandemic, while learning how to adapt and change not only our ways of living but also our ways of thinking, was certainly challenging, both professionally and personally; however, working alongside and with the support of our peers, seniors, and students, the same could take the shape that you witness it in today.

At the very outset, it is important to note the profound role that the academic system and environment of Gujarat National Law University has played in both encouraging the initial festering of this idea in our minds and providing us with the necessary support and resources to enable its growth into something more as a faculty member of the university. The focus that Gujarat National Law University has always placed on helping our students think beyond the rigid dimensions of disciplines and appreciate their interdisciplinary nature has encouraged us as a faculty member to look beyond the traditional modes of teaching and learning and to relearn and relook at our own expertise from a new lens. And it is this relooking and relearning that inspired our own interest in exploring interdisciplinary studies in a more detailed way in the Indian context.

We would be amiss if we did not appreciate the efforts of several scholars and academics who have helped in shaping the very discipline of interdisciplinary studies, and without whose guidance and seminal works, developing this idea would have been impossible for us. This yearbook has been graciously blessed and inspired by a few of these scholars in particular who deserve mention for the immense patience and guidance they have shown to this work – Professor Upendra Baxi and Professor Saul Levmore. Both of these renowned names in the field of interdisciplinary studies have also contributed their works to this venture.

Further, the contributors to this yearbook – Professor Rasananda Panda, Ms. Aneri Patel, Professor Ram Singh, Dr. Joshua Aston, Ms. Cecilia Anthony Das, Professor Jaivir Singh, Ms. Anmol Waraich, Professor Stephanus van Zyl, Mr. Shouvik Kumar Guha, Professor V.S. Elizabeth, Mr. Zaid Deva, Dr. Hiteshkumar Thakkar, and Mr. Anant Agarwal – must also be mentioned herein for the tremendously insightful work produced and contributed by them to this yearbook. Without their insights, the book that you are holding today could never have been produced. It is their brilliant ideas and thoughts that have made this yearbook a true example of pluralistic discourses at their finest.

Additionally, we must also take this opportunity to appreciate the efforts of faculty and student members of the GNLU Centre for Law & Economics. In particular the student members who have greatly assisted us in the creation of this yearbook are– Mr. Swagat Baruah, Mr. Zaid Deva, Ms. Samidha Mathur, Mr. Anant Agarwal, Ms. Niharika Agarwal, and Mr. Kushagra Yadav – who have all through their various commitments demonstrated both interest and drive to see this yearbook in its finished form as it is today.

The publishers of this yearbook have also consistently displayed faith and belief in our vision and supported the creation of India's first yearbook devoted to interdisciplinary studies and law. The incredible insights given by our publishers and the patience displayed by them through the development of this yearbook were indispensable in its creation.

As we stated in the beginning of this section, this yearbook was envisaged and dreamt of as an idea in a world that looked very different from the one we are living in today. Now as this yearbook is on the cusp of publication, the world is facing post COVID dynamics along with critical global sustainability issues and challenges. With incredible flexibility, the world is now learning how to adjust to the so-called 'new' normal; however, this new normal also seems to carry with itself problems that will require incredible flexibility in thinking to resolve. We believe that the new modes of thinking and analysing situations as described in this yearbook offer renewed suggestions to the world to deal with the challenges still ongoing, and yet to come.

INTRODUCTION TO THE YEARBOOK

When the framers of the American Constitution were through with their historic work in Philadelphia, Benjamin Franklin walked out of the Philadelphia Hall and greeted the eager people outside, who asked him, "[W]hat do we have? A republic or a monarchy?" Franklin famously replied, "[A] republic, if you can keep it."[1]

Franklin's statement indicates the dynamic field that is law and a discipline whose contours are framed by other disciplines. Much like Franklin himself who was a renowned polymath, an inventor, a businessman, a lawyer, a writer, an economist, law as a discipline too has several intersections with other disciplines such as economics, psychology, politics etc.[2] In fact, law can rarely be studied in isolation. In fact, for every social, economic and political interaction, there exists a law. The market exchange functions through a set of business laws, contract law, service law, technology law etc.; the political interaction as structured through constitution and administrative law; and social interactions that take place through family law, laws for women and the vulnerable. Therefore, since the object and the subject of law are embedded in interdisciplinary realities, both as shaped in the present times and the evolutionary path of forces that shape them, it is well accepted that an interdisciplinary lens is critical for an objective, evidence-based and impact-oriented study of law.

As the great English barrister Henry Brougham once remarked, "[A] lawyer must know everything about something and something about everything."[3]

A lawyer hence must navigate his or her mind along various subjects in order to arrive at a wholesome understanding of law in action. This approach to study the existing legislations from various perspectives brought by other disciplines has not just remained confined to existing laws but, over time, also influenced policy making and better drafting of laws for the future.

DOI: 10.4324/9781003150565-1

The National Education Policy (NEP) 2020 seeks to bring in this interdisciplinary approach to education in India. The NEP seeks to tackle this by introducing vocational training for students, multi-stream flexibility post class 10, credit transferability in degree-level education etc.[4] This reform will move education from silo tic theoretical study to problem-solving professionals and informed citizenry with interdisciplinary approach playing a pivotal role in the same.

India is a fascinating country with its immense strength along with its multiple challenges, and the most potent force of resolving these challenges is through scientific education – an educational system that is both of the highest standards and accessible. Knowledge and education initiated as an interrelated understanding of the major principles of life and branched out as individual specialised domains of higher knowledge. It appears that this branching out by way of specialisations achieved significant depth of expertise but somewhere created a widening distance between the individual specialised domains. In the developed world, the domains of specialised knowledge, over the past few decades, found robust interactions in terms of the numerous credit-based choices available to students such that it is possible for them to integrate between the areas of their choice and go on to pursue advanced education. In India, we have very recently started on this trajectory, and given some time and a lot of work, India will also equip herself with this deeper strength of knowledge and analysis, which will enable more efficient policy with far-reaching impacts on all facets of the lives of this populous democracy. As a recent example, the Covid-19 phenomenon comes to mind which insistently brings two truths to the fore. First, the architecture of international order and its globalised structure held together by the set of market, societal and political institutions need to be reengineered to meet the demands of the pandemic. Second, it showed the world that every reengineering had its consequences on the varied aspects of human life. We saw state intervention of multiple forms in order to hold together lives and livelihoods. This intervention brought forth multiple ripple effects in the political, medical, social and economic discourses. For instance, is human life more valuable than economic growth? If so, how much more valuable? If more valuable, then what administrative and legal measures best served the objective of saving human lives and livelihoods? What are the long-run law and policy frameworks addressing issues of unemployment (both urban and rural), disruption in education, alarming issues concerning women and the already vulnerable, issues of underprivileged children and malnourishment and concerns relating to public health? Clearly these are big and important questions, answers to which need to be fetched from the interrelated and overlapping learnings in the shape of advanced domains of knowledge and then crafted as laws that reengineer the overall architect of human lives. The most efficient policy decision required, and will keep requiring, an insight into the multiple consequences so as to balance each domain/law related to trade-off optimally. Most importantly, just like the policy and decision makers need the holistic inputs from professionals having an interdisciplinary orientation most suited to a country like India, so does the citizenry need the well-rounded interdisciplinary education and understanding to be able to appreciate and, if required, critically analyse the decisions. In the past, India has been unable to capture the best of terms in multiple international agreements for numerous reasons, one of which is the inability to appreciate the multiple consequences of the terms of the contract/agreement, limited on account of a very narrow orientation of stand-alone domain specialisations. Gradually, efforts have been made to address this constraint by way of the establishment of National Law Universities, which mandate an integrated approach to the study of law embedded in socio-economic, technological and political domains. This academic endeavour envisaged as *The Indian Yearbook of Law and Interdisciplinary Studies: Pluralistic Discourse* is a small step in empowering the present generation of students and professionals in the league of interdisciplinary approaches and studies of law.

In this yearbook, the authors have discussed global issues, such as foreign interference in domestic elections (politics), feminism (social issue), climate change (social issue) and other subjects such as economics, religion, history and literature, from the perspective of law.

The Indian Yearbook of Law and Interdisciplinary Studies: Pluralistic Discourse, acknowledging that not one single approach constitutes the interdisciplinary approach to law, explores this nexus of law and other disciplines using creative and unique approaches to the varied set of laws relevant in the present times. The title has dual reflections. The first that the publication is initiated by Indian academia and second that the chapters focus on law and its interdisciplinarity in India. Ten of the Eleven chapters are dedicated to interdisciplinary studies of law embedded in the context of India, and one chapter i.e., "Anthropogenic Harms" by Professor Upendra Baxi, delves into the overarching scholarly narrative of the biggest question of present times i.e., the catastrophic consequences of climate change, the applicability of which is most relevant across jurisdictions. The thematic congruence of the edited volume is ignited by a quick recollection of the recent few years, which brings to mind a recurring emphasis on certain central tectonic points, which act as powerful levers for change and deep impact on the lives of people. The issues covered are also the central concerns of state policy demanded by a functioning democracy, in terms of democratic quality, aspirations and sustainability. The chapters also resonate the central promise of the Constitution of India pledged towards keeping the spirit of "We the People of India" alive and resonating.[5] The pressing concerns of the climate change and its associated anthropogenic harms, the echoing discourses on democracy and its instrument of elections, the resonating vibrations of autonomy assertive claims under the rubric of federalism, the imperative demands of the marginalised and impoverished in India and thus the need for Universal Basic Income, the growing conundrum of censorship, the potent instrumentality of taxation on environmental impacts in India, the compelling horrors with regard to violence on women in India, the ethos of the Indian Sikh langar and its latitudinal aspects and the humane and factual lens of literature and history for all meaningful understanding, evaluation and interpretation have resonated to the academic mind and thought. Yet sparse literature on the above vibrations from an interdisciplinarity of multiple facets of human life aligning, emanating and eventualising with law finds scholarly expression in the Indian academia. This publication is an effort to broaden the central focus of law foraying into multiple domain-led themes. An ambitious project as this necessitates the setting of its limit. Whereas the scope of every individual theme would require a publication on its own, *The Indian Yearbook of Law and Interdisciplinary Studies: Pluralistic Discourse* aims at an introductory engagement with multiple themes on certain central tectonic points identified, aimed at involving readers of varied interests and training. The purpose is more to explore the multiple domain-led discourses emanating from, culminating in and projecting onwards understanding of law. This approach appreciates the still emerging stage of law and interdisciplinary scholarship in India and acknowledges the fact that both creation and dissemination of interdisciplinary and multidisciplinary approaches to law require academic programmes and platforms. As the scholarship as well as the receivership of this domain matures, initiatives towards more in-depth thematic academic endeavours will find encouragement.

The increasing importance of studying developments in law and jurisprudence is reflected in select recent publications from the interdisciplinary and multidisciplinary approaches. Some recent international publications are *Time, Law, and Change: An Interdisciplinary Study* (2020),[6] by Sofia Ranchordás and Yaniv Roznai, on the multidisciplinary influences of time on the instrumentality of law towards innovation; *Law and Economics as Interdisciplinary Exchange: Philosophical, Methodological and Historical Perspectives* (2019),[7] by Peter Cserne and Magdalena Małecka, on the success, challenges and future possibilities of law and economics; *The Time of Catastrophe: Multidisciplinary Approaches to the Age of Catastrophe* (Law, Justice and Power) (2016),[8] by Christopher Dole and others, on the evolving philosophical redefinitions of catastrophes. *The Indian Yearbook* holds its distinct identity in light of India as the central focus of scholarship.

The select publications traced over the past three years by Indian academia include *Ideas and Methods of Legal Research* (2019),[9] by P. Ishwara Bhatt, with societal dynamics as the evolutionary path of evolution in legal research methodology; *Interdisciplinary Approaches to Public Policy and Sustainability* (2019),[10] by Nivedita Mandal and Rituparna Das, on public policy with central focus on sustainability across sectors; and *Emerging Markets from a Multidisciplinary Perspective: Challenges, Opportunities and Research Agenda* (2018),[11] by Yogesh Kumar Dwivedi, focusing on the unique questions of the digital enterprise in emerging markets. All three Indian publications mentioned here are important in resonating the interdisciplinary approach and are distinct in terms of their domain concentration. They are also strictly differentiated from *The Indian Yearbook of Law and Interdisciplinary Studies: Pluralistic Discourse.*

The volume starts with the chapter on Anthropogenic Harms by Professor Baxi, where the legendry living jurist outlines the seriousness of the advent of The Anthropocene. Professor states that the naming of Anthropocene has already occurred in the many worlds of science, policy, development, governance, resistance, and popular discourse, so much so that the post-Anthropocene has already arrived. Anthropocene occur as a species- planet notion, identifiable with anthropogenic harm, widespread across various human and non-human species resulting in Negative consequences for the world's impoverished and discriminated states and peoples, and world's ecosystems. In addition, "The climate change denial rhetoric" created by U.S. right-wing countermovement nudged by big corporations has amounted to de facto deregulation of regulatory reach and even institutions, preventing new and advanced legislation for adaptation and mitigation. Denialism has added to the large scale existing human rights violations and blinded our obligations of justice owed to future peoples. State non-compliance along with the colluding interest groups has emerged as a major issue and the efficacy of executive policy stances matter. The paper draws attention to the distinction between non-compliance from denialism (especially in the United States) and the resultant renewal of geoengineering policy along with its limitations.[12]

The second chapter looks at the 2019 elections in India where Professor Saul Levmore in "Outside Influence on Democratic Elections" examines the issue of foreign influence on democratic elections in a country by employing law and economics and public choice theory. Professor Levmore considers the case of donors and their logical reasons behind donating to certain candidates and concludes that their interests lie in not so much to influence an election itself but to gain eventual favour with the winner. He further argues that it is difficult to have a consistent policy about outside interference in domestic elections because of a constant friction between what he calls "confidence-in-democracy," which is an idealised version of democracy wherein it is considered sacrosanct that voters themselves must be the sole deciders of an election and that outside groups will most definitely be tilted towards moneyed interests, and a "concern-for-externalities," which is a view that considers the utility of influence of outside jurisdictions.

Professor Levmore concludes by arguing that the task of law is to move towards the first-based solution, in which governments provide useful public goods, and campaigns are limited to providing useful information to voters, assuming that few resources would be used in efficient handing out of payback to those who contribute to the winning party in an election. However, in a case this doesn't work out and there is an inefficient democracy in place, the second-best outcome would be a transfer of wealth from donors to recipients to impact positive policies (positive externalities).

India's Foreign Contribution Regulation Act is one such legislation that seeks to curb foreign influence in the country. The Act empowers the government to regulate, ban and even expel foreign non-governmental organisations (NGOs) from India. Behind the legislation is the government's thinking that "there is no free lunch" and that every foreign donation comes with a hidden agenda, in order to try to influence the democratic process of India. Amnesty International follows the long list of NGOs forced to leave the country under this Act.

The third chapter, by Zaid Deva, looks at the jurisprudence laid down by the Supreme Court in the *Prem Nath Kaul* case, which considers Jammu and Kashmir (J&K) as a sovereign state even after execution of the Instrument of Accession (IoA) and insertion of Article 370 in the Indian Constitution. The chapter considers the consequences on the jurisprudence related to Article 370 when India and J&K are seen as two sovereign states entering into a treaty and the entrenchment of such treaty in the national constitution in the form of Article 370 and the resultant surplus value arising out of the "constitutional bargain." The researcher argues that the IoA scheme represented an efficient zone of possible agreement with adequate surplus value being attained by both the parties with the same subsequently reflected by the constitutional relation defined by Article 370. Moving from the original bargain, i.e. from 1947 to 1950 (Instrument of Accession) and then from 1950 to 1957 (the period when the J&K Constituent Assembly was functioning), up to the abrogation of Article 370 is studied as changing terms of the bargain. The terms of the original bargain are identified as a source of creating surplus value for both the entities. The intervening amendments change the terms of the bargain, and the abrogation of Article 370 leads to increase in costs of both entities to the bargain.

Professor Rasananda Panda and Ms. Aneri Patel's chapter centre around violence against women in India. Although legislations already exist for safety of women in India, why are they still under threat today? The question can be answered by looking into the social conditions and gender relations that exist in Indian society today and our customs and traditions that dictate it. Women's safety can be said to be in threat even today not because laws aren't working but because most women still have access to economic resources and institutional power. Professor SP van Zyl's chapter on a suitable environmental tax regime brings to the light the suitable environmental tax penalties and tax incentive schemes, which can help us realistically realise the goal of sustainable development. Professor Zyl's chapter is an elaborate attempt to understand what kind of an environmental fiscal regime best works in today's India, and he argues that a carrot and stick approach is far better than control and command regime because environmental degradation is inevitable if economic progress is desired, and hence, tax regimes should be structured in a way that doesn't stifle innovation or human progress. Professor Zyl's chapter is an excellent long read into the realities of environmental degradation and a serious take on what can be done to create a sustainable tax regime, which punishes pollutants and creates incentives for non-pollutants.

India's major problem today, which still remains largely unaddressed, is its pollution problem. With majority of its cities ranked as one of the most polluted in the world and some declared as inhabitable, leave alone unliveable places, India needs government intervention in terms of making the polluter actually pay.

While we see each author exploring unique solutions to challenges posed around existing laws, they collectively advocate for the need to allow the law not to be confined to "Black" and "White" but a kaleidoscope of colours that cannot be done with a "one-size-fits-all" approach.

Keeping in mind the recent developments in legal scholarship around each of the niche areas of law, each author makes an attempt not only to reflect upon the impact of the law in polity, economy and society but also to study society as the causal factor for creation of the law. Professor Ram Singh takes up a crucial debate about the proposed basic income support scheme in India. This chapter is highly relevant in light of the ongoing pandemic, which has caused a global economic contraction and has forced even the most capitalist countries of the world to resort to paying financial stimulus to its citizens.

Professor Singh, with an empirical approach, argues that families facing multidimensional poverty should in fact be subject of such interventionary welfare schemes of the government. The pandemic and the subsequent stringent lockdowns in India have plummeted the gross domestic product to a historic −23% with shocking estimate claims of pushing almost 200 million people into poverty. In a country where 45% of its rural households still don't have income enough to meet their basic needs of food and non-food items and with the onset of a catastrophic global pandemic, a basic income support scheme is not necessary but inevitable.

Dr. Joshua Aston and Dr. Cecilia Anthony Das's chapter on censorship in India is an in-depth study on the free speech regime of India and the how art must navigate itself in consonance with the same. They lay out the Indian free speech regime in terms of the provisions, legislations governing it and the jurisprudence preceding and surrounding it. Art has always found itself in the midst of controversy throughout history across societies. Oppressive regimes have detested art and artists and have subjected it to censorship and retaliation. But a society can be truly said to be free only when it listens to its artists, and art can only flourish in freedom.

Dr. Aston and Dr. Anthony Das do a fantastic job tracing the evolving jurisprudence of free speech in India and examining the doctrine of prior restraint in cinema, defamation laws and gag orders, which hinders artistic expression. Free speech is to a democracy what oxygen is to a human body, an intrinsic and indispensable part, and a free speech regime of a country, hence, plays a crucial role in how democracy works out in a country.

With as many as 29 internet shutdowns in 2019 alone, and more specifically in the state of J&K where internet access was shut off for months and is still restricted today, India is reeling under a free speech crisis currently. Social media has become an intrinsic part of democracy because it lets ordinary citizens and previously marginalised and oppressed groups to exercise free speech.

Indian films as recently as 2016 have faced censorship for portrayal of women that goes against the morality of the society. *Lipstick Under My Burkha* was heavily censored because of this reason. In a democratic society, such narratives of moral censorship of free speech are detrimental to new discourse and more so challenging old discourses. In this case, the movie challenged the patriarchal nature of Indian society, and its censorship acted as a barrier to the promotion of the discourse. Thus, the authors have made an attempt to understand law as a cause and/or effect from the developments in society. This has been made possible with the aid of interdisciplinary approaches to law.

The volume also explores unique gaps that arise out of present laws and legal developments in the recent times when searched from an interdisciplinary lens, which otherwise would not arise. The chapter, by Professor Jaivir Singh and Ms. Anmol Waraich, takes us on a unique and insightful ride into the world of gift economy, an economy that is unique to India. They particularly concentrate on the relationship between the gift economy of the Sikh religion called *Guru ka Langar* and the property rights that support it.

Guru ka Langar is a concept of free kitchen emanating from the holy place of Sikhs, Gurudwaras, where everyone could get free food. The authors trace the history of the Sikh religion in India and the emanation of the gift economy, which they argue is a consequence of a moral economy since communities intrinsically rely on giving than on transactions. They also discuss the Sikh Gurudwara Act and how it helps sustaining the gift economy of Sikhs and argue that outlining property rights by way of a legislation helps prevent the "tragedy of commons" in such an economy.

Dr. Shouvik Kumar Guha treats us with a delightful chapter on the nexus between law and literature, taking inspiration from the bestselling series Harry Potter and its references and indictments of law and legal institutions. A short excerpt from the chapter beautifully talks about the parallels between law school and Hogwarts as places where students can learn about power, how to acquire it and use it and that thin but crucial line of difference between Tom Riddle (Lord Voldemort) and Harry Potter and their use of their magical powers. The chapter speaks to a reader personally with its beautiful parallels to the world of magic and law simultaneously, and it reminds us that law as a subject can indeed be fun and shouldn't be taken as a deadly exercise.

Professor V.S. Elizabeth traces the teaching and learning of history in national law schools in India, its foundation, its purpose, its evolution in terms of its work of students and alumni and the evolution of legal history globally and in India to conclude on the importance of history for law students, legal academia and practitioners.

Dr. Hiteshkumar Thakkar and Anant Agarwal study the under-researched perspective of the overlap between gender wage disparity and pay disparity between the organised and the unorganised sector. The authors show through data analysis that there is an increasing statistical trend for the average gender wage differential. Through variables of marginal cost and marginal benefit, the authors analyse the cost-benefit of the level of contractual completeness for unorganised and organised workers. The authors derive a comparative econometric model for comparison between efficiency and equity policy stance, concluding that a balance between equity and efficiency would lead to better convergence between the wage gap, both between males and females and between organised and unorganised sector workers.

Each of the authors goes on to develop the broader, much recognised goals of interdisciplinary legal scholarship. The chapters have proved, first, that it is almost impossible to think of a legal issue in isolation; second, that looking at a legal issue in consonance with a different subject provides us with certain context and improves on our understanding of the issue; and third, that while writing judgements or even passing legislations, a lot has to be taken into account apart from the law itself.

Hence, the yearbook is an ambitious attempt to give its readers such academic insights into issues that prevail in today's world and how an interdisciplinary approach to understand these issues can not only broaden our understanding of these issues but also help us overcome these issues. The task of "keeping a republic," as said by Benjamin Franklin, is a daunting one, and that can be achieved only if we have help from all sides, if we have a broad perspective of things.

- *GNLU Centre for Law and Economics*

Notes

1 Josh Levy, "A republic if you can keep it": Elizabeth Willing Powel, Benjamin Franklin, and the James McHenry Journal, *The Library of Congress Blog*, (January 6, 2022), https://blogs.loc.gov/manuscripts/2022/01/a-republic-if-you-can-keep-it-elizabeth-willing-powel-benjamin-franklin-and-the-james-mchenry-journal/.

2 Walter Isaacson, *Benjamin Franklin: An American Life* (New York: Simon and Schuster, 2003); Janet Weinstein, Coming of Age: Recognizing the Importance of Interdisciplinary Education in Law Practice, *Washington Law Review* 74 (1999): 319.

3 Gerald Uelmen, Lord Brougham's Bromide: Good Lawyers as Bad Citizens, *Loyola of Los Angeles Law Review*, November 1996.

4 Ministry of Education, "National Education Policy 2020," (2020), https://www.education.gov.in/sites/upload_files/mhrd/files/NEP_Final_English_0.pdf.

5 The Constitution of India, 1950, Preamble.

6 Sofia Ranchordás and Yaniv Roznai, *Time, Law, and Change: An Interdisciplinary Study* (London: Bloomsbury Publishing Plc Ann Arbor, Michigan Proquest, 2020).

7 Péter Cserne and Magdalena Małecka, *Law and Economics as Interdisciplinary Exchange: Philosophical, Methodological and Historical Perspectives* (London: Routledge, 2019).

8 Christopher Dole et al., *The Time of Catastrophe: Multidisciplinary Approaches to the Age of Catastrophe* (London Taylor and Francis, 2016).

9 P. Ishwara Bhatt, *Idea and Methods of Legal Research* (New Delhi: Oxford University Press, 2019).
10 Rituparna Das and Nivedita Mandal, *Interdisciplinary Approaches to Public Policy and Sustainability* (Hershey, PA, USA Information Science Reference (IGI Global, 2019).
11 Yogesh Kumar Dwivedi, *Emerging Markets from a Multidisciplinary Perspective: Challenges, Opportunities and Research Agenda* (Cham, Switzerland: Springer, 2018).
12 Colin Moynihan, "A New York Clock That Told Time Now Tells the Time Remaining," *The New York Times*, September 20, 2020, sec. Arts, https://www.nytimes.com/2020/09/20/arts/design/climate-clock-metronome-nyc.html.

References

Christopher Dole et al., *The Time of Catastrophe Multidisciplinary Approaches to the Age of Catastrophe* (London: Taylor and Francis, 2016).

Colin Moynihan, "A New York Clock That Told Time Now Tells the Time Remaining," *The New York Times*, September 20, 2020, sec. Arts, https://www.nytimes.com/2020/09/20/arts/design/climate-clock-metronome-nyc.html.

Janet Weinstein, Coming of Age: Recognizing the Importance of Interdisciplinary Education in Law Practice, *Washington Law Review* 74 (1999): 319.

Josh Levy, "A republic if you can keep it": Elizabeth Willing Powel, Benjamin Franklin, and the James McHenry Journal, *The Library of Congress Blog*, (January 6, 2022), https://blogs.loc.gov/manuscripts/2022/01/a-republic-if-you-can-keep-it-elizabeth-willing-powel-benjamin-franklin-and-the-james-mchenry-journal/.

Government of India, Ministry of Education, "National Education Policy 2020," (2020), https://www.education.gov.in/sites/upload_files/mhrd/files/NEP_Final_English_0.pdf

P. Ishwara Bhat, *Idea and Methods of Legal Research* (New Delhi: Oxford University Press, 2019).

Péter Cserne and Magdalena Małecka, *Law and Economics as Interdisciplinary Exchange: Philosophical, Methodological and Historical Perspectives* (London: Routledge, 2021).

Rituparna Das and Nivedita Mandal, *Interdisciplinary Approaches to Public Policy and Sustainability* (Hershey, PA, USA Information Science Reference, An Imprint of IGI Global, 2020).

Sofia Ranchordás and Yaniv Roznai, *Time, Law, and Change an Interdisciplinary Study* (London: Bloomsbury Publishing Plc Ann Arbor, Michigan Proquest, 2020).

The Constitution of India, 1950, Preamble.

Gerald Uelmen, Lord Brougham's Bromide: Good Lawyers as Bad Citizens, *Loyola of Los Angeles Law Review*, November 1996.

Walter Isaacson, *Benjamin Franklin: An American Life* (New York: Simon and Schuster, 2003).

Yogesh Kumar Dwivedi, *Emerging Markets from a Multidisciplinary Perspective: Challenges, Opportunities and Research Agenda* (Cham, Switzerland: Springer, 2018).

1

ANTHROPOGENIC HARMS AND MARKET FUNDAMENTALISMS

Solar Geoengineering: All Perils, and No Promises?

Upendra Baxi

1.1 Introduction: The Anthropocene as a Shorthand for Notion of Anthropogenic Harm

The Anthropocene is no longer a science fiction fable that was once an entertaining, or terrifying, privileging the individual interpretant of state–corporate performances, forever engaged in infinite corporate semiosis,[1] but is posited as a sociotechnical reality[2] of global warming and climate change.[3] Representations and signifying realities do matter, but so do the experiences of the everyday crisis in coping with the catastrophic consequences of these phenomena.[4] While the International Stratigraphical Commission has yet to officially announce the advent of the Anthropocene,[5] the naming has already occurred in the many worlds of science, policy, development, governance, resistance, and popular discourse, so much so that we already hear of the post-Anthropocene.[6] In a firm sense, we may describe the Anthropocene as a species-planet notion, identifiable with anthropogenic harm. The harm is widespread across various human and non-human species. While the former would be more intensely affected by the spread of global warming and climate change, the depletion of non-human species is alarmingly accelerating, and together with it the loss of habitats.[7] It is also accepted that the warming of the planet due to the greenhouse gas emissions is now a reality and holds a devastating future ahead on planetary scale, besides effecting many changes on social systems at a global scale. Negative consequences are writ large for the world's impoverished and discriminated states and peoples and world's ecosystems.

While anthropogenic harm has been accepted as occurring, and this era has already been named as the period of the Sixth Great Extinction,[8] the problem of causation looms large, and the problems posed by distant or 'delayed' harm have been examined in the literature. It is well known that there is a considerable time

DOI: 10.4324/9781003150565-2

lag between the adverse effect of harms caused by a steady degradation of, and the deterioration in, environment and its real-life impacts – whether on whole communities or individuals and whether measured in terms of core human rights to freedom, well-being, security, health, or subsistence. Further, as Eric Biber has pointed out, such anthropogenic harm recurs even in face of regulation, and there is almost always a 'backlash' against the very paradigm of regulation, which contemporary environmental law innovates and thrives on.[9]

All this is different and distinct (and should be kept so) from the problems posed by climate change denialism, which occurs in its strongest form when the overall validity of the laws and findings of earth (or geological) sciences are themselves denied. But corporate interest groups and vested interests do not need to travel thus far; their job is well performed when they function as (they do in the United States) 'in creating a climate change denial rhetoric' or even a 'so-called denial machine' ('organized by the U.S. right-wing countermovement and made up of big corporations, conservative think tanks, contrarian scientists, and Republican politicians').[10]

Although scientifically denialism does not make much sense, it is politically potent: denialism has a number of consequences. It amounts to de facto deregulation of regulatory reach and even institutions. It prevents new and advanced legislation for adaptation and mitigation. It creates unsuspected distortions in federalism or as the US Constitution put it so felicitously a 'more perfect Union'.[11] It reinforces exceptionalism in international relations.[12] Denialism also adds to a large scale actually existing human rights violations[13] and obligations of justice owed to future peoples.[14] 'Madhouse effect' corrupts the role of experts and makes practices of politics even less transparent and more obtuse.[15] And finally it fosters aggressively disastrous fossil fuel polices, which are human rights unfriendly and remain altogether trade related and market friendly.[16] This short-termism enhances the reality and the potential for further anthropological harm.

The geo-scientific evidence for anthropogenic harm is mounting. No respectable academic scientist today doubts the reality of the facts about such harm. Differences of expert opinion relate to appropriate models, methods, and measurements of specific classes/clusters of anthropogenic harm. Differences may also persist over the types of Anthropocene – such as immediate, median, and distant or dangerous and distant harms. There may also be differences concerning policy prescriptions – about what is to be sectorally done or even to be done overall (as, for example, in the case of solar geoengineering [SRG]). But disagreements about these matters do not mean (as President Trump outrageously commented) that the climate change science is a 'hoax'; this form of denialism is not worthy of the compliment of rational debate.

Similarly, state non-compliance emerges as a major issue (here the differences between climate change litigation[17]), and what the executive policy stances achieve matter a good deal. The reasons for non-compliance need, of course, to be studied and comprehended beyond the criticism of a particular leader or the reason of the state; behind it lie several performances of interest groups who stand to retain or increase their oligarchic power, and one may study this in the light of the play and war among knowledge(s), power, and values.[18] And a Nietzschean analysis may show, in fact, that values are themselves hegemonic constructs, reflecting and reinforcing strategic interests of power-wielders rather than any postulated agreement on values that all people necessarily share.[19] The short point here is that it would advance a clearer analysis to distinguish non-compliance from denialism (especially in the United States), which also paradoxically fostered a renewal of geoengineering policy.[20]

1.2 Geoengineering Techniques: Promise and Perils

Geoenginnering techniques are generally described as 'deliberate, large-scale manipulation of the planetary environment in order to counteract anthropogenic climate change.'[21] Increasing impatience with the slow movement towards anthropogenic harm – manifested in strategies of mitigation and adaptation – some notable governance actors, especially in the United States, are leading the revival of the idea of SRG.[22] Commonly called solar radiation management (SRM), which Baskin now renames simply as SRG (solar geoengineering), this technique is considered more efficient than its alternative CDR (carbon dioxide removal technology). SRM is presented as a cheaper technology, costing estimated as $1 billion annually. When perfected as an applicable technology, it will comprise the injection of about a million of sulphate particles into the stratosphere. Oxidizing for a few weeks to form a sulphuric acid aerosol, the sulphate particles 'would reduce incoming sunlight by a small amount ... The idea is that by reflecting a portion of incoming sunlight before it enters the Earth system, global warming would be reduced or reversed, although to varying degrees in different locations'.[23] Further, 'embarking on SGE is a long-term commitment, a multi-decadal commitment (at minimum) requiring stable and dependable global policy settings. Depending on the dosage, it is not easily terminated without serious climatic "bounce-back" risk'.[24] But there is no precise calculation of adverse climatic effect, which may

> include reduced rainfall, droughts and monsoon disruption, as well as damage to the ozone layer. Moreover, 'the extent of these likely effects, not to mention the associated social effects, is both contested and not reliably known...'. Despised as a 'thoroughly bad idea' and 'regarded with incredulity and something approaching disgust by broad swathes of the public who have been asked their views', Baskin's assessment is that it is currently opposed by most climate scientists.[25]

More specific are the concerns enunciated from the perspectives of human rights. The Malé Declaration on the Human Dimension of Global Climate Change enunciates 'the fundamental right to an environment capable of supporting human society and the full enjoyment of human rights'.[26] The adverse consequences, measurable in terms of human right to health for all, include aggravation of old and obduracy of often life-threatening new diseases, malnutrition, displacement, resettlement in indifferent and distressing locations and camps, and variable and lower food production especially in impoverished and conflict zones. Further, the

> right to private and family life and the right to culture will be affected as increasing warming puts some ecosystems at risk of abrupt and irreversible changes that will reduce economic growth and poverty reduction, erode food security and trigger new poverty traps, particularly in urban areas and hunger hotspots.[27]

Many more social, economic, and cultural rights would be adversely affected, so would be core human rights norms, standards, and doctrines, if not also the very idea of being human and having rights. My purpose here is not merely to archive these actual or imminent feats of human and human rights violations but also to show that human rights sociolect provides one important mode of analysing the impacts of geoengineering. Even when this may not altogether replace the economistic method of rational cost–benefit analysis, a human rights-oriented, or better still a human rights-based, approach to governance and development provides an additional and ethically superior instrument for counting 'costs'.

Among the human rights costs, foremost is the rise of both the prevalence and the depth of impoverishment (I have said elsewhere why I prefer this expression in favour of the more common passive term 'poverty' because it directs attention to people deprived by acts of social indifference and state policy of sustainable means to live with dignity). It is making it harder for people to escape 'poverty' and is increasing their vulnerability to falling into impoverishment, due to price shocks caused by sudden changes in agricultural production, natural disasters, and environmentally triggered health problems. Estimates suggest that even under a low-impact scenario, where powerful mitigation and adaption strategies are successful, between 3 million and 16 million people will be further impoverished by 2030 because of climate change. Under a high-impact scenario, those figures could rise to between 35 million and 122 million.[28]

Climate change is also having an impact on intergenerational inequality. As a recent UN report puts it:

> The disruptions caused by climate change are likely to reduce the livelihood opportunities of future generations, especially in countries hardest hit, and exacerbate downward intergenerational mobility.[29] Climate change is affecting both the prevalence and depth of impoverishment, thereby contributing to inequality. It is making it harder for people to escape poverty and is increasing their vulnerability to falling into poverty,

due to price shocks caused by sudden changes in agricultural production, natural disasters and environmentally triggered health problems.[30]

Assuming powerful mitigation and adaption strategies are successful, it is estimated that 'between 3 million and 16 million people will fall into poverty by 2030 because of climate change', but an upward revision of these figures will be justified under a 'high-impact scenario' giving us an estimate of 'between 35 million and 122 million'.[31] The report carefully identifies vulnerable groups and collectivities including (a) small holder farmers; (b) indigenous peoples; (c) rural coastal peoples;[32] (d) disaster-prone communities; (e) situations of gender injustice and related 'susceptibilities' and 'vulnerabilities'; and (f) systematic climate change policy and action to avoid intra- and intergenerational inequalities, especially for 'future generations, especially in countries hardest hit, and exacerbate downward intergenerational mobility'.[33] The message of the report for all climate policies and actions is simple but critically relevant: in this era, while stressing the normative discursivity of human rights norms, standards, and doctrines may be *necessary*, these are by no means *sufficient*. Different types of disadvantages, dispossession, and affect vulnerabilities of differently situated collectivities, faced by anthropogenic harm and their different coping and survival strategies plus staying powers, need also to be addressed in some existential details in planning amelioration. What is called to attention is not so much the discursive normativity of human rights but rather a close attention to contexts and collectivities and on the basis of urgency, almost on a here-and-now basis. Put another way, the glacial pace at which human rights are enunciated and enforced follow the old *habitus* of very late Holocene remain no longer equal to the urgency of action now summoned by the reality of anthropogenic harm.[34]

Finally, it appears to many that given the overall ecological, human, and human rights costs, as well as probably planetary system costs,[35] this technology while seeming offering a short-term solution may have the effect of exacerbating the anthropogenic harm.

1.3 Non-Use of Solar Engineering Technology?

It has been powerfully argued that future impacts of SRM suggest the ultra-hazardous nature of this intervention. A primary hazard is the unknowability of the future planetary outcomes; additionally, 'moral hazards' are indicated by 'reducing the incentive for states to engage in mitigation and adaptation efforts, for SRM may prove to be faster, cheaper and less difficult to agree upon in international negotiations'.[36] Indeed, it is 'laden with unknowns'.[37] However, the argument against solar geoengineering research and funding seems based upon the 'core dynamic of ... the tension between the continued scientific interest in SRM research and the absence of international governance structures to guide research and to eventually coordinate larger-scale activities'.[38]

Writ large in the recent Open Letter (issued by some leading climate scientists and governance experts and subscribed by a large number of academics in humanities and social sciences),[39] who urge[40] 'an International Non-Use Agreement on Solar Geoengineering' which would be 'timely, feasible, and effective', these will 'inhibit further normalization and development of a risky and poorly understood set of technologies that seek to intentionally manage incoming sunlight at planetary scale', and 'without restricting legitimate climate research'. Further, it would remove 'the false promise of a cheap and feasible alternative' which poses a 'dangerous distraction from current climate policies'.[41] SRG is not 'necessary' or 'desirable' nor is any 'normalization of solar geoengineering research moving on with rapid speed', a strong political message must' come soon to block these technologies is needed'.

It is necessary to clarify what the authors of the appeal want to mean by 'banning research'. An international non-use agreement would not 'prohibit atmospheric or climate research as such, and it would not place exceedingly broad limitations on academic freedom'. Rather, a 'specific set of measures targeted purely at the development of solar geoengineering technologies under the jurisdiction of the parties including outdoor experiments with that specific purpose' may be targeted as a subject of a ban. A 'mutual assurance' not to 'develop or deploy solar geoengineering technologies in the future' will 'suffice to reduce incentives for further research and technology development for solar geoengineering.[42]

The non-use recommendation is based on, and honours, the following commitments: (1) to 'prohibit … national funding agencies from supporting the development of technologies for solar geoengineering, domestically and through international institutions'; (2) to 'ban outdoor experiments of solar geoengineering technologies in areas under their jurisdiction'; (3) not to 'grant patent rights for technologies for solar geoengineering, including supporting technologies such as for the retrofitting of airplanes for aerosol injections'; (4) to 'not deploy technologies for solar geoengineering if developed by third parties'; (5) and to object to 'future institutionalization of planetary solar geoengineering as a policy option in in relevant international institutions, including in assessments by the Intergovernmental Panel on Climate Change'.[43]

This set of basic obligations furnish minimal guidelines for the architecture or ecostructure of a new and appropriate solar engineering regime, as clearly, and poignantly, unilateralism is scarcely a response; it is, from the eye of the present and future humanity, a prime necessity ensuring us all human, species, and nature itself planetary survival in an era of accelerating anthropogenic hurt and harm.

The Open Letter clearly lists several national, industry, and state-sponsored projects for research (for mitigation and adaptation) under way mostly in the developed world. The scientific research potential here is immense and still unfolding. The Open Letter rightly regards these 'proliferating calls for solar geoengineering research and development' as a 'cause for alarm', as they 'risk the normalization of these technologies as a future policy option' in present-day conditions and contexts where 'the risks and efficacy of solar geoengineering are poorly understood'.[44] One cannot but agree that otherwise future peoples may justly blame us for allowing any ill-understood, irreversible, and potentially disastrous course of action like unilateral research and experimentation in SRG.

1.4 Conclusion

Some way ahead seems indicated by the adoption of a code of conduct built on the Oxford Principles,[45] which are held to help mitigate the main 'environmental, social and knowledge risks' associated with geoengineering; the five principles of geoengineering commended thus are as follows. Principle 1 is simply stated: 'the involvement of the private sector in the delivery of a geoengineering technique should not be prohibited and may indeed be encouraged', but it is to be 'regulated as a public good', and such regulation 'should be undertaken in the public interest by the appropriate bodies at the state and/or international ensure that deployment of a suitable technique can be effected in a timely and efficient manner'. Principle 2 recognizes the importance of public participation in geoengineering decision-making but is subjected to two words: 'Wherever possible'. Those 'conducting geoengineering research should be required to notify, consult, and ideally obtain the prior informed consent of, those affected by the research activities.' Of course, any technique 'which involves changing the albedo of the planet by injecting aerosols into the stratosphere will likely require global agreement'. Principle 3 requires

> complete disclosure of research plans and open publication of results in order to facilitate better understanding of the risks and to reassure the public as to the integrity of the process. It is essential that the results of all research, including negative results, be made publicly available.

Principle 4 underscores an independent 'assessment of impacts ... by a body independent of those undertaking the research', and where techniques 'are likely to have transboundary impact, such assessment should be carried out through the appropriate regional and/or international bodies'. Assessments should address both the environmental and socio-economic impacts of research, including mitigating the risks of lock-in to particular technologies or vested interests. And Principle 5 mandates that 'deployment "decisions with respect to" should only be taken with robust governance structures already in place, using existing rules and institutions wherever possible'.[45]

This is scarcely the place to evaluate exhaustively these principles. But it must be said that at least the approach of the Oxford Principles is based on 'robust governance structures already in place'. It is no mere quibble to say that such structures do not exist anywhere in the world, since SRM is a proposed technology framework whose planetary system risks are largely undetermined, and the principles assume that an international framework on 'no first use' and banning SRM research is or will be at hand. The principles further blithely assume that freedom of science and integrational justice (duties to distant future peoples) are ethical priorities that must dictate the future course of climate policy and action, even if it leads to SRM being experimented at unilateral or some regional level.

As against this, it is well argued that SRM is a 'category of political technology': it is 'inherently political' in the sense of being unfavourable to certain patterns of social relations and favourable to others. And if so,

> there is an urgent need to make explicit the ... way in which SRM is being constituted as a technology, to interrogate the embedded assumptions and sociopolitical implications of this constitution, to question whether it might encourage forms of politics that may be incompatible with democratic governance, and to explore the specific challenges that SRM might pose to democracy itself'.[46]

The principal difficulty in any multilevel agreement is the negation of democratic processes, leading to environmental authoritarianism, necessarily inimical to inclusive democratic participation.[47]

They maintain that

> 'the difficulty in modelling climate processes means that it is almost certain that any SRM intervention would not compensate for greenhouse-gas-driven climate change in any straightforward way. SRM interventions will produce novel climate configurations, with both winners and losers, raising complex issues of justice and redistribution. If the climate resulting from an SRM intervention is more unruly than that predicted by geoengineering researchers, the ensuing politics is also likely to be of a different level of disorderliness.

Further, 'the indeterminacy that is endemic to atmospheric and climatic phenomena would mean that the attribution of cause and effect, and of liability and accountability, would be impossible to carry out in any definitive way – even in principle'. See also note 47.

As this rather comprehensive analysis shows, issues concerning free speech are not the only important issues. There is need to address SRM weaponization: 'geoengineering treaty regime should have the power to impose sanctions on nations that fail to comply with prohibitions on weaponization of geoengineering technology'. And any such treaty

> must contain requirements for an Environmental Impact Assessment to identify potential harms and weigh risks and benefits, provide mechanisms for information-sharing to encourage early dispute resolution and compliance with treaty obligations, establish procedural mechanisms to resolve

> transboundary harm disputes, and have substantive legal norms to ensure that transboundary harms are fully compensated (at 218).

Short of a new planetary consciousness and togetherness and comprehensive rejection of all kinds of spiciest thinking, even a framework of international agreement extending basic area of convergence is difficult to come by in near multipolar fractious future.

Notes

1 J. M. Broekman and L. Catà Backer, 'Politics, Semiotics and Law: Person and Thing', in J. M. Broekman and L. Catà Backer (eds.), *Lawyers Making Meaning*, 155 (Dordrecht: Springer Science+Business Media, 2013).

2 Sheila Jasanoff, 'The Idiom of Co-production', in Sheila Jasanoff (ed.), *States of Knowledge: The Co-Production of Science and Social Order,* 1–12 (London and New York: Routledge, 2004); *Ead.* 'Future Imperfect: Science, Technology and the Imaginations of Modernity', in Sheila Jasanoff and Sang-Hyun Kim (eds.), *Dreamscapes of Modernity: Sociotechnical Imaginaries and the Fabrication of Power,* 1–33 (Chicago, IL: Chicago University Press, 2015); see, the further analysis in Jeremy Baskin, *Geoengineering, the Anthropocene and the End of Nature* (London: Palgrave-Macmillan, 2019).

3 See, Will Steffen et al., 'Trajectories of the Earth System in the Anthropocene', *Proceedings of the National Academy of Sciences (PNAS,* August 6, 2018) argue that 'feedback processes within the Earth System coupled with direct human degradation of the biosphere may play a more important role than normally assumed'. They maintain that

> social and technological trends and decisions occurring over the next decade or two could significantly influence the trajectory of the Earth System for tens to hundreds of thousands of years and potentially lead to conditions that resemble planetary states that were last seen several millions of years ago, conditions that would be inhospitable to current human societies and to many other contemporary species.

And they raise four questions: (1) 'Is there a planetary threshold in the trajectory of the Earth System that, if crossed, could prevent stabilization in a range of intermediate temperature rises?' (2) 'Given our understanding of geophysical and biosphere feedbacks intrinsic to the Earth System, where might such a threshold be?' (3) 'If a threshold is crossed, what are the implications, especially for the wellbeing of human societies?' and (4) 'What human actions could create a pathway that would steer the Earth System away from the potential threshold and toward the maintenance of interglacial-like conditions?' [1–2]. And they issue an alert that '[h]umanity is now facing the need for critical decisions and actions that could influence our future for centuries, if not millennia' [6].

4 Such as draughts, floods, desertification, deforestation, rising sea levels, some meltdown of the Arctic glaciers, extreme weather changes, greenhouse gas emissions, alarmingly steady loss of spices, and demographic explosion. Some UN systemwide estimates claim that climate change caused displacement of about 400 million migrants by 2030, and more climate refugees are expected to seek migration in neighbouring regions as the forces of global warming take charge and cause 'disappearing' states, including small island states. Already, internally displaced peoples are fast posing additional problems of intra-state migration. See, Jane McAdam, *Climate Change, Forced Migration, and International Law* (Oxford: Oxford University Press, 2012); Jenny Grote Stoutenburg, *Disappearing Island States in International Law* (Leiden: Brill, 2015).

On the 25th anniversary of their first 'Warning to Humanity', more than 15,000 world scientists issued a second warning, summoning urgent action towards and urging that 'great change in our stewardship of the Earth and the life on it is required, if vast human misery is to be avoided'. They pleaded for the stabilization of world population, the substantial reduction of greenhouses gas emissions, the phasing out of fossil fuel, the diminishment of deforestation, and resistance to the destruction of biodiversity. See, William J. Ripple, Christopher Wolf, Mauro Galetti, Thomas M. Newsome, Mohammed Alamgir, Eileen Crist, Mahmoud I. Mahmoud, and William F. Laurance, 'World Scientists' Warning to Humanity: A Second Notice' (Manuscript in-press with BioScience. The Second Warning Calls for a Thirteen-Point Agenda of 'Sustainability Transitions'. To this we must now add the discourse of Conference of Parties that met at Glasgow: see, IIDS, Glasgow Climate Change Conference, October 31– November 12, 2021 | Glasgow, United Kingdom of Great Britain and Northern Ireland) UN Framework Convention on Climate Change – UNFCCC (2021).

5 See Colin N. Waters, Jan A. Zalasiewicz, Mark Williams, Michael A. Ellis, and Andrea M. Snelling, *A Stratigraphically Basis for the Anthropocene?* (Geological Society, London: Special Publications, 395, 1–21 (2014); Paul J. Crutzen, "Geology of Mankind", *Nature*, 415, 23 (2002); Paul J. Crutzen and Eugene F. Stoermer, "Anthropocene", *Global Change Newsletter*, 41, 17–18 (2000).

6 See, for example, Anne Fremaux, *After the Anthropocene: Green Republicanism in a Post-Capitalist World* (London: the Palgrave Macmillan, 2019); David Chandler, *Ontopolitics in the Anthropocene: An Introduction to Mapping, Sensing and Hacking* (New York: Routledge, 2018); Clare Colebrook, *Death of the Posthuman: Essays on Extinction*, Vol. I. (Ann Arbor, MI: Open Humanities Press, 2014).

7 As is now within at least the elite knowledge, the anthropogenic changes in biodiversity are inevitable, but the exact ratio of extinction is much debated. This rapid loss of species is estimated by experts to be between 1,000 and 10,000 times higher than the natural extinction rate. The experts calculate that between 0.01% and 0.1% of all species will become extinct each year. However, if 'the low estimate of the number of species out there is true – i.e. that there are around 2 million different species on our planet … – then that means between 200 and 2,000 extinctions occur every year': see, wwf.panda.org › our work › biodiversity › biodiversity (last accessed March 3, 2022). The International Union for Conservation of Nature alarmingly estimates that the number of animals and plants facing extinction may rise from more than 28,000 to about 160,000 by 2020.

Very differently, the species extinction is viewed as going beyond mere biodiversity concerns: see, Audra Mitchell, 'Beyond Biodiversity and Species: Problematizing Extinction', *Theory, Culture & Society*, 33:5, 23–42 (2016). Mitchell pluralizes 'extinction' by providing categories 'for several subjects of extinction' and ample grounds for revisiting the doctrines of species encoded in the images of 'biodiversity', 'humanity', 'unloved' subjects, and 'absent or non-relational subjects'. She expounds and explores ingrained hierarchies and violence of the embedded exclusions and inequalities embedded in dominant discourses and identifies possibilities for 'plural ethico-political responses to mass extinction'. She urges that we differentiate between 'the disappearance of the (meta)physical species Homo sapiens and the "figural" extinction … of the normative figure of "humanity" produced by Western European humanism, modernity and capitalism' (at p. 29).

8 Jan Zalasiewicz et al., 'When Did the Anthropocene Begin? A Mid-twentieth Century Boundary Level Is Stratigraphically Optimal', *Quaternary International*, 383–196, 199–200 (2014); Will Steffen et al., 'The Anthropocene: Conceptual and Historical Perspectives', *Philosophical Transactions of the Royal Society A*, 369:842, at 849 (2011).

9 Eric Biber, 'Climate Change, Backlash and the Problem of Delayed Harm', http:/ssrn.com/abstract=1292529 (last accessed February 10, 2022); see pp. 5–10, 22–25, 45–51.

I violate the author's embargo on citation since the points here made are valuable, and this paper is still available on academia.com

10 Núria Almiron and Jordi Xifra, *Climate Change Denial and Public Relations: Strategic Communication and Interest Groups in Climate Inaction*, 1 (New York: Taylor & Francis, 2020). Each chapter in this valuable anthology charts the itineraries of denialism, where various strategies have been deployed to deepen agnotology, see Robert N. Proctor and Linda Schiebinger (eds.) *Agnotology: The Making and Unmaking of Ignorance* (Stanford, CA: Stanford University Press, 2012). See also, Ildiko Ioan, Zamfir Andreea-Ileana, and Constantin Florentina, 'Oil Companies' Climate Change Discourse – Case Study: ExxonMobil's Discourse Analysis', https://ideas.repec.org/a/ora/journl/v1y2009i1p337-342.html (last accessed February 10, 2022); Permanent People's Tribunal, Session on Human Rights, Fracking and Climate Change, May 14–18, 2018; ADVISORY OPINION April 12, 2018, www.permanentpeoplestribunal.org (last accessed February 10, 2022).

There is also much to be learnt in terms of corporate biography and the linkage of governance with deep management styles from Steve Coll's excellent study, *The ExxonMobil and American Power* (New York: The Penguin Press, 2012).

11 The Preamble to the US Constitution says:

> We the People of the United States, in Order to form a more perfect Union, establish Justice, insure domestic Tranquility, provide for the common defense, promote the general Welfare, and secure the Blessings of Liberty to ourselves and our Posterity, do ordain and establish this Constitution for the United States of America.

Initially, it marked a move away from the Articles of Confederation towards a national federal government; later, its meaning was broadened to convey powers to effect significant change in society, and further also to reinforce the federal supremacy clause. Cities, corporations, and states are continuing with the pledges of Paris (notwithstanding the Trump withdrawal; see note 12). For example, 405 municipalities representing 70 million Americans have signed on the Climate Mayors initiative; more than 80 US cities stand pre-committed to 100% renewable energy; several businesses, cities, and states have pledged to follow the Paris goals, in a fight against the withdrawal from Paris Agreement. See, further, Nancy C. Carre, 'Environmental Justice and Hydraulic Fracturing: The Ascendancy of Grassroots Populism in Policy Determination', *Journal of Social Change*, 4:1, 1–13 (2012).

12 The Trump administration has made the United States the only country to have notified withdrawal to the United Nations on November 4, 2019, which will come into effect after a one-year waiting period has elapsed. The American Walkout has been universally criticized and, at the time of the publication of this work, reversed by President Joe Biden.

13 Ronald Moreland, Hans Nelen, and Jan Williams (eds.), *Denialism and Human Rights* (Cambridge: Cambridge University Press, and Intersentia, 2018); Derek Bell, 'Does Anthropogenic Climate Change Violate Human Rights?', *Critical Review of International Social and Political Philosophy*, 14:2, 99–124 (2011).

14 Andrew Linklater, *The Problem of Harm in World Politics: Theoretical Investigations* (Cambridge: Cambridge University Press, 2011); Jorg C. Tremmel, *A Theory of Intergenerational Justice* (London: Routledge, 2009); see also id., 'Climate Change and Political Philosophy: Who Owes What to Whom', *Environmental Values*, 22:6, 725–749 (2013); Burns H. Weston, 'Climate Change and Intergenerational Justice: Foundational Reflections', *Vermont Journal of Environmental Law*, 9:3, 375–430 (2008). Tremmel's article, 'Climate Change and Political Philosophy', attempts rigorously 'to end with a synthesis of the arguments into what can be considered to be the most reasonable and fairest approach to the politics of climate change on a global scale' (at 726). See also, Dale Jamieson, 'Duties to the Distant: Aid, Assistance, and Intervention in the Developing World', *The Journal of Ethics*, 9, 151 (2005).

15 See Steve Coll, Note 10 *supra*, particularly Chapters 23 and 25; Michael Mann/ Tom Toles, *The Madhouse Effect: How Climate Change Denial Is Threatening Our Planet, Destroying Our Politics, and Driving Us Crazy* (New York: Columbia University Press, 2014), See also Núria Almiron and Jordi Xifra Note 10, *supra*; and Michael Thompson and Gregory R. Smulewicz-Zucker (eds.), *Anti-Science and the Assault on Democracy: Defending Reason in a Free Society* (New York: Buffalo, Amherst: Prometheus Books, 2018).

16 See for this distinction, Upendra Baxi, 'Epilogue: Changing Paradigms of Human Rights', in Julia Eckert, Zerrin Ozlem Biner, Brian Donahoe, and Christian Strumpell (eds.), *Law against the State Ethnographic Forays into Law's Transformations*, 266–285 (New York: Cambridge University Press, 2012).

17 See Sabin Center for Climate Change climatecasechart.com (last accessed February 10, 2022); See also 'The Status of Climate Change Litigation: A Global Review United Nations Environment Programme' Columbia University, Sabin Center for Climate Change Law (2017–05), at http://columbiaclimatelaw.com/files/2017/05/ Burger-Gundlach-2017-05-UN-Envt-CC-Litigation.pdf (last accessed March 3, 2022); Suryapratim Roy and Dr Edwin Woodman, 'Situating *Urgenda v the Netherlands* within Comparative Climate Change Litigation', *Journal of Energy & Natural Resources Law*, 34:2, 165–189 (2016); Jacqueline Peel and Hari M. Osofsky, *Climate Change Litigation: Regulatory Pathways to Cleaner Energy* (Cambridge: Cambridge University Press, 2016).

18 See the authoritative study by Jeremy Baskin, *Geoengineering, the Anthropocene and the End of Nature*, 162–240 (London: Palgrave Macmillan, 2019; hereafter referred to as 'Baskin').

19 See Martin Heidegger, *Nietzsche*, 55–56, 66 (Chicago, IL: University of Chicago Press, 1982). See also *The Movement of Nihilism: Heidegger's Thinking about Nietzsche* (London: Continuum, 2011; Laurence Paul Hemming, Bogdan Kostea, Coastas Amiridis Eds).

20 Baskin; Christopher J. Preston (ed.), *Climate Justice and Geoengineering: Ethics and Policy in the Atmospheric Anthropocene* (New York: Rowman & Littlefield International, 2016); Haomiao Du (ed.), *International Legal Framework for Geoengineering: Managing the Risks of an Emerging Technology* (New York: Routledge, 2016); Sam Adelman, 'Geoengineering: Risks, Rights and Justice', *Journal of Human Rights and the Environment*, 8:1, 119–138 (2017). Also see, for a technical analysis, Wei Wu (ed.), *Recent Advances in Geotechnical Research* (Cham, Switzerland: Springer International Publishing AG, 2019).

21 Royal Society, *Geoengineering the Climate: Science, Governance and Uncertainty* 1 (London: The Royal Society, 2009), quoted in Adelman Note 20, *supra*. Perhaps, the best analysis of the history, science, and philosophy subject is presented by Stephen H. Schnider, 'Geo-engineering: Could We or Should We Make It Work?', 1–17, in Brian Launder, J. Michael T. Thompson (eds.), *Geo-Engineering Climate: Change: Environmental Necessity or Pandora's Box?*, 3–26 (Cambridge: Cambridge University Press, 2010). Just to cite one example, we stand to learn a great deal about the histories of justifications for geoengineering via the relation of the changing perceptions of adoption and mitigation strategies of climate changes and global warming.

22 See Baskin who studies the three periods, which he respectively analyses as periods of 'mastery', 'hiatuses', and 're-emergence'. It would take this chapter far afield to note all the views expressed on solar radiation; see, for example, Kerryn Anne Brent, 'The Role of the No-Harm Rule in Governing Solar Radiation Management Geoengineering' (Doctoral Thesis, University of Tasmania, Australia, 2010); and Sanna Joronen, 'Climate Change and Ethics of Geoengineering – Implications of Climate Emergency Ethics' (Finland: University of Turku, 2015).

23 Baskin, at 2.

24 Ibid.

25 But Baskin (p.5) also writes about the 'Janus-like quality' in

> SGE's re-emergence. On the one hand SGE is a response emanating from the centres of global power, rooted in standard practices and epistemologies of science, and purporting to be a solution to the climate change problem. In this sense SGE is part of a hegemonic, or at least preponderant, tale about tackling climate change, in the name of modernity, using big technology. And yet it is simultaneously a subversive story which undermines a great deal in the dominant accounts of modernity, of science and of the human-nature binary.

26 Malé Declaration on the Human Dimension of Global Climate Change, November 14, 2007, http://www.ciel.org/Publications/Male_Declaration_Nov07.pdf, accessed February 29, 2020.
27 Sam Adelman, note 20 *supra*.
28 *The World Social Report 2020: Inequality in a Rapidly Changing World* at 93 (United Nations Publication ST/ESA/372, 2020; cited simply as 'Report'), citing a study by Stéphane Hallegatte, Mook Bangalore, Laura Bonzanigo, and Marianne Fay, 'Shock Waves: Managing the Impacts of Climate Change on Poverty'. Climate Change and Development Series (Washington, DC: World Bank Group, 2016). Id., 'Unbreakable: Building the Resilience of the Poor in the Face of Natural Disasters'. Climate Change and Development Series (Washington, DC: World Bank, 2017).
29 *Report* at 8.
30 Id., at 3.
31 Id., at 8.
32 *Report* at 93–99. See also the description and analysis of adaptation and mitigation policies at 99–104 and the road ahead, stressing the need for a 'system perspective' at 105–106. Ibid., citing a study by Stéphane Hallegatte, Mook Bangalore, Laura Bonzanigo, and Marianne Fay, *Shock Waves: Managing the Impacts of Climate Change on Poverty. Climate Change and Development Series.* Washington, DC: World Bank Group, 2016). Id., *Unbreakable: Building the Resilience of the Poor in the Face of Natural Disasters. Climate Change and Development Series* (Washington, DC: World Bank, 2017).
33 Report, at 8.
34 Tracey Skillingon rightly observes (invoking Walter Benjamin's imageries of 'now-time' and 'empty time') that 'the realization of a more equitable and ecologically sustainable world cannot be confined to some future project of humanity' but 'rather must be located in the energies, the experiences, and critical reflexive capacities of the 'now-time' of the present. What is immediately required to 'make real … alternative future are said to require an equally alternative conception of the historical intelligibility of our civilizational development' is a movement away from the current dichotomization of a relatively stable, even if fragile, ecological present, confronting a distant and endangered future to an understanding of how our actions today intricately shape the 'not yet' moment of collective futurity'. The starting point of this new phase of critical thinking is the realization that we are all trapped in what Beck … describes as 'a shared global space of threats – without exit'. Occupying this space in a sort of 'empty time'… of ecological destruction… will not will these problems away, neither will responding to them through a national defence of difference.

> The transborder nature of shared ecological problems means that, as a subject of a collective willing, climate solutions cannot be limited de facto to members of one particular community but, rather, must be the concern of a more indefinite commons, in both geographical and generational terms; see her, *Climate Justice and Human Rights* (New York: Palgrave Macmillan, 2017) See also, Upendra Baxi, 'Towards a Climate Change Justice Theory?', *Journal of Human Rights and the Environment*, 7:1, 7–31 (2016).

35 As to these, see, generally, Victor Galaz, 'Planetary terra incognita', in Victor Galaz (ed.), *Global Environmental Governance, Technology and Politics: The Anthropocene Gap*, 1–15 (London: Elgar, 2014). He issues a

> modest call to appreciate existing controversies about the Anthropocene and 'planetary boundaries' as a normal state of scientific discovery. … Scientific theories evolve over time *because* they are debated, not the other way around. … While there certainly are areas of strong disagreement, few global change scholars would question the claim that humanity has entered a new era of rapid environmental change. The human enterprise has drastically changed Earth's climate dynamics, fundamentally modified marine and land- based ecosystems at very large scales, and even changed the course of biological evolution. These changes, in combination with insights about how complex systems behave, pose extremely challenging risks at unprecedented temporal and spatial scales.
>
> (at 15)

36 Masuko Hamaguchi et al., *Human Intervention in the Earth's Climate: The Governance of Geoengineering in 2025+"*, at 6 (supported by the Robert Bosch Stiftung. Stuttgart, 2015).

37 Id., 13.

38 Id., 16. However, and in the abstract, some researchers point to a conflict between freedom of speech and expression and justice across generations. Even if the former, while being near-absolute, may be subject to some reasonable restriction, it remains an open question whether intergenerational justice standards may apply here. But it has been argued that might be the case: Holly 'Jean Buck, a professor at the University of Buffalo and an expert in geoengineering, wrote on Twitter:

> Can you not imagine someone in, say, 2050, who is suffering from extreme heat, wondering why their parents' generation decided to forbid research on something that might be able to cool the climate and save them from a dangerous heat wave?

As reported by *Grist*, 'Should the world ban solar geoengineering? 60 experts say yes', https//grist.org/science/should-the-world-ban-solar-geoengineering-60-experts-say-yes/ (last accessed January 21, 2022).

39 See, Frank Biermann, Jeroen Oomen, Aarti Gupta, Saleem H. Ali, Ken Conca Maarten A. Hajer, Prakash Kashwan, Louis J. Kotzé, Melissa Leach, Dirk Messner, Chukwumerije Okereke, Asa Persson, Janez Potocˇnik, David Schlosberg, Michelle Scobie, and Stacy D. Van Deveer, 'Solar Geoengineering: The Case for an International Non-Use Agreement', *Wire's Climate Change*, 1–8 (2021).

40 In the concluding para of the appeal at page 6 above.

41 By 'removing the Decarbonization of our economies is feasible if the right steps are taken, leading also to innovation opportunities through economic transformation and ecological benefits beyond climate change mitigation'.

42 At p. 5.

43 Ibid.

44 Open Letter, 1. See, for further detail, Scott Barrett et al., 'Climate Engineering Reconsidered', *Nature Climate Change*, 4, 527–529 (2014). https://doi.org/10.1038/nclimate2278

45 Oxford Martin School, Oxford Geoengineering Programme, www.geoengineering.ox.ac.uk/oxford-principles/principles. See, further Steve Rayner, Clare Heyward, Tim Kruger, Nick Pidgeon, Catherine Redgwell, and Julian Savulescu, 'The Oxford Principles', *Climatic Change*, 121, 499–512 (2013) at 500. They conclude:

> The development of technology-specific research protocols is the first step of the bottom-up process of building a flexible governance architecture. Through the development of the protocols, the Principles will be translated into specific content, recommendations and regulations, appropriate to different technologies as they

> develop. For example, they could serve initially as a code of conduct by scientific researchers and research councils. The more specific regulations generated in the research setting could then be adopted and modified by other institutions, including, where necessary, formal mechanisms such as legal regulation.
>
> (at 509)

46 Bronislaw Szerszynski, Matthew Kearnes, and Phil Macnaghten, 'Why Solar Radiation Management Geoengineering and Democracy Won't Mix', *Environment and Planning A*, 45, 2809–2816 at 2811 (2013).

47 See, Upendra Baxi, 'The Future of Dissent in the Anthropocene' –*Mainstream*, November 17, 2020; mainstreamweekly.net/article8604.html ¼ (being the text of the Second Rabi Ray Memorial Lecture). See also, Vishal Garg, 'Engineering a Solution to Climate Change: Suggestions for an International Treaty Regime Governing Geoengineering', *Journal of Law, Technology & Policy*, 2014, 197–218 (2014).

2

OUTSIDE INFLUENCE ON DEMOCRATIC ELECTIONS

Saul Levmore[1]

2.1 Introduction

The 2019 Indian general election, and especially the enormous amount of money spent on campaigning and befriending voters during the election season, has drawn attention to the question of whether and when "outside" support (in the form of money and other assistance) from companies and persons not directly involved in an election should be forbidden, tolerated, or even encouraged. Common reactions to outside influence are negative but ultimately and necessarily inconsistent. The losing side (or sides) is likely to regard vote buying through any means as anti-democratic, as well as a practice that fosters corruption. It is unusual for the losing party (or parties) to have collected more money,[2] or more outside money, than the winning party, but this alone hardly proves that money brings about victory in a political campaign. Outsiders regularly try to influence local elections within a country, whether by transferring money or individual labor. Donors, as we might call them, are often looking for rewards and thus are more likely to support the perceived winner and the incumbent party.[3] When in doubt, it is not unusual for donors to give to multiple contestants. Their goal is often not so much to influence the election but to gain favor with the eventual winner or even with the incumbent during the period prior to the election.

As Section 2.2 will show, it is difficult to fashion a consistent policy about outside, or cross-border, influences on politics. The discussion considers arguments based, first, on an idealized version of democratic rule and then on one driven by the reality that what happens in one country, or jurisdiction, often affects another. These sensible approaches, labeled here as "confidence-in-democracy" and "concern-for-externalities," are shown to be in tension with one another. Section 2.3 then develops the somewhat surprising case for allowing or even encouraging outside interventions, especially in the form of money. It touches on

DOI: 10.4324/9781003150565-3

ideas about decision-making outside of general elections, including the question of whether elected legislators ought to be able to pay one another for votes and whether there is an argument for allowing judges on multi-member panels to do the same. Section 2.4 concludes and suggests that allowing or even welcoming limited interference in politics, whether from inside or outside a jurisdiction, may be a second-best solution for some democracies. The idea is strengthened if law requires transparency.

2.2 Democracy and Externalities

2.2.1 Confidence-in-Democracy

There are at least two important arguments against outside influence.[4] First, the very idea of democracy is that those who are governed should decide things for themselves, normally by majority vote or by delegation to representatives or their delegates. The matter is complicated in India because many people remain registered in constituencies where they grew up rather than in jurisdictions in which they live and where voting has a direct impact; voters rarely return to their home districts to cast votes.[5] Indian law seems aimed at preserving long-term affiliations or ensuring that elected representatives will have strong ties to their original home constituencies.[6] This is less so in other democracies; in some, people have a choice and can return "home" to vote (or vote by mail) or can vote where they now reside "temporarily." A second principle, or claim, is that outside interest groups are likely to be tilted in favor of moneyed interests and so should be limited or forbidden to interfere. Democratic decision-making, and majority vote in particular, is an alternative to markets; a critical decision for a democracy is to decide what should be allocated to markets as opposed to voting – and then to judges or other government decision-making bodies appointed by elected officials or elected in direct fashion. Some of this allocation between markets and democratic decision-making is written into constitutions, but some is decided by democratic decision-making itself, as when governments decide to privatize some government functions or – to the contrary – to forbid private ownership of weapons and to monopolize law and order in the hands of the government.[7] Even when we understand that the government (or the Constitution) decides what is allocated to governmental decision-making, there is the underlying question of whether some form of market is available to influence elections, and thus the lawmaking itself. Every democracy allows candidates for office to hire advertising firms and to rely on polls run in the private sector, to take two simple examples, so there is always some outsourcing to private markets. All democracies permit neighbors to try to influence one another through conversation so that a one-person-one-vote principle is subject to rules or market mechanisms that influence how voters are informed. Any system that penalizes citizens who try to influence fellow citizens' political judgments would be derided as illiberal. It is probably impossible to completely separate politics from markets.

Still, some countries, like the United States, forbid money contributions from outside the country (but not from other jurisdictions for more local elections within the country) to political parties or candidates for office, while other countries do not.[8] India permits limited contributions from foreign entities and places various limits on contributions, especially to individuals rather than parties, but enforcement of these rules is difficult and rare.[9] Most of these countries allow domestic contributions, though sometimes these are subject to limits.[10] It is apparent, but also usually attractive, that each jurisdiction (or nation) decides the degree to which markets and wealth are permitted to influence democratic decision-making. Outright bribes and vote buying might be forbidden, whether from inside or outside a jurisdiction, and we can imagine that each jurisdiction is trusted to decide its own rules consistent with democratic, self-rule principles. Each decides on the allocation between markets and politics and then also about the degree to which money is allowed to influence politics (from inside or outside). Confidence-in-democracy is consistent with a view that each jurisdiction will do a good job if allowed to decide these rules for itself.[11] It leads to the principle that each jurisdiction should decide in some democratic way how much, and what kind of, outside influence to permit. For example, and quite relevant to India and several other nations, a country might decide to allow citizens who "intend" to return home to vote while they are abroad, even though this presents obvious problems of enforcement. An alternative is to require citizens to return "home" in order to vote, as is the case in Israel.[12] With respect to this and other matters, the more one has confidence-in-democracy, the more one is inclined to trust a state to decide its own rules.

We might expect institutions that are liberal in this regard to require transparency, which, in this case, means the disclosure of the source of funds that affect political outcomes. Just as some jurisdictions require candidates for office to announce the source of their campaign funds and their approval of campaign advertisements, they might be even more insistent that the voters know when influence has come from outside the jurisdiction. Such revelation might help or disadvantage a candidate running for office, but if the idea is to abide by the confidence-in-democracy idea, then voters need all the knowledge that can be mustered. I will return below to the question of why voters might like direct contributions from abroad, whether or not disclosed to their compatriots. Similarly, each jurisdiction can decide in democratic fashion how much its government or its citizens are permitted to try and influence *other* jurisdictions. Interference is an export as well as an import. No symmetry is required, and there is certainly no need for a balance of trade. Americans and Europeans may be horrified at the prospect of Russian influence on their elections, but they take as given their own newspapers' and politicians' freedom to try and influence Russia's government or Israel's elections. A trade imbalance is considered desirable and even moral, when the observer is confident about right and wrong.

There is an analogy here – or even a direct symmetry in law – to boycotts. Most democracies feel free to boycott the goods of another nation, much as individuals feel free to choose one store over another, and even to advertise a private boycott, whether for personal or political reasons. An example of political aims was the wide boycott of Apartheid-era South Africa, beginning in the 1960s and ending in the 1990s when true elections began. Nations feel free to ban both exports and imports, often for political reason, and they may do one and not the other. They may forbid their citizens from visiting another country while not refusing entry to citizens from that country. Correspondingly, foreign trade is used to encourage political regimes abroad, or to encourage instability. The conflict between externalities and democratic thinking disappears in the minority of cases where the cross-border intervention can be said to promote democracy in the foreign country, for the point is to advance confidence-in-democracy.

2.2.2 Externalities

A second, often opposing, view is that it is fair and efficient to allow outside influence because the confidence-in-democracy idea does not fully consider the utility of people in other jurisdictions. One country might want to encourage another to pollute less or to save an endangered species, and it might do so by trying to influence political decisions across borders. Readers who start out intuitively opposed to outside intervention, usually because it favors the wealthy or because it interferes with the confidence-in-democracy idea, should consider two counterpoints. First, many democracies, including India, allow internal money to be used for advertisements and other campaign expenses.[13] This can be defended as necessary to inform voters, to allow for free speech, or to allow for the expression of intense preferences. Second, nothing stops a democracy from limiting or banning inside and outside money, unless there is a constitutional restraint on free speech grounds.[14]

Law-and-economics suggests a third reaction, based on the external effects of one jurisdiction on the citizens of another. If, for instance, the United States is worried about climate change so much that its government or several of its citizens use their wealth to encourage India to use different fuels, or to "pay" for India to pass legislation that limits the use of certain kinds of coal, would anyone really object on the grounds of a distaste for outside influence and a tampering with India's democratic process? Both sides would be better off – as is true of most transactions – as one side's greater wealth would benefit the less-well-off recipient. The benefit comes in the form of the transferred resources and might be enhanced by long-term environmental benefits. There is a familiar moral objection to one country paying another to *accept* pollutants, or simply trash, but it is unlikely that there would be a similar objection to payments made in order to improve the environment rather than to transfer unwanted materials from one country to another. These examples nearly dispose of the argument that it is always offensive for wealth to affect cross-border arrangements.

It remains, however, for us to consider the claim that cross-border interference on grounds of externalities is only acceptable when wealth serves to advance a common good, at least as perceived by the international community. Most people look back on the international anti-Apartheid movement with admiration, and most regard cross-state Freedom Riders (civil rights activists in the United States who went from northern to southern states in the 1960s to promote the cause of civil rights) as heroes rather than as persons who could afford to travel to other states and thus impose their preferences regarding racial equality. Had it been the reverse, with rich southerners in the United States traveling north to encourage race discrimination, we might well frame the objection as one based on using wealth to influence politics in another jurisdiction. In the case of cross-border externalities within one country, there is also an escape offered by the national government; in the United States, the national government can impose rules regarding the environment as well as racial discrimination so that there is a substitute for cross-border political influence. In any event, the larger claim is that interference from other jurisdictions is simply based on the politics or preferences of the observer so that there is no right answer to the general question about outside intervention and influence. This claim is stronger when the interference is in the hands of wealthier countries or people so that we cannot be sure that their utility can be compared with that of poorer people or jurisdictions. If a group thinks that a policy or candidate in its own jurisdiction is morally offensive, it will disapprove of foreign interference that solidifies this policy or candidate. And if the foreign interference is an attempt to undo what is regarded as offensive, then suddenly foreign interference will be welcomed by the global community.

But imagine that we can put wealth aside, as when there is a serious limit on individual politically directed contributions, or when two jurisdictions, or adherents to opposing viewpoints, have similar per capita wealth. In this case, there is a reasonable argument for foreign interference because of external, or cross-border, effects. Consider the case where one state, O, has factories that employ many people but that also pollute the atmosphere; prevailing winds drive these pollutants to the east, to a neighboring jurisdiction, P. Voters in O might rationally prefer laws that permitted the pollution because they do not take the cost and preferences of P's citizens into account. An even more interesting case is where P's citizens value scenic beauty that for some reason does not appeal to citizens of O. O will not take P's (pure) preferences into account. If there is some negative externality running in the other direction, O and P might simply agree that each will behave in a way that satisfies the other. If not, a law-and-economics reaction, beginning with the Coase Theorem, is that the government of P could buy the factories in O and install better smokestacks, or shut them down with some payment to employees.[15] But the more interesting application of the bargaining idea is for P, or interest groups in that jurisdiction, to pay O to enact laws that reduce the pollution or save the scenic view. Another version of this kind of foreign interference or influence would be to finance the election of political candidates in O, who promise to reduce the pollution. Finally, and somewhat equivalently, P or some of its offended citizens might pay voters in O to change the outcome; these recipients would vote for new environmental laws or for politicians who are dedicated to reducing the problem that largely affects the neighboring state, P. Payments from across the border can in this way change the political outcome and take account of the negative externality suffered by nonvoting, foreign citizens. It is apparent that voters in O (and especially poorer voters, though the discussion here has tried to eliminate the issue of wealth disparities) might be better off with a rule that allows or even encourages payments from abroad, and this is especially so if some of the transferred money is directed to workers in O who are made worse off. This is the essence of the concern-for-externalities argument in favor of allowing foreign payments, or other intrusions.

The assumption, or trick, of eliminating wealth effects is not entirely fanciful, but size effects must also be considered. It is common, for example, though perhaps tongue in cheek, to hear citizens of The Netherlands or of Canada say that they ought to vote in American elections, because American policies, and especially its trade and tax policies, have a great impact on these smaller countries. To be sure, this impact is less than that experienced by residents of New York or other domestic groups in the United States, but at least these groups have votes. Presumably, the Dutch would be happy with an arrangement that gave each Dutch voter one-fifth of a vote in U.S. elections, though it is hardly clear how the right percentage would be calculated and adjusted over time. The suggestion is fanciful for several reasons. Dutch and Canadian citizens do not pay taxes to the United States; they would hardly agree that the United States could draft them in case of war; and they would hardly agree that Americans should get comparable votes in elections in their countries, if only because the vast number of U.S. voters, even if each is given a mere fraction of a vote, would overwhelm the voters who live in Canada and The Netherlands. Relative size does not, however, explain much; it seems absurd to say that residents of Pakistan should vote in Indian elections, though there are even greater externalities in that setting. Cross-border externalities or conflicts are better decided by discussion, by international agreements and delegation, or even by payments or threats of a sort. Externalities do not translate well to votes, though they surely influence votes within each jurisdiction.

It is important to see that the "confidence-in-democracy" and "concern-for-externalities" approaches are not always in conflict, however easy it is to see particular cases of conflict. The more we have faith-in-democracy, the more a country like O, in the stylized example just presented, should be trusted when it allows or disallows payments or other interference from abroad. But a slightly weaker form of the confidence-in-democracy approach takes differing wealth into account and suggests that democracy is itself a choice *not* to have a market and thus not to allow the buying and selling of policies, politicians' power, or votes. In the case of O and P, and depending on how money arriving from P is allocated to government projects or voters in O, people in O can be made better off by allowing outside interference from P. And yet, there is something startling and offensive about the prospect of vote buying. If it really benefits recipients, even as it permits citizens of P to express their preferences, then why not favor markets for votes quite generally? This question is addressed in Part III.

There is, it should be noted, a different kind of political solution that sometimes discourages P from paying O, or even encourages O to lose the option of encouraging P to pay for the right to impose costs on some citizens of O. Instead of bargaining, either can go to a superior legislature. If, for example, P and O are states within a single nation that has the power to create binding national rules, then P might coordinate with other states that pay taxes from wealth created by their (polluting) factories and obtain from the national legislature the "right" to pollute up to some level. Citizens of O will now have lost the advantage that tort law might give them, although they can still pay P to reduce the pollution heading toward O. Similarly, O might find it difficult to extract payment from P sufficient to compensate O, and O might coordinate with other states suffering from wind-blown pollutants, and they might have the votes to get a national anti-pollution rule. This power to obtain national legislation might reduce some of the problems emphasized here, unless the national legislature is also captured by wealth effects. In the case where O and P are not states within a nation, but sovereign and separate nations, the possibility of law taking charge is diminished. Countries like O might seek international treaties, but these can be ignored; they might try to involve the United Nations in the same way that states try to combine interests and impose rules by a national government, but again these rules have much less power. The European Union is a nice example of an intermediate "solution," and it is no surprise that some of its rules are welcome by some member countries but much resented by others.

In sum, there is something of a conflict between confidence-in-democracy and a concern for positive and negative externalities. Within the United States, and in other countries that allow cross-border contributions to political campaigns, it is common for residents of one state to contribute to candidates or causes in another. It is even more common for individuals to refuse to buy goods from other states, or to go out of their way to visit or patronize other states. The usual justification draws on externalities; people are affected and sometimes simply morally offended (or thrilled) by what happens in other jurisdictions. We have already seen that it is difficult to limit this argument and that it is often in conflict with a faith-in-democracy in the receiving jurisdiction. The conflict can be eliminated as an intellectual matter if we take the confidence-in-democracy argument further than is usually done, by reasoning that a jurisdiction can simply legislate that it welcomes – or forbids – outside contributions, with or without limits. In any event, when applied to real cases, such attempts to resolve the tension between democratic principles and worrisome externalities lead to the observation that one's views on cross-border contributions, whether in-kind or in cash, and even contributions within a single jurisdiction (which is to say debates about the wisdom of limiting private financing of political campaigns), quickly reflect the observer's preferences about the winners and the losers. Those who contribute to causes that are later seen as obviously correct and moral are regarded as heroes, while those who fund causes or officials who come to be seen as destructive are regarded as reprehensible or even criminal. As before, the continuing task here is to identify nonpolitical arguments for one rule or another.

2.3 Money in Politics

Consider first the familiar problem of vote buying. It is unlawful in virtually every jurisdiction for one judge to pay another to change his or her vote. Similarly, it is generally regarded as wrongful for me to pay my neighbor in cash so that he or she will vote for my favorite candidate, though secret ballots make enforcement, and therefore such agreements, difficult. On the contrary, I may discuss the coming election with my neighbor and even take time off from work (and thus lose money) to try to influence my neighbor to vote as I prefer. An economist would point out that, in this last example, my sacrifice along with the fact that my neighbor does not receive anything of value shows that I have a strong belief or preference, while the neighbor is only receiving information. Payment in such a case might truly satisfy intense preferences and thus increase overall utility. It might be acceptable to let a neighbor know that "I want you and others to vote for X, and if X wins the election, I will give $1,000 to a charity that I know you like." My intensity and the fact that the voter is not personally enriched seem decisive – though it is acceptable to invite the neighbor to a celebration dinner if a preferred candidate wins an election. Generally speaking, it is socially and politically unacceptable to pay one's friends in order to satisfy one's own preferences at the expense of the friend's; this is especially the case where wealth inequality is apparent.

The discussion thus far is in preparation for seeing campaign finance issues within a single jurisdiction in a new light. Current law in virtually every jurisdiction forbids direct vote buying but permits and even protects a willing buyer who is eager to buy votes indirectly through advertising and other campaign expenditures. If direct vote buying were permitted, we would expect buyers to look first to unlikely, unmotivated, or simply indifferent voters, as a source of eager sellers.[16] These citizens do not place great value on their votes and would likely sell a vote at a very low price. If buyers need a great number of votes, they will eventually need to buy from more motivated voters, who either enjoy voting or are more likely to have stronger preferences about the outcome and, irrationally perhaps, believe their votes might be decisive. If this second group can be identified and tends to be the same from election to election, then its members will, by virtue of their strong preferences and constant participation in elections, set the legal rules over time. It is, therefore, not surprising that this group establishes rules against vote buying. It is as if the group knows that its votes will be less influential if a buyer can amass the votes of the unmotivated voters, who would otherwise be likely to stay home or randomly distribute votes in ways that do not affect the outcomes in most elections. Only rarely will very highly motivated buyers of votes need to go so far as to buy the more expensive votes held by the highly motivated voters, who are typically dispersed or only loosely coordinated. If the unmotivated citizens have some say in the initial rules, or the government or the Constitution sets the rules early on, with an eye on their later impact, it would not be surprising to see laws protecting the unmotivated voters against whipsaw, as it is called in the corporate and securities law literature.[17] As a practical matter, they should be expected to constitutionalize restrictions against vote buying. The unmotivated voters are numerous but not organized. If only they could combine forces, they would see that a party that bought many of their votes has purchased something quite valuable, and the sellers would therefore design a rule that gave each seller an amount equal to the highest price, paid to any seller.[18] Alternatively, the motivated voters might (and do) develop a rule that banned the purchase of votes, knowing they would be outvoted by a party that bought a substantial set of votes from those who attached a lower value to voting.

The analysis is more complicated, but perhaps more rather than less convincing, when wealth differentials are added more completely to the picture. If poorer voters are as motivated to vote as more fortunate citizens, they might still favor a rule that allows the sale of votes, because some interest groups will offer more money (or other benefits) than the vote is worth to any individual. This is especially so when each voter knows that solving the collective action problem among voters is difficult. If I know that my vote is just one of many, I will surely accept a dollar for my vote, for it is essentially worth nothing to me, unless I think that holding out will raise the price. What drives up the price is likely to be competition from other potential buyers. The buyer of votes like mine needs to offer enough to discourage competitors from an auction for votes like mine. In public choice terms, the result is interesting and close to what we observe. Those who can solve the collective action problem, like a large corporation that stands to gain from a specific government policy, will find it worthwhile to give money to the candidate or party it expects to win. The recipient needs this money to defeat opponents or simply to enjoy life. In turn, the receiving party will spend much of this money "buying" votes from those who cannot solve their collection problem. No one will pay $3 to a CEO for his vote and expect much in return. But the CEO might pay thousands of dollars to gain favor with a person or party that is capable of awarding contracts or other favors, knowing that the recipient will use this money to pay $3 per vote to voters who are not organized and not particularly motivated.

There is more to the story from the point of view of those who are not particularly motivated and who have little expectation of forming coalitions. As we have seen, they will benefit if parties or other entities compete for their votes, but we have not yet touched on the question of whether they (rather than the empowered voters or interest groups) benefit from a ban on vote buying. If there is an effective ban of this kind, interest groups will turn to nonmonetary benefits.

They may make extravagant campaign promises, invite people to lavish retreats, or pay for campaign workers to go from home to home to try to convince (what I have called) unmotivated people to vote one way or another. All this is less attractive to the recipients than is cash; it is also, and perhaps of greater interest to see that it is, an inefficient waste of resources. The money spent on nonmonetary inducements is largely a waste of resources compared to cash. Cash allows each recipient to spend on goods he or she truly wants. From the point of view of poorer voters who are not organized, it is likely that vote selling is more attractive than its likely alternatives. To be sure, this claim ignores other arguments including the idea that many poor people, along with their more fortunate fellow citizens, think of voting as a matter of dignity and thus favor its inalienability. As is apparent, the discussion here has focused on two important arguments, labeled as confidence-in-democracy and concern-for-externalities, and it has not insisted that there are no other reasons to fear even limited vote buying. As emphasized shortly, the case for vote buying is a second-best argument.

2.4 Conclusion

When democracy works well, significant resources are spent providing public goods that benefit the citizenry. Few resources should be wasted on campaign strategies or on inefficient favors eventually handed out as payback to those who contribute to the winning party in an election. But when the private interests of politicians and donors are unlikely to move in this direction, the second-best outcome could conceivably be a transfer of wealth from donors to those recipients who will accept small payments for their support. They may do so because they are unmotivated voters – because they know that one vote makes little difference, because they are not well organized into groups, because they have lost faith in government, or for a host of other reasons. The task of law is surely to move toward the first-best solution, in which governments provide useful public goods, and campaigns are limited to providing useful information to voters who can benefit from the wisdom of crowds in choosing elected officials and public projects to pursue. But when law has not succeeded in bringing a democracy to this state, it should be no surprise to see payments intended to impact politics in the ways described here. When compared to the most desirable forms of democracies, it is painful to see, but it may be a kind of second-best result, especially when seen from the eyes of those who are paid, in one way or another, for their political support. This second-best result is more likely if voters are well informed about contributions to campaigns because it enables voters to evaluate the likelihood that elected officials will respond to interest groups they find unattractive.

Notes

1 Thanks to Paresh Lal for help with the details of and insights regarding Indian law.
2 There is a strong correlation between electoral success and fundraising. *See* Wesley Lowery, "91% of the time the better-financed candidate wins. Don't act surprised."

The Atlantic (2014). The correlation holds in many countries, though it is hard to ignore the obvious selection effect; donors may prefer to give to candidates expected to win. *See* Gary W. Cox and Michael F. Thies, How Much Does Money Matter? "Buying" Votes in Japan, 1967–1990, 33 *Comparative Political Studies* 37–57 (2000); Myungsoon Shin, Youngjae Jin, Donald A. Gross, and Kihong Eom, Money Matters in Party-Centered Politics: Campaign Spending in Korean Congressional Elections, 24 *Electoral Studies* 85–101 (2005).

3 *See* Taylor C. Boas, Daniel Hidalgo, and Neal P. Richardson, The Spoils of Victory: Campaign Donations and Government Contracts in Brazil, 76 *Journal of Politics* 415–429 (2014); Michael Barber, Donation Motivations: Testing Theories of Access and Ideology, 69 *Political Research Quarterly* 148–159 (2016). For an interesting proposal to reduce the influence-based incentives of political donations, see Ian Ayres and Jeremy Bulow, The Donation Booth: Mandating Donor Anonymity to Disrupt the Market for Political Influence, 50 *Stanford Law Review* 837–891 (1998).

4 To be sure, there are many other arguments that can be developed against vote buying. Perhaps votes should be inalienable because they are personal and reflect a core human capacity. It is impossible to take on all such arguments here, as conceded in Part III, but the discussion concentrates on the two arguments noted in the text. As for an argument that voting is about human dignity, and must therefore never be commodified, note that few democracies make voting mandatory, and this is perhaps an indication that it is something that belongs to the individual, who can set it aside or sell it. The argument against any one entity or person having multiple votes is more difficult to develop or defeat. Democracies allow coalitions and political parties, and these are devices for combining votes and are rarely criticized on the basis of dignity-based arguments.

5 *See* Anupama Roy, Identifying Citizens: Electoral Rolls, the Right to Vote, and the Election Commission of India, 11 *Election Law Journal: Rules, Politics, and Policy* 170–186 (2012). Nevertheless, for the purposes of the discussion here, it is easier to think of a democratic model as opposed to an externality model while keeping in mind that the democratic model is imperfect, or can be subdivided, because of voter registration systems.

6 *See* Representation of the People Act 1951 (Part II – Acts of Parliament), Chapters I–II.

7 Political elections, as currently organized, have not only many defects but also some obvious virtues. Among these virtues is that no voter or contributor who prefers candidate G has reason to vote for, or to support, H. In contrast, a market in votes will create the risk that voters, while holding out for higher prices or waiting to buy at lower prices, will vote or sell perversely. This does not rise to the level of a paradox, because it is not as if the rational voter is expected to vote for the candidate he or she least prefers (at the offered price), but it does amount to a serious danger that markets will do harm rather than good, even when measured on their own terms. Another, perhaps overwhelming, defect of a market in voting rights is that wealth effects might dominate preference intensities, just where a majority is inclined to limit the effects of unequal wealth. But there are ways of limiting wealth effects. Eventually, limited markets may retain the quality of avoiding perverse voting behavior even as they remain simple enough to provide a sense of legitimacy.

8 For U.S. law, see 52 USC § 30121. India, as of 2016, relaxed its legal definition of "foreign" for purposes of foreign contributions, which are still unlawful. See Milan Vaishnav, Political Finance in India: Déjà Vu All Over Again, Carnegie Endowment for International Peace (2019). Canada, France, Israel, Mexico, and Brazil do not allow any foreign corporations or entities, or domestic corporations, to make political donations. At the other extreme, South Africa has no campaign restrictions, and Italy does not restrict foreign donations. In the middle are Germany and Russia, which allow corporate giving if firms are not majority foreign-owned. Japan has recently

legalized foreign corporate contributions. Jieun Lee, Foreign Direct Investment in Political Influence, Working Paper, 2018. https://www.internationalpoliticaleconomysociety.org/sites/default/files/paper-uploads/2018-10-28-21_42_07-leejieun@umich.edu.pdf. Within the United States, Alaska now restricts partially foreign-owned corporations from spending in its election process. *See* Alaska Stat. § 15.13.068 (2018), 132 *Harvard Law Review* 2402–2409 (2019).

9 *See* Ellen L. Weintraub and Samuel C. Brown, Following the Money: Campaign Finance Disclosure in India and the United States, 11 *Election Law Journal: Rules, Politics, and Policy* 241–266 (2012).

10 Canada, for instance, does not allow corporate campaign contributions at the federal level, though some provinces allow corporations to contribute to parties. For the federal Canadian rule, see Canada Elections Act, S.C. 2000, c. 9, 363(1). For a discussion of provincial rules, see D. M. Brock and H. J. Hanson, Raising, Spending, and Regulating Party Finances in the Provinces, 9 *Canadian Political Science Review* 55–74 (2015). Israel does not allow campaign contributions by corporations to national political candidates. LOC https://www.loc.gov/law/help/campaign-finance/israel.php. France has a nearly total ban on entity contributions other than political parties and certain groups. https://www.loc.gov/law/help/campaign-finance/france.php.

11 A country might decide to allow citizens, who "intend" to return home, to vote while they are abroad, though this presents obvious problems of enforcement. As emphasized in the text, the more one believes in democracy, the more a state ought to be trusted to decide its own rules.

12 *See* Rainer Baubock, Expansive Citizenship: Voting beyond Territory and Membership, 38 *PS: Political Science and Politics* 683–687 (2005).

13 *See* David Gilmartin and Robert Moog, Introduction to "Election Law in India," 18 *Election Law Journal: Rules, Politics, and Policy* 136–148 (2012); M. V. Rajeev Gowda and E. Sridharan, Reforming India's Party Financing and Election Expenditure Laws, 18 *Election Law Journal: Rules, Politics, and Policy* 226–240 (2012).

14 The United States remains an anomaly in this regard. See *Buckley v. Valeo*, 424 U.S. 1 (1975); *Citizens United v. Federal Election Commission*, 558 U.S. 310 (2010).

15 *See* R.H. Coase, The Problem of Social Cost, 3 *Journal of Law and Economics* 1–44 (1960); Fred S. McChesney, Rent Extraction and Interest-Group Organization in a Coasean Model of Regulation, 20 *Journal of Legal Studies* 73–90 (1991). For a re-interpretation of Coase's case study of lighthouses, which argues that public–private bargaining reaches an efficient result, rather than private–private bargaining as Coase originally indicated, see Elodie Bertrand, The Coasean Analysis of Lighthouse Financing: Myths and Realities, 30 *Cambridge Journal of Economics* 389–402 (2005). Readers might notice a moral hazard in the text's example: savvy businesses in jurisdiction O might threaten to start businesses in order to extract payments from P.

16 A more expansive version of the argument found in this part can be found in Saul Levmore, Voting with Intensity, 53 *Stanford Law Journal* 159 (2000).

17 See Levmore, supra note 16. Inasmuch as voter turnout in India is relatively high, they are referred to here as unmotivated, while the cited literature thinks of them as "unlikely."

18 This is what happens in securities law in many countries, as in the United States' Williams Act.

Bibliography

Ayres, Ian, and Jeremy Bulow, The Donation Booth: Mandating Donor Anonymity to Disrupt the Market for Political Influence, 50 *Stanford Law Review* 837–891 (1998).

Barber, Michael, Donation Motivations: Testing Theories of Access and Ideology, 69 *Political Research Quarterly* 148–159 (2016).

Bauback, Rainer, Expansive Citizenship: Voting beyond Territory and Membership, 38 *Political Science and Politics* 683–687 (2005).
Bertrand, Elodie, The Coasean Analysis of Lighthouse Financing: Myths and Realities, 30 *Cambridge Journal of Economics* 389–402 (2005).
Boas, Taylor C., Daniel Hidalgo, and Neal P. Richardson, The Spoils of Victory: Campaign Donations and Government Contracts in Brazil, 76 *Journal of Politics* 415–429 (2014).
Brock, D. M., and H. J. Hansen, Raising, Spending, and Regulating Party Finances in the Provinces, 9 *Canadian Political Science Review* 55–74 (2015).
Coase, Ronald H., The Problem of Social Cost, 3 *Journal of Law and Economics* 1–44 (1960).
Cox, Gary W., and Michael F. Thies, How Much Does Money Matter? "Buying" Votes in Japan, 1967–1990, 33 *Comparative Political Studies* 37–57 (2000).
Gilmartin, David and Robert Moog, Introduction to "Election Law in India," 18 *Election Law Journal: Rules, Politics, and Policy* 136–148 (2012).
Gowda, M. V., and E. Sridharan, Reforming India's Party Financing and Election Expenditure Laws, 18 *Election Law Journal: Rules, Politics, and Policy* 226–240 (2012).
Lee, Jieun, Foreign Direct Investment in Political Influence, Working Paper, 2018. https://www.internationalpoliticaleconomysociety.org/sites/default/files/paper-uploads/2018-10-28-21_42_07-leejieun@umich.edu.pdf.
Levmore, Saul, Voting with Intensity, 53 *Stanford Law Journal* 159 (2000).
McChesney, Fred S., Rent Extraction and Interest-Group Organization in a Coasean Model of Regulation, 20 *Journal of Legal Studies* 73–90 (1991).
Shin, Myungsoon, Youngjae Jin, Donald A. Gross, and Kihong Eom, Money Matters in Party-Centered Politics: Campaign Spending in Korean Congressional Elections, 24 *Electoral Studies* 85–101 (2005).
Vaishnav, Milan, Political Finance in India: Déjà Vu All Over Again, Carnegie Endowment for International Peace (2019)
Weintraub, Ellen L., and Samuel C. Brown, Following the Money: Campaign Finance Disclosure in India and the United States, 11 *Election Law Journal: Rules, Politics, and Policy* 241–266 (2012).

3

JAMMU & KASHMIR'S CONSTITUTIONAL STATUS

Constitutional Bargain and 'Erosion' of Article 370

Zaid Deva

3.1 Introduction

Knowledge and knowledge production can never be achieved in silos. Disciplines interact and mould each other in ways that make interdisciplinary studies not just essential but inevitable.[1] That is one of the purposes of this project – to highlight the importance of interdisciplinary legal research in the Indian context and enable future research on topics that have remained underexplored – and mine is a modest contribution to the set of chapters published in this volume.

In this chapter, I look at Kashmir from a constitutional lens[2] and specifically explore why scholarship on Kashmir will gain if constitutional realities of Kashmir are taken into account. By constitutional realities, I mean the nature and dynamics of constitutional systems in place in Kashmir before accession to India and the systems enacted post-accession.[3] One of the limitations of the existing constitutional scholarship on Kashmir is that any question on its constitutional status tends to inevitably and singularly focus on Article 370 of the Indian constitution.[4] In doing that, the constitution of 1939[5] (which governed Kashmir at the time of accession) and later on the presidential orders of 1950[6] and 1954[7] and the state constitution of 1957 (and how these constitutional documents interact with the Indian constitutional space)[8] are overlooked. Another problem (this is an outcome of the aforementioned limitation) that this strain of scholarship suffers from is that there is an inherent presumption that the relation between India and Kashmir is federal[9] in nature. And, federalism, even though it may be asymmetrical in the context of Kashmir as is argued, tends to be hierarchical.[10]

What is idiosyncratic about Kashmir's constitutional status that arguably might keep it outside the federal union? And, how would one go about describing (without over-doing) a Kashmir-centric constitutional account but at the same time remaining conscious of the Indian constitutional realities? While

DOI: 10.4324/9781003150565-4

there are multiple ways of doing this, in this chapter, I rely on bargain theory and set theory to first point out that constitutional orders[11] in Kashmir and India are independent of each other and at once interactive, but the latter one does not subsume the former,[12] and second, by 'eroding' Article 370, Kashmir's constitutional space is brought within the sphere of India's constitutional space leading up to the events of August 5, 2019. Even though the terminology in vogue has been erosion/amendments/changes of Article 370,[13] the object of analysis has remained this one provision and not the consequences its erosion has had on Kashmir's constitutional space or the skewed shifting of surplus value after such changes are imposed on the original bargain.

The scheme of the chapter is as follows: in Section 3.2, I describe the constitutional relations between Kashmir and India using bargain theory and make my argument that there are two legal orders at work, building on my previous work on the topic. In Section 3.3, I use set theory to illustrate how the two constitutional orders work independently of each other while at the same time interacting with each other. This is divided into six phases to study the tilt in the surplus allocation in favour of India that leads to slow and steady incorporation and dissolution of Kashmir's legal space in India. Section 3.4 concludes the discussion.

3.2 Sheikh, Nehru, and Bargain Theory

3.2.1 Law and History

We start, not from 1947 or 1935 but from 1939, when the constitution act of Jammu & Kashmir (J&K) was enacted.[14] This marked the ruler's 'first adventure to democratise the state'.[15] The constitution vested the ruler with inherent and absolute powers to make laws in the state. Even though the government of India Act of 1935[16] had no applicability, paramountcy of the British Crown operated vis-à-vis J&K through both informal and formal arrangements.[17] Therefore, internal matters were governed by the ruler, and subjects like foreign affairs and defence came under the jurisdiction of the British.[18] Even though the demarcation could be fluid at times, the roles were performed in two spaces – hence the establishment of two legal orders.

Until 1947, the two legal orders were interacting informally. With the implementation of the Cabinet mission plan through the Indian Independence Act, British paramountcy over the princely states ended, and the powers exercised by the British vis-à-vis princely states returned back to the states.[19] This logic applied to J&K as well – hence the need for standstill agreements.[20] With the end of paramountcy, the interface between the two legal orders ceases, and the two become separate from each other. From the end of paramountcy and the signing of accession, many have argued, including the Supreme Court (SC) in the *Prem Nath Kaul* case, that the state existed as an independent entity.[21] This is the point at which the bargain theory becomes relevant. Before proceeding, it's worth pointing out that even though the object of analysis here are the two legal orders, the interests that govern the bargain are those of Sheikh Abdullah and Jawaharlal Nehru. Even though Nehru's interests in integrating J&K in India were shared by many (the means differed though),[22] Sheikh's interests in J&K's accession to India were restricted to himself and his close aides in the National Conference.[23] Therefore, the two parties I use in describing Article 370 as a constitutional bargain are not India and J&K, but Nehru and Sheikh.

Foreseeing the consequences of a divided polity, the Indian state undertook a humongous task of integrating the princely states within the union.[24] The terms of the initial bargain were set by the Indian state by demanding instruments of assession from princely states that would vest India control over defence, foreign affairs, and communications.[25] Under duress, the ruler of J&K signed the Instrument of Accession (IoA) giving control to India over the three subjects.[26] But at the time the instrument was executed, the 1939 constitution that vested the ruler with absolute powers was still in force in J&K. So, what would become of the IoA? The J&K High Court answered this question in a lesser-known case by holding that the IoA only 'created' legislative power in the Indian dominion over the three subjects while the ruler continued to retain full ambit of the same power himself as well.[27] Therefore, as per Shagoo, no power was ceded to the union; rather, the IoA only led to a concurrent exercise of law-making over the three subjects. In the *Prem Nath Kaul* case, the SC, on similar lines, held that neither the IoA nor Article 370 affected the legislative, executive, or judicial powers of the ruler, which he possessed after the lapse of paramountcy.[28] In fact, the court also recognised that there are two independent legal orders at work by observing:

> It would not be permissible or legitimate to hold that, by implication, this Article sought to impose limitations on the plenary legislative powers of the Maharaja. These powers had been recognised and specifically provided by the Constitution Act of the State itself; and it was not, and could not have been, within the contemplation, or competence of the Constitution-makers to impinge even indirectly on the said powers.[29]

As I argue elsewhere, this implied that the two orders derived authority from different sources and were interlocked due to elements like the IoA or Article 370 without one order fully controlling (or subsuming) the other.[30] This acts as the premise of my argument and develops into how the J&K legal order was eventually and systemically subsumed in the Indian legal order.

By 1949, seeing no progress with the United Nations Security Council involvement in the Kashmir dispute, the governments of J&K and India began negotiations over a provision that would govern the relationship in the future constitutional setup.[31] Many drafts were discussed between the two sides, and the final draft that was passed in the Indian constituent assembly was very different from the first one proposed by the government of J&K.[32] It's worth noting that Article 370 is only a procedural provision and remains substantive only to the extent that it applies itself and Article 1 of the Indian constitution to J&K. It lays down a scheme for extending of Indian legal authority over J&K. For extending Indian legal authority in J&K in respect of subjects that are covered under the IoA, the Indian president is required to consult the state government before. And, for subjects that go beyond the IoA, concurrence of the state government is required. A similar drill is required to be followed for the Indian constitutional provisions: consultation with state government for provisions corresponding to the IoA and concurrence for provisions going beyond the IoA. Further, the provision also specifies that anything done under concurrence of the state government would be required to be placed before the constituent assembly of J&K (J&KCA) whenever it would convene for drafting the state constitution for any decision it may take thereon. Finally, when the constitution-making process would be over, it was envisaged that the J&KCA would recommend to the Indian president to cease the operation of Article 370 or continue its operation with modifications. Since no such recommendation was made, the Indian president has, from time to time ever since, employed Article 370 to extend the Indian jurisdiction over the state, and finally, the provision was abrogated in 2019.[33]

3.2.2 The Bargain

Now I turn to bargain theory and show how Article 370 establishes the bargaining zone by surplus allocation in the form of legislative competences and making provision for application of the Indian constitution in J&K. A functional account of the bargain theory would mean that two parties enter into a contract because both gain from such bargain, thus creating a net surplus for each other.[34] To agree to a bargain, the parties have to identify their reservation points and the bargaining zone.

Reservation point is the maximum amount that a buyer and the minimum amount that a seller would be willing to pay for a service.[35] And, if the reservation point of the buyer is higher than the seller's, the distance between the two points is called the bargaining zone.[36] Therefore, the bargaining zone is fixed by the reservation points of both the parties.[37] For example, if A is willing to pay 5 lacs for a car to B, while B prefers anything over 4 lacs, then the bargaining zone of 1 lac is created between the two prices. The reservation point for Nehru is defined in the IoA (since the subjects enumerated in the union list of the Indian constitution mostly pertain to the three subjects[38]) and includes the probability of widening the quantum of accession eventually.[39] For Sheikh, the reservation points are also the same three subjects as he understands the limitations of his position as the prime minister and the need for patronage of the Indian state for continuing his authority.[40] Both reservation points are reflected in Article 370 as, one, it reinforces the IoA's distribution of competences, and two, at the same time, it provides pathways for widening the jurisdiction of the Indian state. Looking at Article 370, the bargaining range is the maximum value desired by Nehru and the minimum value attainable by him against the maximum value desired by Sheikh and the minimum value attainable by him.[41] Quite contrary to the example of A and B stated above, the reservation points of both the parties are flexible and are liable to change as both wanted to avoid a no-bargain scenario when Article 370 was being drafted.

The reservation points of Nehru and Sheikh are set off against the costs of 'No bargain'. Here, the costs of no bargain are the very ground realities of J&K[42] and the possibility of holding of a plebiscite in the region that has the potential to threaten both Nehru and Sheikh's positions.[43] Hence, the individual interests that define the bargain and get transposed on the two legal orders are, in essence, attempts at self-preservation. In case of a no-bargain scenario, for Nehru, India loses a strategic region. For Sheikh, in case a plebiscite is held, and J&K votes in favour of Pakistan (which many suspected it would), he loses his position of power as in his own words, he expected a 'short shrift' from Jinnah in case J&K went to Pakistan.[44] The bargain here is, therefore, the aggregate of the costs of no bargain that are saved and shared between both the parties. The bargain zone, therefore, becomes the respective minimum target surplus value possible for both the parties, having taken the costs of no bargain into consideration. Also referred to as the zone of possible agreement (ZOPA), it is the range in which the respective minimum targets of the parties overlap. When ZOPA is broad, the parties design strategies to influence distribution in the ZOPA range. As the ZOPA range reduces, it becomes more difficult to identify terms of the bargain in which both gain.[45] The changing ZOPA from a broad to a narrow one and finally to a position of negative bargaining zone (NBZ) is identified post 1953.

3.2.3 Implementing the Bargain

With the passage of Article 370 in the Indian constituent assembly, the processes of constitution-making in J&K were initiated.[46] On the eve of the adoption of the Indian constitution, the Regent of J&K issued a proclamation which read as follows: *[T]he Constitution of India shortly to be adopted by the Constituent Assembly of India shall in so far as it is applicable to J&K govern the constitutional relationship between this State and the contemplated Union of India.*[47] This has two implications: one, the Indian constitution, in so far as it is applicable i.e., Article 370, performs the function of governing the constitutional relations between India and J&K; two, the Indian constitution does not comprise J&K's constitutional space, and therefore, J&K cannot be considered as a federal unit (since in federal relations generally, the legal order tends to remain the same[48]). But, are the two legal orders created as a result of Article 370, or do the constitutions exist in a continuum? What I mean by that is, is the new legal order in J&K succeeding the previous one just like the Indian legal order enacted in 1950 replaced the Government of India (GOI) Act of 1935?

First, the origins and the source of authority are different. While in the case of India, the source of authority for the creation of the new legal order was the Indian Independence Act of 1947,[49] in the case of J&K, the source of authority was the ruler and his proclamation calling for the J&KCA.[50] Second, similar to how the Indian constitution ended the authority of the GOI Act of 1935 and the Indian Independence Act of 1947,[51] the state constitution of 1957 ended the constitution act of 1939 and abolished monarchy.[52] Article 370 could not have envisaged to do that as it was merely a procedural provision and was limited in scope and content. Finally, the seamless transition of sovereignty from the princely order to the J&KCA does not involve the Indian legal order. I will unpack this point below using Article 370.

The provision makes a distinction between subjects based on whether the state government's 'consultation' or 'concurrence' is required. And, the consultation–concurrence distinction is premised on the distribution of competences enumerated in the IoA. Subjects that have been transferred to the union by the ruler under his sovereign decision-making are beyond the review of the J&KCA (however, the J&KCA did revisit the 1950 order and made alterations to the subjects that had been applied on consultation of the state government, which were technically speaking outside the authority of the J&KCA[53]). Whereas for subjects other than the ones mentioned in the IoA, for which concurrence is required, the J&KCA is the final arbiter. This implies that as sovereignty shifted form the monarch to the J&KCA, there was, in some sense, a continuity and a discontinuity as well. In so far, Article 370, under the assumption that the sovereign's decision need not be revisited by the future sovereign, made a distinction between consultation and concurrence based on the nature of subjects to be applied to the state, and there exists a seamless transition of sovereign authority from the monarch to the J&KCA. But, since a sovereign cannot limit a future sovereign's authority and, in that sense, marks a discontinuity between two consecutive sovereigns, to that extent also, the J&KCA fulfils the criteria of a sovereign since it did revisit the subjects applied on consultation of the state government and made some alterations to them. Not just restricted to making changes, under the J&KCA's authority, the 1950 order was revoked and superseded, and then all the subjects applied to the state through the 1954 order were applied on concurrence of the J&KCA. Therefore, whatever distinction existed because of the concurrence/consultation processes were at once done away with, when the 1954 order was passed in the J&KCA.[54]

Therefore, the constitutional regime existing in J&K comprises the state constitution of 1957 and the 1954 order. It's worth noting that as per the Regent's proclamation, the 1954 order is purposed for governing the constitutional relations with the Indian union.[55] This means that the provisions contained in the 1954 order exist in J&K's constitutional space but are not indigenous to it. There are two kinds of provisions in the 1954 order: (1) provisions that are applied to J&K without any modifications and (2) provisions that are applied with modifications and exceptions and, as a consequence, are not in force in the Indian constitutional space. The existence of the two constitutional orders and the distinction between the provisions in the 1954 order will become clearer with the help of the set theory and Venn diagrams.

3.3 Set Theory and the Two Legal Orders

Set theory[56] is applied to formulate the genesis of the bargain relation between India and J&K and the evolving bargain relation between the two. Set theory complements the argument about bargain theory because it allows us to mark a distinction between the two legal orders and illustrate how they exist independent of each other while at the same time showing how the surplus application keeps tilting towards India constantly. The use of set theory also allows us to make a distinction between the two kinds of provisions in the 1954 order as pointed before and situate them in the two legal spaces. As sets are 'well-determined collections',[57] the elements included in each set studied here are the constitutional documents governing the two entities. The point here being that J&K's constitutional set is not a subset of the Indian constitutional set.[58] Another point to be noted here is that even though there might be multiple overarching documents governing the two spaces, legislations, executive orders, and ordinances, I consider them part of the constitutional order, and therefore, they are included in the two constitutional regimes.

Coming to the phases in which the set theory is employed: Phase I is situated in the pre-independence phase, which was governed by formal (by formal arrangements I mean treaties, etc.) and informal arrangements between the Ruler of J&K and the British Crown; Phase II – the lapse of paramountcy and how it impacts the two legal orders; Phase III – the execution of the IoA and the resultant bargain along with the distribution of surplus value through Article 370; Phase IV looks at the relationship by taking into account the 1954 order and the state constitution; Phase V is the phase of the dissolution of J&KCA and the ensuing 'erosion' of Article 370; and Phase VI is the abrogation of Article 370 and how it impacts the original bargain.

3.3.1 Phase I

In Phase I, the elements of two sets include the proto-constitutional documents governing J&K and India.

Set I – {Government of India Act, 1935}
Set J&K – {Constitution Act of 1939}

Even though both exist independently of each other, paramountcy connects the two through formal and informal arrangements. Therefore, the intersection of the two sets includes paramountcy that itself entails authority over defence and foreign affairs of J&K (Figure 3.1).[59]

The two sets, when looked at from the point of the legal orders that exist, share the same law and policy on foreign affairs and defence. So, even though the princely states and British Indian provinces were conceptually very different from each other, on matters such as these, the two were on the same plane and

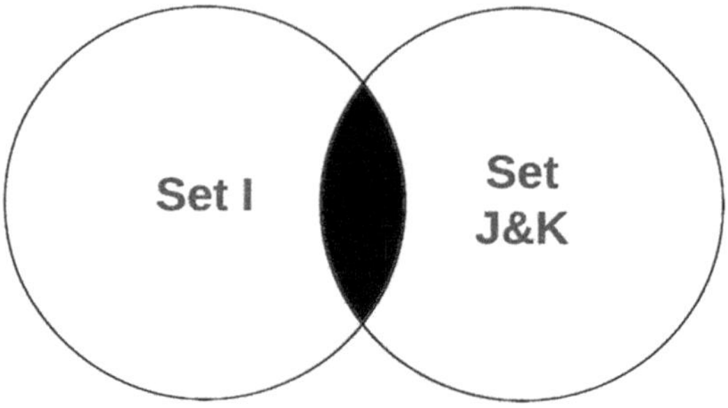

FIGURE 3.1 Illustration of the intersection of the two sets, I and J&K, during the colonial rule.

hence this intersection. Apart from control on the two subjects, paramountcy also ensured that the princely states functioned under the overall supervision of the British government. So even though legally speaking, the two had separate rules of government, practically speaking, both were under the control of the British (the control was direct in the case of provinces and indirect in the case of princely states).[60]

3.3.2 Phase II

This phase covers the period in which the British paramountcy had ended and just before the IoA had been signed by the ruler. As pointed out by many scholars,[61] and by the SC[62] as well, this was the period in which J&K existed as an independent entity since its legal linkages with the British had ended as a consequence of the Indian Independence Act. Recall that paramountcy was not inherited by either of the dominions – hence the need for the standstill agreements. While J&K was able to execute one with Pakistan, India wanted more

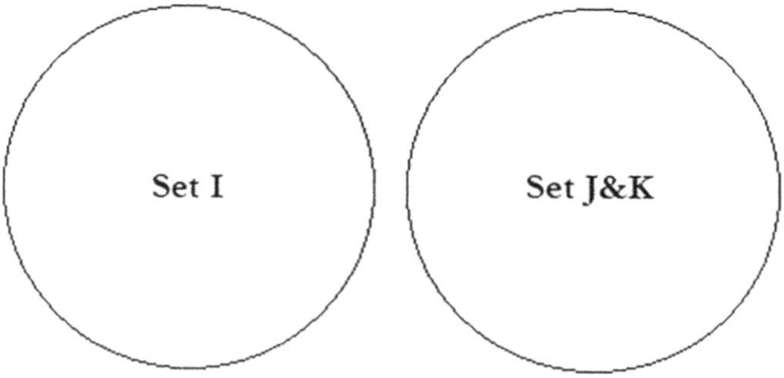

FIGURE 3.2 Illustration of the disappearance of the grey area implying the end of paramountcy and those informal and formal arrangements that kept J&K under the control of the British.

deliberations.[63] Therefore, in this period, the sets of the two legal orders would appear as follows (Figure 3.2):

Set I – {Government of India Act, 1935 and the Indian Independence Act, 1947}
Set J&K – {Constitution Act of 1939}

The separation of the two legal orders in this phase also buttresses the point that it is not Article 370 that gives rise to the two legal orders, but the very existence of two legal orders necessitate the creation of a provision like Article 370. The two sets, therefore, in this phase become a disjoint set.[64]

Set I ∩ Set J&K = ∅

3.3.3 *Phase III*

The third phase looks at IoA and its impact on the two legal orders. Legally speaking, the IoA only led to transfer of law-making powers on the three subjects to the Indian dominion.[65] As per Shagoo, however, it wasn't a transfer of law-making powers (since the ruler retained these powers) but only creation of legislative power in the Indian parliament.[66] In this phase, the two legal orders start interacting again, much like they did in Phase I. The difference here being that the interaction was governed by a formal instrument and not by an informal arrangement. This also implied that the interaction would be limited since the limits would be imposed by the formal instrument, whereas informal arrangements would keep the limits fluid. The two sets would comprise (Figure 3.3):

Set I – {Government of India Act, 1935 and the Indian Independence Act, 1947}
Set J&K – {Constitution Act of 1939, relevant parts of the GOI Act of 1935}

Therefore, Set I ∩ Set J&K = {relevant portions of the GOI Act of 1935}

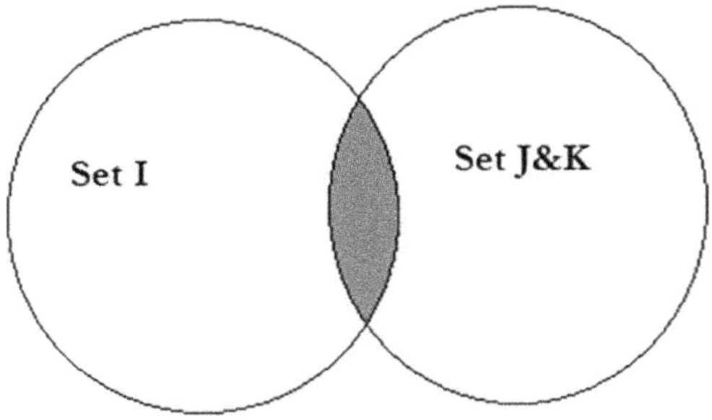

FIGURE 3.3 Illustration of how the India–J&K shared constitutional space comes into being in the aftermath of the execution of the IoA. Here the grey area represents the same shared constitutional space.

Even though the IoA makes this linkage possible, the shared constitutional space is not occupied by this instrument alone. In the main, this space gets occupied by the intersection of the two sets i.e., the relevant parts of the GOI Act of 1935 that become applicable to J&K as a consequence of the IoA.[67] Once Article 370 is inserted into the Indian constitution and the 1950 order is passed by the Indian president on consultation with the state government, there is a change in the elements of the two sets and the shared constitutional space. But, as the SC has pointed out in the *Prem Nath Kaul* case, the status of J&K after the IoA and after the insertion of Article 370 remains the same.[68] Therefore, the area occupied by the shared constitutional space is constant because the 1950 order was complying with the IoA and Article 370.

The two sets, however, reflect as follows:

Set I – {Constitution of India, 1950}
Set J&K – {Constitution Act of 1939, Article 370 of the Constitution of India, 1950 (1950 order)}

There are certain modifications that are made to the provisions of the Indian constitution through the 1950 order, which do not exist in the Indian constitutional space, but since the 1950 order got superseded by the 1954 order, I consider the impact of such modifications on the two legal orders in the next phase.

3.3.4 Phase IV

In the fourth phase, the elements of J&K's set are replaced by the postcolonial constitutions. The 1950 order gets superseded by the 1954 order, which increases the quantum of the accession by increasing the legislative power of the Indian parliament. Therefore, the two sets appear as follows:

Set I – {Constitution of India, 1950}
Set J&K – {The Presidential Order of 1954, Constitution of J&K, 1957}

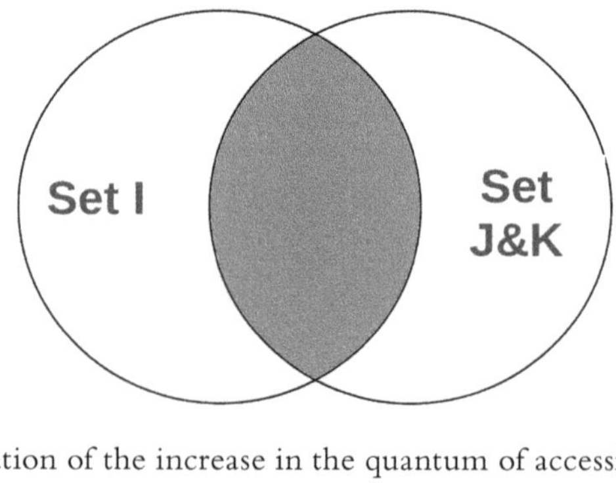

FIGURE 3.4 Illustration of the increase in the quantum of accession as a result of the enactment of the 1954 order and the state constitution of 1957.

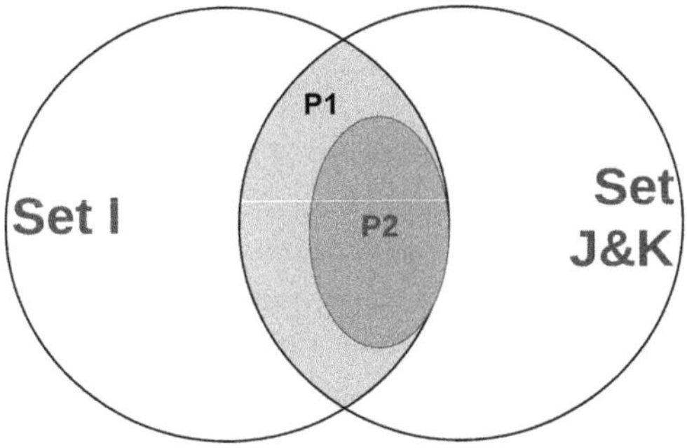

FIGURE 3.5 Illustration of the difference between the P1 and P2. Even though both form part of the shared constitutional space, certain features of P2 demand this distinction from P1.

And, the intersection (the grey area in Figure 3.4) of the two sets yields those provisions of the Indian constitution that are applicable to J&K without any modifications (P1) plus the provisions that are applied with modifications (P2). The latter part of the provisions enjoy a dual existence. Even though they are lumped together in the term 'Constitution of India as applicable to J&K', functionally, they are not part of the Indian constitution and do not find place in the Indian constitutional space. Therefore, I have represented them separately from those provisions that have been applied without modifications (Figure 3.5).

Set I ∩ Set J&K = {P1 + P2}

P1 here also includes Article 370. Because of this distinction between P1 and P2, Article 370 could not have been employed to affect any change to Article 367 (that formed part of P2) that had the effect of changing Article 370 itself.[69] This is not to say that Article 370 can be used to change the P1 provisions once they have been applied. In fact, under Article 370, there is no scope for promulgating amendment orders.[70] These powers have been read into the provision using a statute that remains an extrinsic aid to interpretation.[71] It's also worth pointing out that even though P2 provisions are seen as amendments to the Indian constitution (like Article 35A), for J&K's constitutional space, they are part of the constitution as originally applied in 1954 and, hence, are not considered as amendments but an original provision of the constitution.

3.3.5 Phase V

In Phase V, the systemic erosion of Article 370 is studied and its impact on the two legal orders. With the execution of more than 50 presidential amendment orders, the constitutional space of J&K was squeezed out, and J&K's legal authority was also limited. In its place, the Indian constitution and the Indian legal authority came to occupy the space. This erosion is effected by expanding the scope and content of the 1954 order, and at the same time, limiting the content and authority of the state constitution. Therefore, the shared constitutional space gets burgeoning, and the original bargain is replaced by a NBZ. In essence, every amendment that was passed post dissolution of the J&KCA amounted to a unilateral decision in violation of the original bargain. As the surplus of J&K eroded, so did the ZOPA incrementally reduce. When ZOPA reduces from a broad range to a narrow range, negotiations break down, and the bargain moves into the NBZ (Figure 3.6).

With the application of the second amendment order of 1958[72] and the second amendment order of 1965,[73] the entire Indian constitution (as it then stood) was applied to J&K while retaining the P2 provisions and the J&K's own constitution. Once this happens, J&K's own legal order as a separate entity ceases to exist, while P1 becomes Set I. The Set J&K becomes part of the Set I. Even though there are provisions of the constitution that are still not applicable to J&K, its existence as a separate set ends because the rules of the game are changed at this stage. J&K's legal authority gets steadily reduced, while, at the same time, the Indian legal authority over J&K is systematically increased. Even though the set elements remain the same, the quantum of the 1954 order keeps steadily increasing. In many ways, the 1954 order is repurposed from governing constitutional relations between J&K and India to becoming the dominant constitution in J&K's constitutional space (Figure 3.7).

As more and more amendment orders are enacted, J&K's legal space shrinks. Terming this process as 'erosion of Article 370', therefore, is a mask that keeps this sinister and systemic process hidden (Figure 3.8).

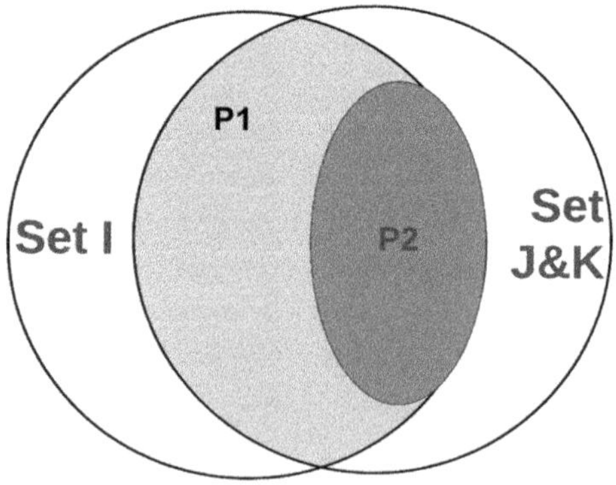

FIGURE 3.6 Illustration of the burgeoning of the shared constitutional space and the squeezing out of the J&K's own constitutional identity.

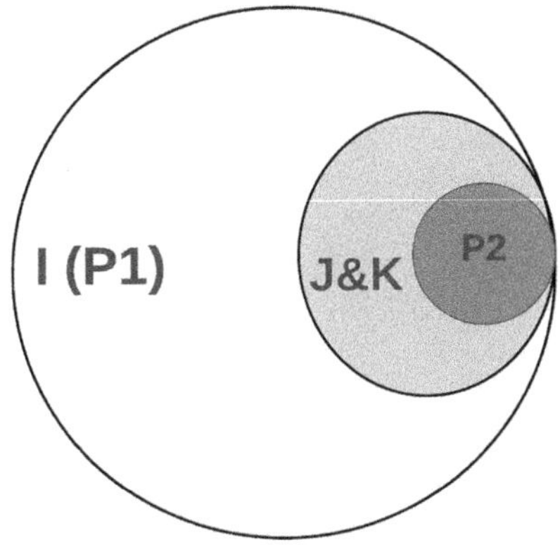

FIGURE 3.7 Illustration of how the J&K legal order was incorporated in the Indian one.

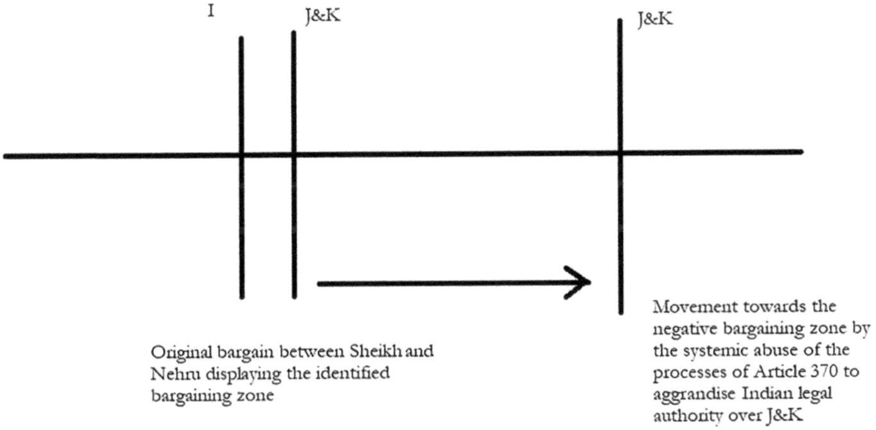

FIGURE 3.8 Illustration of the establishment of the NBZ.

3.3.6 Phase VI

The Phase VI looks at the post-abrogation of Article 370 impact on Set I and subset J&K. Article 370, as such, has no implications since it is a procedural provision and not a substantive one. Therefore, what is abrogated, in essence, are the state constitution of 1957 and the 1954 order. Here, the bargain formally enters the NBZ. The subset J&K disappears here, and the Set I reigns supreme (Figure 3.9).

It's worth pointing out that had just Article 370 been abrogated, then the two sets would have become disjointed once again on the lines of Phase II. This is because the shared constitutional space would no longer exist. But since abrogation of Article 370 was accompanied (or rather primarily driven) by the

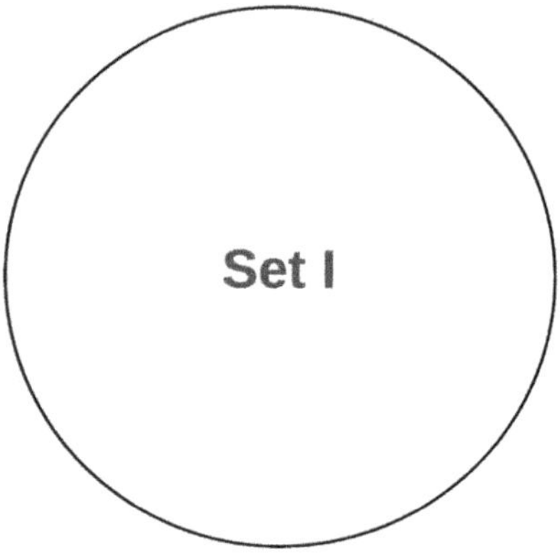

FIGURE 3.9 Illustration of the end of J&K's legal order and the formal occupation of the legal space by the Indian legal order.

motivation to abrogate the state constitutional law and apply the Indian constitution in totality, J&K's own constitutional space disappears as a consequence.

3.4 Conclusion

The ideal outcome for Nehru would have been to have J&K merged into the Union, and the ideal outcome for Sheikh would have been to continue J&K's complete autonomy after the British relinquished its suzerainty. The compelling conditions for both made them come together in a strategic cooperative bargain in the form of Article 370. Article 370 involved erosion in individual gains (Nehru would have preferred wider application of federal jurisdiction, and Sheikh would have preferred autonomous status for J&K), but by inserting Article 370 and through it limiting the Indian legal authority, a bargaining range was identified. However, this range subsequently entered the NBZ once Sheikh was dismissed from office and arrested, allowing Nehru to initiate the 'erosion' of Article 370. As I pointed out in this chapter, terming this abuse as merely 'erosion of Article 370' is misleading since it masks what actually is happening underneath, i.e., aggrandisement of the Indian legal authority at the cost of J&K's legal authority.

Notes

1 Lydia Nkansah and Victor Chimbwanda, 'Interdisciplinary Approach to Legal Scholarship: A Blend from the Qualitative Paradigm' (2016) 3(1) *Asian Journal of Legal Education* 56, 59–60.

2 In recent times, there has been a significant literature on Kashmir from an international law lens, but constitutional analysis of the dispute has remained minimal. Exception to this remains Noorani's works in the Indian context and Hayat's

recent work in the Pakistani context. See, generally, A. G. Noorani, *Article 370: A Constitutional History of Jammu & Kashmir* (Oxford University Press 2011) and Javaid Hayat, *Azad Jammu & Kashmir: Polity, Politics, and Power-Sharing* (Oxford University Press 2020). On international law analyses of the Kashmir dispute and its varied facets, see, Fozia Lone, *Historical Title, Self-determination, and the Kashmir Question* (Brill Nijhoff 2018).

3 For J&K's Instrument of Accession, see, Venkatesh Nayak, 'The Backstory of Article 370: A True Copy of J&K's Instrument of Accession' The Wire (August 5, 2019) https://thewire.in/history/public-first-time-jammu-kashmirs-instrument-accession-india accessed December 20, 2021.

4 See Madhav Khosla, *The Indian Constitution* (Oxford University Press 2012) 74. See also Louise Tillin, 'Asymmetric Federalism' in Sujit Choudhry, Madhav Khosla and Pratap B. Mehta (eds.), *Oxford Handbook of the Indian Constitution* (Oxford University Press 2017) 576–578.

5 See The Constitution Act of 1939 in MK Teng, RK Bhatt & S Kaul, *Kashmir: Legal & Historical Documents* (Light & Life Publishers 1977) 66.

6 See The Constitution (Application to Jammu & Kashmir) Order 1950 as quoted in Ministry of States, Government of India, White Paper on Indian States (1950) https://archive.org/details/in.ernet.dli.2015.207474/mode/2up accessed December 21, 2021 378–383.

7 See The Constitution (Application to Jammu & Kashmir) Order 1954 https://egazette.nic.in/WriteReadData/1954/E-2227-1954-0111-103041.pdf accessed December 23, 2021.

8 For an analysis of how the documents interact, see Zaid Deva, 'Basic without Structure?: The Presidential Order of 1954 and the Indo-Jammu & Kashmir Constitutional Relationship' (2020) 4(2) *Indian Law Review* 180–194.

9 Federalism, as understood in the Indian context, which sought to create a unified and a centralised legal order, see, Khosla (n 4) and Tillin (n 4).

10 See State Bank of India v Santosh Gupta & Others (2017) 2 SCC 538 where the court concluded that J&K's constitution was subordinate in nature to the Indian constitution. Anand, in his commentary on the J&K constitution, goes one step further and points out that power to 'confer' special status on J&K flows from Section 2 of the Indian constitution; see, Ashok Desai, 'The Constitution of Jammu & Kashmir: Its Developments and Comments by A. S. Anand' (1995) 37(3) *Journal of the Indian Law Institute* 409. This completely overlooks the implications of the IoA on the future constitutional relationship and misses the point that the special status was not conferred but rather was inherent in the state or at least negotiated between the two parties.

11 I use the terms 'constitutional orders', 'legal orders', and 'constitutional spaces' interchangeably to mean the spaces that the constitutions create in which the legal regime exists.

12 Provincial constitutions tend to form part of the federal legal order; see, Cheryl Saunders, 'The Constitutional Credentials of State Constitutions' (2011) 42 *Rutgers Law Journal* 853. However, this logic cannot be extended to India–J&K shared constitutional space.

13 The recalibration of the relationship through abuse of Article 370 was first described as 'erosion' by Jawaharlal Nehru; see, Jawaharlal Nehru on the 'Erosion' of Article 370, Lok Sabha, vol XII Lok Sabha Debates, November 27, 1963.

14 See The Constitution Act of 1939 (n 5).

15 Desai (n 10) 408.

16 Government of India Act 1935, http://www.legislation.gov.uk/ukpga/Geo5and1Edw8/26/2/contents> accessed December 21, 2021.

17 On paramountcy, see, Report of the Indian States Committee 1928–1929 (London, 1929).

18 Josef Korbel, *Danger in Kashmir* (Gulshan Books 2021) 14.

19 See Indian Independence Act 1947, s 7 http://www.legislation.gov.uk/ukpga/Geo6/10-11/30/contents accessed December 12, 2021.
20 Had the paramountcy been inherited by the Indian or the Pakistani state, then there would have been no reason to sign standstill agreements with the two dominions calling for continuation of existing arrangements until a final settlement could be made. While Pakistan agreed to a standstill agreement, India wanted more deliberations; see, VP Menon, *Integration of the Indian States* (Orient BlackSwan 1956) 395. For J&K-Pakistan standstill agreement, see, Teng et al. (n 5) 231.
21 Prem Nath Kaul v State of Jammu & Kashmir (1959) Supp (2) SCR 270.
22 See Nehru (n 13). Also see, Ayynagar's speech to the Rajya Sabha where he stated that Article 370 could be 'wiped off the Constitution' as quoted in Sheikh Abdullah's letter to Nehru dated June 28, 1953, in Noorani (n 2) 230.
23 Sheikh Abdullah, Jammu & Kashmir Constituent Assembly Debates, vol I (November 5, 1951). On why Sheikh's stance was limited to him and his party ilk, see, generally, Pandit Prem Nath Bazaz, *The History of Struggle for Freedom in Kashmir* (Naya Hindustan Press 1954).
24 See generally, Menon (n 20); Also see, White Paper on Indian States (n 6).
25 See White Paper on Indian States; id. This also meant that the relationship between the princely states and the Indian dominion was inherently unequal.
26 See the IoA (n 3). Also see, Puranlal Lakhanpal, *Essential Documents and Notes on Kashmir Dispute* (2nd edn., International Books 1965) 47.
27 Rehman Shagoo and Ors. v. State of Jammu and Kashmir 1958 CriLJ 885.
28 Prem Nath Kaul (n 21).
29 id.
30 Deva (n 8) 179–180.
31 See Noorani (n 2) 50–63.
32 See the first draft of the provision as prepared by the government of J&K in id. 52.
33 See Noorani (n 2) 303–316.
34 *See* Todd Lowry, 'Bargain and Contract Theory in Law and Economics' (1976) 10(1) *Journal of Economic Issues* 6.
35 Russell Korokbin, 'A positive Theory of Legal Negotiation' (1999) 88 *The Georgetown Law Journal* 1792.
36 id. 1792.
37 id. 1797.
38 The idea being that J&K should almost be similarly placed with respect to the Union as other states.
39 Of course, the reservation point for Nehru increases as he eventually demands widening of the quantum of the accession i.e., vesting of more subjects in the union and applicability of more provisions of the Indian constitution. See Sheikh Abdullah's letter to Maulana Azad dated July 16, 1953, as quoted in Noorani (n 2) 232–236.
40 On Sheikh's precarious position as the prime minister, see, Aijaz Ashraf Wani, *What Happened to Governance in Kashmir* (Oxford University Press 2019) 117.
41 Korokbin (n 35).
42 See Bazaz (n 23).
43 As Noorani has pointed out, Nehru was all long dishonest about plebiscite in Kashmir, see, A. G. Noorani, 'Review: How and Why Nehru and Abdullah Fell Out' (1999) 34(5) *Economic and Political Weekly* 268.
44 Wani (n 40) 117.
45 *See* Mariusz Jerzy Golecki, 'Bargaining within the Shadow of Fairness: Economic Analysis of Article 4.109 of the Principles of European Contract Law' (2009) 4 *International Journal of Economic Policy Studies* 162.
46 Proclamation of the Regent calling for a constituent assembly in J&K, 1951 as quoted in Noorani (n 2) 95–96.
47 Proclamation for the State of Jammu & Kashmir, November 25, 1949, as quoted in White Paper on Indian States (n 6) 371–372.

48 Cheryl Saunders, 'The Constitutional Credentials of State Constitutions' (2011) 42 *Rutgers Law Journal* 854.
49 See Indian Independence Act of 1947 (n 19).
50 See the Regent's proclamation (n 47).
51 See Article 395 of the Indian constitution. By ending the authority of these colonial-era legislations, the constitution marked a break from the colonial legal order.
52 See Section 157 of the J&K constitution. On the abolition of monarchy, see, Mirza Beg, vol I J&K Constituent Assembly Debates (November 10, 1952) and The Constitution (Application to Jammu & Kashmir) Order, 15 November 1952 passed under Article 370 (3) in Noorani (n 2) 225.
53 Many subjects that were applied to J&K on consultation of the state government were modified with the 1954 order by the J&KCA as pointed out by the SC in the *Prem Nath Kaul* case (n 21).
54 See the preamble to the Constitution (Application to Jammu & Kashmir) Order, 1954 (n 7).
55 See the Regent's proclamation (n 47).
56 Joan Bagaria, '*Set Theory*' Stanford Encyclopedia of Philosophy https://plato.stanford.edu/entries/set-theory/ accessed December 21, 2021.
57 id.
58 A subset is a set whose elements are part of another set as well. For example, if A includes 1, 2, and 3 and B includes 1, 2, 3, and 4, then A is called a subset of B.
59 See Korbel (n 14). Intersection of sets implies the common elements comprising two sets.
60 See generally the White Paper on Indian states (n 6).
61 Noorani (n 2).
62 Prem Nath Kaul (n 21).
63 See Teng (n 20); Also see Menon (n 20).
64 A disjointed set is a pair of sets in which none of the elements are common.
65 Prem Nath Kaul (n 21).
66 Rehman Shagoo (n 27).
67 See clause 2 of the IoA (n 3).
68 Prem Nath Kaul (n 21).
69 See 'The Constitution (Application to Jammu and Kashmir) Order 2019' (August 5, 2019) http://egazette.nic.in/WriteReadData/2019/210049.pdf accessed December 22, 2021.
70 The 'erosion' of Article 370 has been carried out by promulgating such amendment orders. See Noorani (n 2) 337–388.
71 Sampat Prakash v The State of Jammu and Kashmir and Anr. 1969) 2 SCR 365.
72 See Noorani (n 2) 339.
73 See Noorani (n 2) 351.

Bibliography

A. G. Noorani, *Article 370: A Constitutional History of Jammu & Kashmir* (Oxford University Press 2011)

A. G. Noorani, 'Review: How and Why Nehru and Abdullah Fell Out' (1999) 34(5) *Economic and Political Weekly* 268.

Aijaz Ashraf Wani, *What Happened to Governance in Kashmir* (Oxford University Press 2019) 117.

Ashok Desai, 'The Constitution of Jammu & Kashmir: Its Developments and Comments by A. S. Anand' (1995) 37(3) *Journal of the Indian Law Institute* 409.

Cheryl Saunders, 'The Constitutional Credentials of State Constitutions' (2011) 42 *Rutgers Law Journal* 853.

Fozia Lone, *Historical Title, Self-Determination, and the Kashmir Question* (Brill Nijhoff 2018).
Government of India Act 1935, http://www.legislation.gov.uk/ukpga/Geo5and1Edw8/26/2/contents, accessed December 21, 2021.
Indian Independence Act 1947, s 7, http://www.legislation.gov.uk/ukpga/Geo6/10-11/30/contents, accessed December 12, 2021.
Javaid Hayat, *Azad Jammu & Kashmir: Polity, Politics, and Power-Sharing* (Oxford University Press 2020).
Jawaharlal Nehru on the 'Erosion' of Article 370, Lok Sabha, vol XII Lok Sabha Debates, November 27, 1963.
Joan Bagaria, '*Set Theory*' Stanford Encyclopedia of Philosophy, https://plato.stanford.edu/entries/set-theory/, accessed December 21, 2021.
Josef Korbel, *Danger in Kashmir* (Gulshan Books 2021) 14.
Louise Tillin, 'Asymmetric Federalism' in Sujit Choudhry, Madhav Khosla and Pratap B. Mehta (eds.), *Oxford Handbook of the Indian Constitution* (Oxford University Press 2017) 576–578.
Lydia Nkansah and Victor Chimbwanda, 'Interdisciplinary Approach to Legal Scholarship: A Blend from the Qualitative Paradigm' (2016) 3(1) *Asian Journal of Legal Education* 56, 59–60.
Madhav Khosla, *The Indian Constitution* (Oxford University Press 2012) 74.
Mariusz Jerzy Golecki, 'Bargaining within the Shadow of Fairness: Economic Analysis of Article 4.109 of the Principles of European Contract Law' (2009) 4 *International Journal of Economic Policy Studies* 162.
Mirza Beg, vol I J&K Constituent Assembly Debates (November 10, 1952).
Pandit Prem Nath Bazaz, *The History of Struggle for Freedom* (Naya Hindustan Press 1954).
Prem Nath Kaul v State of Jammu & Kashmir (1959) Supp (2) SCR 270.
Puranlal Lakhanpal, *Essential Documents and Notes on Kashmir Dispute* (2nd edn., International Books 1965) 47.
Rehman Shagoo and Ors. v. State of Jammu and Kashmir 1958 CriLJ 885.
Report of the Indian States Committee 1928–1929 (London, 1929).
Russell Korokbin, 'A Positive Theory of Legal Negotiation' (1999) 88 *The Georgetown Law Journal* 1792.
Sampat Prakash v The State of Jammu and Kashmir and Anr. 1969) 2 SCR 365.
Sheikh Abdullah, Jammu & Kashmir Constituent Assembly Debates, vol I (5 November 1951).
State Bank of India v Santosh Gupta & Others (2017) 2 SCC 538.
The Constitution (Application to Jammu and Kashmir) Order 2019 (August 5, 2019), http://egazette.nic.in/WriteReadData/2019/210049.pdf, accessed December 22, 2021.
The Constitution (Application to Jammu & Kashmir) Order 1950 as quoted in Ministry of States, Government of India, White Paper on Indian States (1950), https://archive.org/details/in.ernet.dli.2015.207474/mode/2up, accessed December 21, 2021 378–383.
The Constitution (Application to Jammu & Kashmir) Order 1954, https://egazette.nic.in/WriteReadData/1954/E-2227-1954-0111-103041.pdf, accessed December 23, 2021.
The Constitution Act of 1939 in MK Teng, RK Bhatt & S Kaul, *Kashmir: Legal & Historical Documents* (Light & Life Publishers 1977) 66.

Todd Lowry, 'Bargain and Contract Theory in Law and Economics' (1976) 10(1) *Journal of Economic Issues* 6.

Venkatesh Nayak, 'The Backstory of Article 370: A True Copy of J&K's Instrument of Accession' The Wire (August 5, 2019), https://thewire.in/history/public-first-time-jammu-kashmirs-instrument-accession-india, accessed December 20, 2021.

VP Menon, *Integration of the Indian States* (Orient BlackSwan 1956) 395.

Zaid Deva, 'Basic without Structure?: The Presidential Order of 1954 and the Indo-Jammu & Kashmir Constitutional Relationship' (2020) 4(2) *Indian Law Review* 180–194.

4

VIOLENCE IN PUBLIC AND PRIVATE SPACES

A Behavioural Economic Analysis of Women-Specific Legislation in India

Rasananda Panda and Aneri Patel

> Human law becomes the law of the time, and the law of the moment becomes the law of human beings. During the period of transition, the lives of the people who are key to the change go haywire.
>
> – Volga, *The Liberation of Sita*

4.1 Introduction

Ancient Indian scriptures worshiped women as the embodiment of 'Shakti' or power. Sanskrit shlokas conveyed that societies where women were respected prospered. Mythological insights also reveal the position of respect and reverence Indian women enjoyed in the ancient Indian society.[1] The *Rig Veda* identified many women sages as treasurers of knowledge and foresight. Hindu and Buddhist texts during Indus Valley civilization revealed liberal views on marital sex. Women had inheritance rights, which were exercised at the time of their marriage. Violent practices like dowry did not exist at the time, and both sexes seemed to enjoy equal status in the society.

During the post-Vedic period, however, *Manusmriti* – an ancient legal text – was translated by Sir William Jones and came to form the basis of the Hindu law. It dichotomized the private and public spheres, confining women to the former, and was responsible for the derogatory position accorded to them in society. Women were portrayed as dependent and requiring constant protection by men in their lives. Unmarried, menstruating women were ostracized and considered religiously polluted. Repercussions of Imperialism and the Bible shaped the conservative norms, which exist in the modern republic of India. The strong influence of Islamic dominance also contributed to this hegemonic heterosexuality and oppression of women.

DOI: 10.4324/9781003150565-5

These internalized misogynist beliefs formed the backbone of patriarchy in India and were further reinforced by the presence of a complex caste–class nexus. Cultural forces, which existed to preserve this patriarchy, committed violence in the name of tradition to maintain male dominance and female subjugation in the society. Violence was thus rooted in historically unequal power relations between men and women.[2]

The women's movement in India began as a social reform movement back in the 19th century. In the post-independence era, the movement concerned itself with issues of violence against women. National discourse of increasing poverty and class differentiation till then had excluded gender-related dialogue in the country and rendered women powerless victims of systemic discrimination and violence.[3]

Legislative power was used as a dominant tool to tackle various forms of oppression prevalent in the Indian subcontinent. It was prominent in addressing the women's question and in bringing about constitutional equality by granting women the right to education, to vote and entry into the professional landscape. Indian women were now permitted to actively participate in public spaces, working under the assumption that such access would result in equality of the sexes in the society. After all, the Indian woman was no longer confined to her household.

The 1980s were considered a golden era for women's movement in India. During this decade, significant protective laws resulting from campaigns related to violence against women were passed.[4] The Department of Women and Child Development was set up in the year 1985 as a part of the Ministry of Human Resource Development. In 2006, it was upgraded to a fully functional ministry, with the aim of holistic development of women and children. The ministry now has six autonomous organizations, including the National Commission for Women, working under its aegis. Protective laws passed by such organizations, along with the constitutional provisions, exist to safeguard the fundamental rights of women and protect them against violence perpetrated in both public and private spaces. Such provisions have resulted in significant improvements in the rates at which these crimes are reported. However, certain violent acts continue to be disguised as tradition, and many crimes often go unreported or undocumented due to cultural values and beliefs upheld in the country. This brings forth the larger question of the extent and effectiveness of laws in bringing about social change.

This chapter explores gender-based violence in the two dominant spheres of households and public spaces by situating the relevant legislation for the same. The issues are viewed from a heterosexual lens, taking into account 'gender' as either male or female. The chapter is divided into three parts: 'Theorizing Violence', 'Analysing Women-Specific Legislation' and 'Violence in Private and Public Violence: A Comparative Analysis'.

4.2 Theorizing Violence

To understand the intricacies of women-related legislation, it is of paramount importance to first understand what is construed as violence against women and the various forms it takes in India.

Violence against women has persisted across the world as a pervasive violation of fundamental human rights and as an impediment to gender equality and development. It takes up various forms and affects women at different stages of their lifespan and cuts through categories of socio-economic class, caste, race and nationality. According to the United Nations (UN) Declaration on Violence against women, Article 1[5] defines it as:

> violence that results in, or is likely to result in, physical, sexual or psychological harm or suffering to women, including threats of such acts, coercion or arbitrary deprivation of liberty, whether occurring in public or in private life.

Gender-based violence includes both single, isolated acts of violence and a continuum of resource deprivation and discrimination. In this section, such violent acts are classified under the categories of 'Violence within the Household' and 'Violence within the Community'. Prominent forms of violence within these groups are further elaborated upon by linking them with appropriate theories to gain a more comprehensive understanding of the same. Principles of behavioural economics with the backing of sociological and feminist literature provide a foundational base to successfully theorize violence.

4.2.1 Violence within the Household

Violence within the household, or private violence, according to Article 2 of the UN Declaration,[6] includes physical, sexual and psychological violence occurring in the family. Battering, sexual abuse of female children, dowry-related violence, marital rape, female genital mutilation and other traditional practices harmful to women, non-spousal violence and violence related to exploitation all come under this category. Domestic violence is often described as a 'seed for other kinds of violence', as it tends to normalize violence from an early, impressionable age and is surrounded by a culture of silence. Dowry-related violence and intimate partner violence rampant within the Indian context are discussed below.

4.2.1.1 Dowry-Related Violence

Dowry was historically given to the daughter as a form of bequest due to India's skewed inheritance laws. Economic theory[7] suggests that in a perfectly competitive marriage market, individuals choose partners who maximize their utilities and create optimal partnerships. Becker (1991)[8] points out that marriage markets in the real world are imperfect, and thus, compensation transactions in the form of dowry or bride price are used to get the desired partners. If the bride's share of family income is above her 'shadow' price, a dowry is paid to the in-law's family in order to attract grooms from higher socio-economic class.

As a result of 'marriage squeeze' and the greed of the husband's family to maximize their utility out of the marriage contract, dowry price has inflated over the years.[9] Limited procurement of human capital due to household-oriented skills and forced transfer of assets to family-in-law put women in situations where they rely on marriage for economic sustenance. The bride's parents thus pay for the status associated with the groom and access to the groom's economic resources and human capital accumulation. The dowry amount should give the female higher bargaining power, but it has come to serve as a tool of harassment by the groom and his family.

Dowry-related violence occurs when the woman's utility is minimal, especially when she has provided for a male heir or is unable to provide for one, resulting in violent acts like female infanticide and forced abortions. Application of social exchange theory suggests that the groom's family will use violence to increase the groom price/dowry when the rewards of the dowry exceed the cost of being violent.[10] Dowry murders take place when expected gains resulting from elimination of a man's current wife exceed the gains in continuing his marriage with her. The opportunity cost of staying with her is the cost of dowry, which could be extracted from a second marriage. Wife abuse is also used to acquire more dowry from the existing marriage or to induce women to leave the marriage, allowing the man to appropriate dowry from a second marriage. Cultural spill-over theory[11] also suggests that the use of physical force for non-sexual, socially acceptable reasons gets generalized to relationships and interactions between the sexes, making the act of dowry by itself violent.

4.2.1.2 Intimate Partner Violence

Intimate partner violence can be explained as male coercion and oppression of women within the household. This includes physical, sexual, economic and psychological abuse imposed on the woman. It results from unequal power relations within their intimate relationships and in society. Patriarchal culture condones and justifies such acts of violence.

Contemporary socio-biology and Neo-Darwinism suggest that evolution of male violence and aggression stems from their need to maintain female fidelity and secure reproductive control.

Men use the social, personal and economic resources available to them to establish their dominance in their family and society. Resource theory posits that when these resources are exhausted, they turn to violence as a resource to establish their dominance on women.[12] Men of low self-esteem may attempt to boost their image and nourish their ego by carrying out acts of violence on their partner, expecting her to comply with her role of being the 'nurturing' one.[13]

Abuse in relationships does not occur as a single, isolated incident but is part of a larger continuum of physical and psychological abuse. According to the theory of cycle of violence, after a violent episode, the batterer profusely apologizes and assures the victim that he won't be abusive again.[14] This acts as positive reinforcement for women to remain in violent relationships, and the cycle continues. The behaviour of women is also characterized by endowment effect where given that they are bound by marital contracts, they may overvalue their relationships with their husbands. When the woman has invested too much into the relationship, she continues investing due to sunk-cost fallacy. Time becomes both an investment and an expense. Women employ loss aversion strategy, believing that breaking the cycle would involve dissolution of the relationship. They stay in an abusive environment to avoid such a loss, which to them is greater than the freedom and well-being gained from leaving. In a society where marriage is the norm, the benefit of staying in an abusive relationship is higher than the cost of leaving the relationship.

4.2.2 Violence within the Community

Violence within the community, or public violence, manifests as physical, sexual and psychological violence. This includes rape, sexual abuse, acid attacks, sexual harassment and intimidation at work, and elsewhere, trafficking of women, forced medical treatments and abusive medication. Exploitation and commercialization of women's bodies and forced prostitution are outcomes of increasing poverty and economic liberalism.[15]

Violence is also perpetrated by the state when custom and tradition are prioritized over fundamental freedom of women. The rise of religious fundamentalism in the country can adversely affect a woman's economic autonomy and freedom of choice. It also results in social exclusion of women. In armed conflict, such violence is also exercised as a weapon of war and takes various forms including rape, murder, sexual slavery and so on.[16] It impedes women's access to safe public spaces and essential services. The internet age has also led to increased commercialization of women's bodies. With their incidence and reporting rates consistently increasing, rape and sexual harassment, along with commercialization of women's bodies, have become major areas of concern and thus will be the focus of this section.

4.2.2.1 Rape

Rape is a form of sexual assault involving sexual intercourse or penetration carried out without the person's consent. According to Thornhill (1999),[17] from a biological perspective, rape is explained as a desire for differential reproductive success through inter-individual selection. The overcompensating benefits of rape to male reproductive success exceed the large costs of raping. In patriarchal societies, rape and the fear of rape are used by men to assert power over women and maintain their subordination. Women are seen as sexual possessions, which exist to be controlled and exploited by men using aggression and violence. The desire to dominate a woman also stems from an insecure sense of masculinity.

Social exchange theory[18] posits that sexual activity by a woman has an exchange value. A heterosexual community is a marketplace where females can provide sex in exchange of benefit from men. The perceived value of sex from a female is more than the perceived value of sex from a male. As per the female control theory, women gain from restricting the supply of sex and thus increasing its price. In the market for sex, rape becomes a property crime as sex is stolen from the woman to whom it belongs.[19] When sex becomes a resource, rape is a violation of the rules of exchange. In the process, the woman incurs potential costs in the form of pain, trauma and unwanted pregnancies.

Use of force is also justified because of the culturally held belief that the woman is owned by the man. Commodification of sex then leads to a sense of entitlement to sex. Due to this entitlement, men may perceive the price of sex with a woman as free. According to zero price effect,[20] this results in the rise in intrinsic value of a woman's sexual activity, thereby making it even more desirable to men. Rape becomes normalized in settings where manipulation, coercion and violence are valid ways of conducting social relationships.

4.2.2.2 Sexual Harassment

Sexual harassment can be 'quid pro quo', which involves sexual favours or sexual contact from an employee on a conditional basis. It can also take the form of hostile work environment created due to sexual advances resulting in an intimidating, threatening and abusive work environment.

Sexual harassment is a product of culturally sanctioned power and status differences between the two sexes, which boil down to the organizational level and lead to misuse of power to coerce or intimidate women. Men dominate public spaces and assert their authority via a combination of ascribed, achieved and situational power. Opportunity structures, sex ratios and organizational norms make the working environment more conducive to sexual harassment. In both traditional and non-traditional work roles for women, power distance and attitudes interact to determine the likelihood of sexual harassment. When the power distance between women and their superiors is high, it results in quid pro quo and hostile environment for sexual harassment.[21]

A favourable sex ratio in work spaces encourages men to carry over gender-based expectations for behaviour, which may be irrelevant or inappropriate for the opposite gender. When women constitute a minority of the work group, their gender becomes an identifying characteristic and is subject to gender-based categorizations. This also leads to stereotypical evaluations of female employees. Mcleod's social identity theory[22] recognizes that interpersonal differences result in in-group–out-group perspective of the work environment and in devaluation of the out-group. This serves to reinforce gendered modes of power within the larger society and maintains that men control all economic resources. In cases of unintended sexual harassment, men associate power with sex and assume that sex with a woman implies her submission to his control and power. The polite and submissive behaviour of a woman is interpreted as being sexually receptive. She views herself as a victim, while he sees himself as being 'lead on'.[23]

4.2.2.2 Commercialization of Women in Media

Portrayal of women as sexual objects in mass media to increase the appeal of the media or product is a form of exploitation and commercialization of their bodies. Hypodermic Needle model (Oladejo & Agwanwo, 2015) suggests that all messages portrayed in the media are received and wholly accepted by the viewers as a true representation of reality.[24] Such portrayals then have a tendency to misrepresent reality through a flawed depiction of women and reinforce their subjugation. Overly sexualized representation of women sets impossible beauty standards for them while creating stereotypes about their bodies and expectations of how they are to behave around men. It may also act as a precursor to sexual violence and promote the idea that women are mere puppets existing to meet their sexual/leisure needs.

Nudity and sexualization of a woman in mass media also meet the erotic needs of the audience and tend to substitute a real sexual experience.[25] Such commercialization of the human body in the advertisement sector is backed by capitalist tendencies to use sex appeal in order to maximize sales. This results in normalizing objectification of women's bodies as a means of increasing income and leads to their commercialization.

Prominent forms of violence within households and within the community are theorized in this section. Upon application of theory and behavioural economics principles, it becomes evident that violence manifests differently between the two aforementioned groups. Dowry-related violence and intimate partner violence are understood as means employed by perpetrators to extract maximum resources from women. In cases of rape, sexual harassment and commercialization of women's bodies, women are seen as sexual objects entitled to men. Men then go to extreme ends to gain control over women's sexuality. This understanding forms a theoretical foundation of further analysing women-specific legislations.

4.3 Analysing Women-Specific Legislations

According to a global poll conducted by Thomson Reuters, India is the most dangerous country for women in the world.[26] In 2015, one of the sustainable development goals adopted by the UN General Assembly for their 2030 Agenda was to 'eliminate all forms of discrimination and violence against women in the public and private spheres and to undertake reforms to give women equal rights to economic resources and access to ownership of property'.[27] It is in this context that dialogue around women's legislation in India becomes important given that the state predominantly uses its legislative power to correct unjust and oppressive behaviour that women are often subjected to.

This section analyses the major women-specific legislations by grouping them into two categories: 'Laws Governing Private Spaces' and 'Laws Governing Public Spaces', with the help of theoretical explanations of violence from the previous section. Various other principles of behavioural economics are also employed to gain an insight into these legislations.

4.3.1 Laws Governing Private Spaces

4.3.1.1 The Dowry Prohibition Act, 1961 (Amended in 1986)

Under the Dowry Prohibition Act, 1961, the act of giving or taking dowry, or abetment of the same, was penalized with imprisonment of minimum five years and a fine of Rs 15,000 or net worth of dowry received, whichever was higher.[28] Demanding of dowry was also penalized albeit with a relatively lenient punishment. It did not cover cash and gifts exchanged during the marriage and monetary transactions occurring after the marriage. In its 1986 amendment, the onus of proof was shifted on the accused, and dowry was made a non-bailable offence.[29] Section 304B of the Indian Penal Code (IPC) further categorized dowry deaths as deaths of women occurring under abnormal circumstances such as those caused by burns or bodily injury. An offence under this section results in severe punishment of seven years to lifetime.

Among other reasons, the stringent punishment related to dowry deaths can be understood as a need from the bride's family to avenge her death and retrieve the gifts. Although dowry deaths have harsh penalties, the punishment under Dowry Protection Act is relatively negligible. Minimal expected punishment for legal violations concerning dowry and absence of negative socio-economic consequences for men at dissolution of marriage results in dowry-related violence.[30] Curbing of dowry-related violence and dowry deaths requires elimination of the practice of dowry itself. But given its roots in the Indian tradition, the practice of dowry is not considered an area of concern.

Economic theory suggests that low conviction rates due to harsh penalties also reduce the cost of condoning acts of violence to extract maximum dowry or to resort to killing/burning the first wife and thus increase its likelihood. Remedial provisions could be provided for the bride to successfully lodge a complaint considering her family values and the norms of marriage over the harassment she faces in the due process. Appropriate actions should be taken to reduce the opportunity cost of dowry-related violence by successfully prohibiting the practice of dowry, inclusive of gifts and money exchanged before or after the wedding.

4.3.1.2 Protection of Women from Domestic Violence Act, 2005

Protection of Women from Domestic Violence Act (PWDVA), 2005, is a civil law directed towards providing relief to the aggrieved woman (wife or female live-in partner or any other female family member) who faces violence in her home. It provides temporary relief and secure housing to the woman and protects her right to reside in her matrimonial or shared household.[31] Behavioural principles suggest that independence-seeking behaviour such as seeking help from the police may be punished by the abuser who wishes to assert dominance over the woman by controlling her access to resources. Protection officers are thus assigned to guide them through legal proceedings and provide them with medical counselling and other support services.

Till 1983, no special provisions existed to curb violence in households, and abusers were convicted under the provisions of criminal law. General criminal remedies did not pay heed to this specific situation where the victim is economically and emotionally dependent on the abuser.[32] Contrary to criminal proceedings, PWDVA does not require for the rules of evidence to be strictly followed, and the woman can reach out for protection even before the abuse took place. Under the act, however, the respondent can only be subject to a restraining order but does not face jail time. Criminal law is only sanctioned when the accused violates the protection or residence order.

Compensation for expenses and losses incurred along with monthly payments of maintenance from the respondent are imposed by the magistrate. Such remedies provided by the act reduce the perceived cost of leaving the abusive relationship by decreasing the dependency of the woman on the abuser. To break the cycle of violence, a no-drop policy of prosecution should be passed. As per this policy, once an abuser is charged for domestic violence, the charges cannot be dropped even if the victim wishes otherwise.[33] This helps counteract the endowment effect and loss aversion, which make women stay in abusive relationships. Since the 2016 Supreme Court ruling, as per the demands of men's rights activist groups, the words 'adult male' have been struck down from the definition of respondent in the act. Women can now file domestic violence complaints against other women.[34]

4.3.2 Laws Governing Public Spaces

4.3.2.1 The Criminal Law (Amendment) Act, 2013

Popularly called the Anti-Rape law, the Criminal Law (amendment) Act, 2013, amended laws related to sexual offences in IPC, Indian Evidence ACT and Code of Criminal Procedure, 1973. These provisions broadened the definition of rape to include certain non-penetrative acts including sodomy and also defined consent, further clarifying that absence of resistance would not imply consent. The act also made an exception of medical examination for rape survivors.

The punishment extended from seven years up to life imprisonment and in some cases included death penalty. The victim is always assumed to be female while the perpetrator male; this lack of gender neutrality may be due to an availability heuristic[35] as theorized by Tversky and Kahneman. People can recall incidents of male perpetrators relatively easily.

Provisions were made for acts of violence ranging from acid attacks, gang rape cases to stalking, voyeurism and so on. The amendments, however, did not recognize marital rape in ongoing marriages and continued to protect the members of Armed Forces (Special Powers) Act from prosecution for rape and assault by requiring a sanction to prosecute an army personnel. It also raised the age of consent from 16 to 18 years.[36]

According to behavioural economics principles, confirmation bias[37] occurs when people evaluate information in a manner that fits with their existing thinking. The draconian punishment of death penalty in the amendment bill reinforces the patriarchal notion that rape is worse than death. Such a notion approaches legal proceedings with a preconceived bias that rape is a crime against the family's honour and not one that violates female bodily autonomy.[38] Confirmation bias of the prosecutors may have an adverse impact on criminal proceedings related to rape considering their orthodox views on the subject matter. A seven-year minimum punishment along with the expanded definition of rape can also be problematic as it may lead to higher rate of acquittals. Women's rights groups have suggested that expansion of the definition of rape be accompanied with different gradations of sexual assault, which coincide with different punishments.[39]

4.3.2.2 The Sexual Harassment of Women at Workplace (PREVENTION, PROHIBITION and REDRESSAL) Act, 2013

The Sexual Harassment of Women at Workplace Act, 2013, defines sexual harassment in work spaces and provides the mechanism for redressal of complaints by setting up local complaint committees. Education and sensitization programmes should be conducted by employers, and a separate set of policies must be developed against both quid pro quo and hostile work environment for sexual harassment. Although the act exists for prevention and redressal purposes, Section 354 of IPC facilitates one to three years imprisonment and/or a fine for the accused. Employers are also obligated to report all sexual harassment offences occurring in their firm. The act covers all types of workplaces and also includes students in educational settings and patients in hospitals.[40]

The burden of proof falls on the woman who files the complaint. In case of false accusations, the woman faces the risk of being prosecuted.[41] This acts as a deterrence in reporting the offence since it induces fear into the aggrieved woman. The lack of gender neutrality of the act has also been under scrutiny. It fails to take into consideration minimal liability of the employer in case of employee–employee harassment. According to economic theory, this act increases the cost of lawsuits and settlements to the organization. It also increases indirect cost of reduced performance, decreased goodwill in the market, reduced employee turnover and increased absenteeism as a result of harassment. Since sexual harassment at workplace stems from systemic oppressions of women, the act shifts accountability from individuals to institutions. Given that sufficient proof must be provided and women may hesitate to file complaints due to risks of confidentiality breach, the act has proved to be quite ineffective.

Attributional bias,[42] a systematic error made while evaluating one's own or others' behaviour, is extremely pervasive in the workplace. When a woman participates in the workplace, the harasser evaluates this as her non-conformity to the role attributed to her gender. Since harassment is seen as a correction of inappropriate behaviour clubbed with out-group hostility, often the perpetrator may be unable to comprehend that he is making the woman uncomfortable or violating her rights. The woman might also be unaware that she is being harassed. This explains the emphasis of the act on prevention rather than punitive action and the mandatory clause for conduction of sexual harassment workshops.

4.3.2.3 The Indecent Representation of Women (Prohibition) Act, 1986

The Indecent Representation of Women (Prohibition) Act, 1986, aims to prevent depiction of women that may be derogatory or likely to corrupt public morality. This implies prohibition of indecent portrayal of women in media via advertising, writings and illustrations.[43] Given the time of enactment, the focus was primarily on print media. Punishment for first conviction extended up to two years along with a fine of Rs 2,000 and for a second conviction extended from six months to five years with a fine ranging from Rs 10,000 to Rs 1,00,000.[44]

The concept of default option can be applied to understand the normalization of such exploitation. Commodification of women also influences the social value placed on them by the masses. The broad definition of indecent representation is ambiguous, making way for misuse of the provisions of the act.[45] When the standard of indecent portrayal is not categorically defined, it leaves room for judging the same via orthodox morality. The act also penalizes prostitutes, reinforces the puritanical concept of policing a woman's sexuality and dichotomizes women as either 'good' or 'bad'. The importance of this act has been largely debated in the internet age with some suggesting the need for an amendment.

4.4 Violence in Public and Private Spheres: A Comparative Analysis

The preceding sections reiterate the initial premise of the chapter that violence manifests differently in households and public spheres. In household or private settings, gender roles of a bread-earning father and a housewife mother are defined on an individual level.[46] The resulting power imbalance is due to the lack of access of economic resources by the woman. Her work within the household has no economic value and is considered invisible labour. The utility of the woman is thus dependent on her reproductive resources, which help carry forth the male lineage in the family. Violence in these spaces takes the form of a continuum of resource deprivation and exploitation. Violent acts are carried out to extract maximum resources from the woman through birthing only male children, dowry extraction and nourishing of aggressive male ego.

Public violence, on the contrary, involves perpetuation of gender bias at a macro level. Institutional structures while permitting women to join the public sphere continue to control them via subordination and segregation.[47] Power imbalance here is not due to in-access of economic resources but due to the quest for equal access. Moreover, sexualization of the female body is valued over her economic contribution to the workplace and society at large.

While in private spaces, women are considered vessels through which resources are acquired and exploited, in public spaces, women themselves become the resources that are exploited. Due to this, relatively harsher punishments are given for extreme acts of violence like rape and exploitation of women's bodies, while laws related to household violence take the protective, preventive approach in an attempt to reduce resource extraction and exploitation. Domestic violence and dowry-related laws do not hold such draconian punishment. Instead, the law attempts to curb such behaviour rather than correct it. Legislation regarding public violence, by contrast, are framed with the objective of correcting oppressive behaviour and thus may be gender-biased. In this manner, violence in public and private spheres manifests differently, and legislation framed to tackle this violence is dependent on the manifestation of violence itself.

4.5 Conclusion

Constitutional provisions and protective legislation, though considered progressive at the time of their framing, have proved to be quite ineffective overtime. Given the harsh criminal sentences and onus of proof placed on women in some laws, conviction rates are not satisfactory. One of the reasons for this ineffectiveness is the callous framing of the laws, which has allowed for loopholes that could be easily exploited by the convicts. At the time of their framing, mere passing of such laws was seen as a stepping stone for the women's movement in the country, and questions pertaining to how these laws were framed and who was framing them were seldom asked. The skewed pressure on the legislative body to be the sole guardian and promoter of women's rights has led to indifference at the executive and judiciary levels to successfully interpret and implement these laws.

Behavioural economic insight into theories of violence against women and related legislation have enabled a thorough understanding of why, how and for whom these laws are framed. Evidently, laws are framed differently for violent acts occurring in public and private spaces since violence manifests differently in these spaces. Successful enactment of laws in the two dominant spheres is not sufficient to bring about feminist justice. This is because punishments or formal sanctions often have no effect on the criminal if he holds the belief that he is morally correct in his behaviour and has not committed a crime. Laws would thus be ineffective till cultural norms are incongruent with the larger legal framework.

Thus, cultural norms need to consider women as active members of the society, and laws need to reinforce the same rather than emphasizing on age-old patriarchal fallacies of women as objects. Policy preferences need to be such that women can maintain their bargaining power in relationships and in public without having to use the traditional female resources. This can be achieved by ensuring equal access of economic resources to women in the public space, which would also reduce their dependency in private spaces.

Notes

1 Department of Economic Affairs, Economic Survey 2018–19 (2019), https://www.indiabudget.gov.in/budget2019-20/economicsurvey/doc/echapter.pdf/.
2 In-depth Study on All Forms of Violence against Women, (2006), https://documents-dds-ny.un.org/doc/UNDOC/GEN/N06/419/74/PDF/N0641974.pdf?OpenElement
3 Rekha Pande, The Public Face of a Private Domestic Violence, 4 *International Feminist Journal of Politics* (2002).
4 Flavia Agnes, *Protecting Women against Violence? Review of a Decade of Legislation, 1980–89*, 27 EPW17 (1992).
5 A/RES/48/104. Declaration on the Elimination of Violence against Women (1994), United Nations, https://undocs.org/en/A/RES/48/104.
6 Id.
7 Tonushree Jaggi, *The Economics of Dowry: Causes and Effects of an Indian Tradition*, 5 UAUJE (2001).
8 Gary S. Becker, A Treatise on the Family*: Enlarged edition*. Harvard University Press (1991).
9 Tonushree Jaggi, *supra* note 7.
10 Kathryn Seifert, *Youth Violence: Theory, Prevention and Interventions*, 50 (2012).
11 Larry Baron & Murray Straus, *Legitimate Violence, Violent Attitudes, and Rape: A Test of the Cultural Spillover Theory*, 528 Annals of the New York Academy of Sciences (1987).
12 Ram Ahuja, *Violence against Women*, 175 (1998).
13 Russell Geen & Edward Donnersten, *Human Aggression: Theories, Research and Implication for Social Policy*, 112 (1998).
14 Lenore Walker, *The Battered Woman*, 94 (1980).
15 *supra* note 2.
16 *Supra* note 6.
17 Randy Thornhill, *The Biology of Human Rape*, 39 ABA 137 (1999).
18 *Supra* note 10.
19 Katharine K. Baker, *Once a Rapist? Motivational Evidence and Relevancy in Rape Law*, 110 Harvard Law Review 563 (1997).
20 Kristina Shampanier, Nina Mazar, & Dan Ariely, *Zero as a Special Price: The True Value of Free Products*, 26 Marketing Science 742 (2007).
21 Gary L. Whaley & Shirley H. Tucker, *A Theoretical Integration of Sexual Harassment Models*, 17 Equal Opportunities International 21–29 (1998).
22 Saul A. McLeod, *Social Identity Theory* (October 24, 2008), http://www.simplypsychology.org/social-identity-theory.html.
23 Id.
24 Abiodun O. Oladejo & Destiny E. Agwanwo, *Media Entertainment and Commercialization of the Body*, 15 GJHSS (2015).

25 Id.
26 Press Release by WCD, *World's Most Dangerous Country for Women 2018 by Thomson Reuters Foundation* (2018), https://wcd.nic.in/sites/default/files/Reuters_poll_PR.pdf
27 UN General Assembly, *Transforming Our World: The 2030 Agenda for Sustainable Development* 18 (2015), https://www.un.org/ga/search/view_doc.asp?symbol=A/RES/70/1&Lang=E.
28 Dowry Prohibition act of 1961 (1961), https://wcd.nic.in/act/dowry-prohibition-act-1961.
29 *Supra* note 4, at 5.
30 Vageshwari Deswal, *Dowry Prohibition Act: Attempting Legal Solution to a Social Problem* (May 7, 2019), https://timesofindia.indiatimes.com/blogs/legally-speaking/dowry-prohibition-act-attempting-legal-solution-to-a-social-problem/
31 The Protection of Women from Domestic Violence Act of 2005, MLJ (2005), https://wcd.nic.in/sites/default/files/wdvact.pdf.
32 *Supra* note 4, at 6.
33 John Balz, *What Behavioural Economics Has to Say about Domestic Violence*, Nudge Blog (September 11, 2008), http://nudges.org/what-behavioral-economics-has-to-say-about-domestic-violence/.
34 Utkarsh Anand, *Women Can Also be Prosecuted Under Domestic Violence Law: SC* (2016), https://indianexpress.com/article/india/india-news-india/women-can-also-be-prosecuted-under-domestic-violence-law-sc-3071493/
35 Amos Tversky & Daniel Kahneman, *Judgment under Uncertainty: Heuristics and Biases*, Science- New Series 185 (1974).
36 Niveditha Menon, *Seeing Like a Feminist* (2012).
37 Shahram Heshmat, *What Is Confirmation Bias?* (April 23, 2015), https://www.psychologytoday.com/us/blog/science-choice/201504/what-is-confirmation-bias
38 Niveditha Menon, *The Gap between the Feminist Understanding of Sexual Violence and the Law* (February 24, 2019), https://thewire.in/women/sexual-violence-rape-law-india
39 Id.
40 Sexual Harassment of Women at Workplace Act of 2013, MLJ (2013), https://wcd.nic.in/sites/default/files/Sexual-Harassment-at-Workplace-Act.pdf
41 Id.
42 Gibran Naushad & Susanah Naushad, *Sexual Harassment of Women at Workplace*, https://www.indialawjournal.org/archives/volume8/issue-1/article9.html
43 Indecent Representation of Women (Prohibition) Act (1986), https://wcd.nic.in/act/indecent-representation-women
44 Id.
45 *Supra* note 4, at 10–11.
46 Sylvia Walby, (1989). Theorizing Patriarchy, *Sociology, 23* (2), 213–34.
47 Id.

References

A/RES/48/104. (1994). *Declaration on the Elimination of Violence against Women*. United Nations. Retrieved August 2, 2019, from https://undocs.org/en/A/RES/48/104

Agnes, F. (1992). Protecting Women against Violence-Review of a Decade of Legislation, 1980–89. *Economics & Political Weekly, 27*(17). Retrieved August 2, 2019, from https://www.epw.in/journal/1992/17/review-womens-studies-review-issues-specials/protecting-women-against-violence

Ahuja, R. (1998). *Violence against Women*. Rawat Publications. Jaipur and New Delhi.

Anand, U. (2016, October 8). *Women Can Also be Prosecuted under Domestic Violence Law: SC*. The Indian Express. Retrieved August 2, 2019, from https://indianexpress.com/article/india/india-news-india/women-can-also-be-prosecuted-under-domestic-violence-law-sc-3071493/

Baker, K. K. (1997). Once a Rapist? Motivational Evidence and Relevancy in Rape Law. *Harvard Law Review, 110*(3), 563. Retrieved August 2, 2019, from https://doi.org/10.2307/1342241

Balz, J. (2008, September 11). *What Behavioral Economics Has to Say about Domestic Violence*. Nudge Blog. Retrieved August 2, 2019, from https://nudges.org/what-behavioral-economics-has-to-say-about-domestic-violence/

Baron, L., Straus, M. A., & Jaffee, D. (1987). Legitimate Violence, Violent Attitudes, and Rape: A Test of the Cultural Spillover Theory. *Annals of the New York Academy of Sciences, 528*(1), 79–110. Retrieved August 2, 2019, from https://doi.org/10.1111/j.1749-6632.1988.tb50853.x

Becker, G. S. (1991). *A Treatise on the Family: Enlarged edition*. Cambridge: Harvard University Press.

Department of Economic Affairs. (n.d.). *Economic Survey 2018–19*. India Budget | Ministry of Finance | Government of India. Retrieved August 2, 2019, from https://www.indiabudget.gov.in/budget2019-20/economicsurvey/doc/echapter.pdf

Deswal, V. (2019, May 7). *Dowry Prohibition Act- Attempting Legal Solution to a Social Problem*. Times of India Blog. Retrieved August 2, 2019, from https://timesofindia.indiatimes.com/blogs/legally-speaking/dowry-prohibition-act-attempting-legal-solution-to-a-social-problem/

Dowry Prohibition Act, 1961. (1961). Ministry of Child and Women Development. Retrieved August 2, 2019, from https://wcd.nic.in/act/dowry-prohibition-act-1961

Geen, R. G., & Donnerstein, E. D. (1998). *Human Aggression: Theories, Research, and Implications for Social Policy*. Elsevier.

Heshmat, S. (2015, April 23). *What Is Confirmation Bias?* Psychology Today. Retrieved August 2, 2019, from https://www.psychologytoday.com/us/blog/science-choice/201504/what-is-confirmation-bias

Indecent Representation of Women (Prohibition) Act. (1986). Ministry of Women and Child Development. Retrieved August 2, 2019, from https://wcd.nic.in/act/indecent-representation-women

In-depth Study on All Forms of Violence against Women. (2006). United Nations. Retrieved August 2, 2019, from https://documents-dds-ny.un.org/doc/UNDOC/GEN/N06/419/74/PDF/N0641974.pdf?OpenElement

Jaggi, T. (2001). The Economics of Dowry: Causes and Effects of an Indian Tradition. *University Avenue Undergraduate Journal of Economics, 5*(1). Retrieved August 2, 2019, from https://digitalcommons.iwu.edu/uauje/vol5/iss1/2

Mcleod, S. A. (2008, October 24). *Social Identity Theory*. Study Guides for Psychology Students – Simply Psychology. Retrieved August 2, 2019, from https://www.simplypsychology.org/social-identity-theory.html

Menon, N. (2012). *Seeing Like a Feminist*. Penguin UK.

Menon, N. (n.d.). *The Gap between the Feminist Understanding of Sexual Violence and the Law*. The Wire. Retrieved August 2, 2019, from https://thewire.in/women/sexual-violence-rape-law-india

Naushad, G., & Naushad, S. (n.d.). Sexual Harassment of Women at Workplace. *Indian Law Journal*. Retrieved August 2, 2019, from https://www.indialawjournal.org/archives/volume8/issue-1/article9.html

Oladejo, A. O., & Agwanwo, D. E. (2015). Media Entertainment and Commercialization of the Body. *Global Journal of Human-Social Science: A Arts & Humanities – Psychology, 15*(2). Retrieved August 2, 2019, from https://doi.org/10.17406/GJHSSAVOL15IS2PG5

Pande, R. (2002). The Public Face of a Private Domestic Violence. *International Feminist Journal of Politics, 4*(3), 342–367. Retrieved August 2, 2019, from https://doi.org/10.1080/14616740220000031535

Press Release by WCD. (2018). *World's Most Dangerous Country for Women 2018*. Thomson Reuters. Retrieved August 2, 2019, from https://wcd.nic.in/sites/default/files/Reuters_poll_PR.pdf
Seifert, K., & Ray, K. (2012). *Youth Violence: Theory, Prevention, and Intervention*. Springer Publishing Company.
Sexual Harassment of Women at Workplace Act of 2013. (2013). Ministry of Law and Justice. Retrieved August 2, 2019, from https://wcd.nic.in/sites/default/files/Sexual-Harassment-at-Workplace-Act.pdf
Shampanier, K., Mazar, N., & Ariely, D. (2007). Zero as a Special Price: The True Value of Free Products. *Marketing Science*, *26*(6), 742–757. Retrieved August 2, 2019, from https://doi.org/10.1287/mksc.1060.0254
The Protection of Women from Domestic Violence Act. (2005). Ministry of Law and Justice. Retrieved August 2, 2019, from wcd.nic.in/sites/default/files/wdvact.pdf
Thornhill, R. (1999). The Biology of Human Rape. *American Bar Association*, *39*(2), 137. Retrieved August 2, 2019, from https://www.jstor.org/stable/29762595
Tversky, A., & Kahneman, D. (n.d.). Judgement under Uncertainty: Heuristics and Biases. *Science- New Series*, 185. Retrieved August 2, 2019, from https://doi.org/10.1126/science.185.4157.1124
UN General Assembly. (2015). *Transforming Our World: The 2030 Agenda for Sustainable Development*. United Nations. Retrieved August 2, 2019, from https://www.un.org/ga/search/view_doc.asp?symbol=A/RES/70/1&Lang=E
Walby, S. (1989). Theorizing patriarchy. *Sociology*, *23*(2), 213–34.
Walker, L. E. (1980). *Battered Woman*. William Morrow Paperbacks.
Whaley, G. L., & Tucker, S. H. (1998). A Theoretical Integration of Sexual Harassment Models. *Equal Opportunities International*, *17*(1), 21–29. Retrieved August 2, 2019, from https://doi.org/10.1108/02610159810785485

5

THE STICK AND CARROT APPROACH TOWARDS ENVIRONMENTAL FISCAL REFORM IN INDIA

Stephanus van Zyl

5.1 Introduction

Environmental issues such as climate change dominate international debate. Governments are encouraged, by environmentalists and conservationists, to impose legislation to curb global warming, eliminate greenhouse gases, and reduce the exploitation of natural resources. It is trite, in a changing society, that it is not always advisable for governments to intervene in social or public structures by imposing new legislation, taxes, or regulations. Occasionally, existing laws, regulations, or taxes can be implemented to achieve the desired outcome. In the case of environmental reform, not all forms of intervention are successful in combating climate change or promoting environmental reform.[1] Careful consideration should be given to ensure the intervention is not overly prescriptive.[2] The majority of these laws adopt the command-and-control approach.[3] This approach is premised on the conjecture that human behaviour impacting on the environment can be regulated by prescribing a range of legislative standards, prohibitions, and restrictions and to further sanction any person who contravenes them.[4] It has, however, become a concern the world over that the command-and-control approach towards environmental management is ineffective.[5] This is mainly as a result of costly implementation and administration of command-and-control legislation and the general inability to enforce compliance adequately. In addition, in many cases, the private sector has adopted measures to regulate environmental reform sufficiently. In these cases, additional government intervention often leads to market distortions.[6]

Market-based instruments in the form of environmental fiscal reform have shown to be more effective in furthering environmental goals than command-and-control measures. The main purpose of market-based instruments is to cure market failure caused by externalities, which follow because of

DOI: 10.4324/9781003150565-6

environmental cost for which no payment is made.[7] For example, where a paint manufacturer dumps harmful elements in the sewerage system that ends up in rivers, it leaves a cost on the environment. When no payment is made to compensate for this "bad", an externality occurs because the cost to the environment is not compensated for. Economic or market-based instruments are intended to encourage environmentally beneficial behaviour by shifting the price of environmental resources upwards to reflect more accurately the environmental cost of production and/or consumption.[8] In the current example, by putting a cost on the pollution, the externality is removed, and the polluter is encouraged to adapt to production methods that are more environmentally friendly. Market-based instruments should, in principle, encourage behaviour that goes beyond mere compliance with existing environmental laws.

Corrective taxes or Pigovian taxes have shown to be more effective in correcting or changing human behaviour (in general) than the command-and-control mechanism.[9] Environmental taxes have a dual purpose: It can penalise the environmental "bads" through additional taxes and nurture the environmental "goods" through tax incentives (also known as the stick and carrot approach).[10] The range of environmental tax reform instruments is wide, and no one instrument has proved more successful than the other.[11] In the main, these instruments can be subdivided into the following categories: (a) taxes on products pollutants and emissions, (b) user charges and levies, (c) environmental subsidies, (d) tradable permits, and (e) deposit-refund systems.[12] While the government of India has realised the importance of environmental fiscal reform in achieving environmental goals, very little environmental fiscal reform has seen the light.

The objective of this chapter is to analyse, document, and evaluate the general principles of the stick and carrot approach towards effective environmental fiscal reform in India with specific consideration of the existing tax framework. Carbon tax or any other cap-and-trade system as an environmental tax measure falls outside the scope of this chapter and, as such, is not discussed.

5.2 Environmental Tax Penalties

5.2.1 Source of Revenue

Environmental taxes have the potential to create revenue.[13] The cost of environmental incentives can be reduced or wholly eliminated with the introduction of a collateral environmental levy. In India, where taxpayers are already overburdened with high taxes, environmental taxes can substitute a portion of personal taxes to alleviate the tax burden on taxpayers created by personal taxes on labour. However, Oates argues that environmental tax rates must be determined by environmental objects and not by revenue considerations.[14] Put differently, an environmental tax penalty must not be implemented as an extra stream of revenue.

5.2.2 Revenue Extrapolative

Revenue from environmental levies is based on predictions in behavioural patterns. A change in behavioural patterns can erode the tax base.[15] For example, an environmental tax or levy on certain products or services may be effective enough that the demand for the product is completely suppressed within a short period of time. As a result, the taxes levied on the product is also diminished. This phenomenon is not restricted to environmental taxes as most taxes are influenced by behavioural patterns.[16] The legislator must, therefore, consider behavioural patterns carefully before environmental taxes are introduced. In this regard, studies in behavioural science in countries where environmental taxes have been introduced may be helpful. However, as the circumstances, social background, traditions, and cultures differ, the results in one country may not necessarily repeat in India. Further, it is suggested that taxes on relatively inelastic commodities such as energy will not result in drastic changes in human behaviour so as to eliminate consumption to levels that would result in the erosion the tax base.[17] For example, consumers may reduce electricity consumption by adopting energy-saving behaviour or installing energy-saving equipment, but the consumption for electricity will not be eliminated completely by higher energy levies.

5.2.3 Must Not Result in Poverty

The economic impact of environmental taxes on all the income groups must be considered before the actual tax rate or implementation thereof is finalised.[18] Environmental levies on inelastic consumer products could lead to poverty.[19] Lower-income households are dependent on electricity and transport.[20] Renewable energy generators are expensive, and it is most likely that only higher income earners will benefit from levies on inelastic products. This is known as the "free-rider" phenomenon.[21] These well-off households are more likely to afford renewable energy generators. The lack of capital prevents lower-income households from investing in energy-efficient appliances.[22] In India, where most citizens live in poverty, an environmental levy on electricity is likely to increase the need for other non-renewable energy sources such as paraffin or wood, which is not only more harmful to the environment but also carries a health risk. This can put an even greater monetary pressure on the *fiscus* when these citizens apply for state medical care or other social grants because of ill health. Mitigation or compensation measures must be considered to alleviate the burden on lower-income groups.[23] Tax recycling in the form of subsidies or compensatory grants can eliminate the regressive nature of environmental taxes.[24] For example, where the environmental levy on electricity is earmarked for environmental reform, government must apply revenue to install renewable energy heaters or generators at no cost to lower-income households to balance the economic inequity created by the levy. Environmentally friendly low-energy consumption products such as LED lamps could be exempted from value-added tax (VAT) or goods and services tax (GST). Incentives on energy-efficient products in Europe have shown to be more effective than energy taxes.[25] Of course, general VAT/GST exemptions on energy-efficient products will benefit the free-rider phenomenon as explained above. In this regard, Kasonen and Nicodème suggest that specific targeted incentives to poorer households will be more effective.[26] They further opine that direct incentives will be more visible than a general VAT/GST exemption, resulting in political support for a concomitant environmental levy.[27] However, the administrative cost and burden associated with direct subsidies make a general VAT/GST exemption on energy-efficient products a more attractive option.

5.2.4 Must Not Disturb International Competitiveness

International competitiveness can be disturbed where domestic products subject to high environmental taxes compete with international products not subject to similar taxes.[28] This is even more so when domestic products compete against established international brands. For example, where a carbon tax is levied on the Mahindra and Tata motor companies,[29] they will struggle to compete internationally against established brands not subject to the same levies. This could result in further economic distortions, ultimately leading to job losses and greater poverty.[30] Competitiveness can be restored by the introduction of tax incentives like carbon emissions credit incentives. Government must, however, be cautious to lower income tax rates for certain manufacturers (or to exempt manufacturers from an environmental levy altogether) in an attempt to balance the cost of manufacture as this will defeat the overall environmental objective of the tax.[31] For example, where a manufacturer is subject to carbon emissions tax of INR 10 million per month, but, at the same time, its income tax liability is reduced by INR 10 million, the cost of manufacture will not be adversely affected, and the manufacturer will not put any measures into place to reduce carbon emissions. Similarly, exempting energy-intensive producers of inelastic products is not a viable option as it undermines the polluter-pays principle.[32]

Studies by Barker and Johnston reveal that taxes on energy and carbon have no significant impact on competitiveness.[33] In the main, the fear of competitiveness is raised and exaggerated by energy-intensive manufacturers.[34] However, this does not mean that the trade implications of environmental taxes must be ignored altogether. The studies were all conducted in developed economies. The impact of energy taxes, and more specifically carbon tax, on developing economies remains to be tested. As such, competitiveness remains one of the stumbling blocks for the introduction of new environmental taxes in developing nations.

At domestic level, competitiveness in the international realm can be restored by way of basic tax-free thresholds, export rebates, and border tax adjustments.[35] At international level, competitiveness can theoretically be resolved through international harmonisation of environmental tax rules.[36]

In the case of carbon tax, manufacturers may opt to move their manufacturing plants to neighbouring countries where no or low carbon tax rates apply. This phenomenon is known as "carbon leakage".[37] The Organisation for Economic Co-operation and Development (OECD) recommends that governments should negotiate and implement uniform regional carbon taxes to prevent carbon drain.[38] Regional fiscal co-operation in the form of uniform environmental tax regimes will prevent manufacturers in the region from tax hopping. In Europe, there has not been any significant trace of carbon leakage recorded, but this can be attributed to the exemption (from carbon tax) of the most vulnerable local industries.[39]

As an alternative to even-out international competitiveness, strict import regulations or higher import taxes may be introduced on imported products not subject to the same domestic environmental levy. However, such measures may have a ripple effect as it may result in international trade distortions or violation of international public relations. Due to the sensitive nature of trade regulations and the effort-intensive process to negotiate them, it is not advisable for India to impose increased import taxes or strict import regulations unilaterally.

A further alternative is to provide for a transition period to allow manufacturers to implement mitigation measures.[40] An escalating tariff can be introduced to ease the initial burden of the environmental tax to allow manufacturers to alter the way they manufacture goods without significantly increasing the cost of production.

5.2.5 Must Not Increase Cost of Distribution Significantly

Fuel levies, carbon tax on vehicles, and environmental toll fees all result in increasing cost of distribution of domestic produce. These costs are reflected in higher consumer prices leading to further impoverishment of low-income households. This is especially evident in dense urban areas where basic food stuffs like milk, bread, and vegetables are transported from distant rural areas and where manufactured goods are transported to distant rural areas. The OECD does not recommend exempting poorer households from the environmental levy or to exempt the transportation of certain goods from a fuel levy as it will defeat the purpose of the environmental levy.[41] Instead it recommends that other mitigation measures such as green cheques or relief from income tax should be implemented.[42] However, as pointed out above, a mere shifting of funds will not enhance the ultimate environmental objective of the penalty.

5.2.6 The Tax Penalty Must Be Appropriate

Where an environmental levy has been identified as potentially beneficial, a detailed analysis is required to determine the appropriateness thereof. For example, a flat-rate levy might be less effective in changing human behaviour than a progressive levy. Where the flat-rate levy is more affordable to the taxpayer compared to adopting environmentally beneficial behaviour, the taxpayer is likely to pay the tax without attempting to change the behaviour. In this case, the tax serves no purpose but to raise revenue.

The appropriateness of a tax is further influenced by the administrative cost and burden of its application.[43] For example, measuring and taxing the carbon emissions of individual vehicles is an administrative nightmare. Furthermore, in the absence of technology, it is impossible. In this case, a general environmental levy on fuel is more appropriate to discourage the use of individual motor vehicles and to encourage the use of public transport. In contrast, where the aim is to reduce sulphur dioxide emissions in vehicles, a general fuel levy will be ineffective. However, taxing the sulphur content in fuel will reduce the need for fuel with high sulphur content and encourage the use of cleaner fuels, which would ultimately lead to a reduction in sulphur emissions.[44]

VAT/GST has the advantage of an enormously wide tax base.[45] Instead of developing and implementing new environmental tax systems altogether, the existing VAT/GST rules can be amended to factor in the environmental impact of consumption. Albrecht recommends that environmentally detrimental consumption must be taxed at a higher VAT/GST rate than environmentally beneficial consumption.[46] However, the administrative burden of variable VAT/GST rates is costly resulting in the cost of tax collection exceeding actual revenue.

5.2.7 Must Subscribe to an Environmental Object

Patterson points out that the environmental tax must be closely linked to the environmental "bad" that it aims to control.[47] Where the linkage between the tax and the pollution is weak, the tax is likely to fail in having an impact on pollution and may result in costly distortions to production and consumption decisions.[48] Where the linkage is poor, additional or alternative pollution control measures may be appropriate. This can take the form of additional regulation, subsidies, or tax incentives.[49]

5.2.8 Object to Alter Behaviour

Ideally, environmental taxes and levies must be implemented with the objective of altering patterns of behaviour that would ultimately reduce the damage inflicted on the environment.[50] Despite extensive market research, results are often based on predictions and mostly overstated.[51] In some cases, the introduction of environmental levies only results in temporary alteration in behavioural patterns. In these cases, additional measures must be implemented to alter damaging behaviour. These measures typically include demand-and-control measures in the form of additional restrictive legislation or trade restrictions.

Consumers are often not aware of the damaging effect of their behaviour.[52] Proper education will not only result in political support for the tax but also ultimately lead to behavioural change.[53]

Although the state-level ban on plastic bags has resulted in a reduction of plastic bag pollution, pollution in general is still high.[54] Apart from GST on plastic-coated jute bags and sacks, no environmental tax is levied on plastic bags. However, many retailers charge between INR 10 and 20 for a plastic bag or supply environmentally friendly jute or material bags only.

5.2.9 Ideally, Revenue Must Be Earmarked to Achieve Object

In public finance theory, the model recommendation is that the government should separate its spending decisions from its taxation decisions so that spending can be undertaken unrestricted and mainly based on benefit–cost considerations.[55] However, Buchanan and Goetz argue that when there is a significant connection between the taxpayer and the beneficiary of taxes, earmarking shows taxpayer preference for public services.[56] While there may not necessarily be an economic rationale for earmarking, it makes good political sense to gain public acceptance for the introduction of new taxes.[57] In fact, an international poll of 22,000 people in 21 countries revealed that 50% supported higher energy taxes and that this support rose to 70% if the revenues were earmarked for the promotion of energy-saving and cleaner fuels.[58] Taxpayers often reject the imposition of new taxes where they believe that revenue will be spent wastefully or that a substantial part of it goes for a service that they disapprove altogether.[59] A lack of trust that the government would do with the revenue as they promised remains a fundamental problem confronting successful environmental tax reform.[60] Many people also believe that taxation on its own will not achieve the desired environmental behavioural change.[61] Oates remarks that strict earmarking may result in increased spending.[62] He argues that certain environmental projects will be undertaken just because funds are available.[63] Instead, environmental projects must meet the same economic and budgetary requirements as any other government project or expenditure.[64] Earmarking of revenue, so it is believed, will improve the state of the environment.[65] Barde and Owens argue that as the object of the environmental tax is to alter human behaviour, earmarking is unnecessary.[66] This argument is only valid where it can be established that the environmental tax genuinely alters human behaviour on its own. In cases where a levy becomes ineffective or the consumption of the dutiable product is inelastic, the revenue must still be used towards achieving the objective. For example, where a levy is charged on electricity (an inelastic commodity), the levy must be used towards the roll-out of renewable energy generators. The OECD recommends that revenue from environmental taxes should be treated as general government revenue.[67] The OECD suggests that it is unlikely that revenue from environmental levies can be sustained to fund a specific environmental policy.[68] This is evident in cases where environmental levies on elastic products significantly alter behavioural patterns resulting in a diminishing tax base. However, this does not prevent governments from linking new taxes to general environmental expenditure or soft earmarking.[69] Soft earmarking allows for better fiscal planning and regular policy reform.

The Indian government is not against the earmarking of taxes. In recent developments in the taxing of tobacco, both the national government and state-level governments introduced the earmarking of excise taxes and cess levies on tobacco.[70]

5.2.10 Purpose Not to Enrich Government

It must not be the object of environmental levies to replenish government's finances. An environmental tax is not a miracle cure for government's financial problems.[71] Governments often impose environmental levies under the misconception that residents would not be disinclined to pay an environmental levy. This is based on the political propaganda that the environmental tax is for the greater good of the environment. Where the revenue from environmental taxes will not be earmarked, this approach must not be followed. The lack of transparency and publicity on environmental expenditure will lead to the perception that the imposition of environmental taxes is just another method to fill government money coffers.[72] This may result in a culture of non-compliance and the rise in tax avoidance schemes.

5.2.11 Should Not Encourage More Damaging Behaviour

In some cases, an environmental tax penalty could result in an increase in environmentally damaging behaviour.[73] For example, where the dumping of hazardous material is taxed, dumping itself may be reduced, but some taxpayers may avoid these taxes by dumping the hazardous material illegally.[74] The risk can be reduced by imposing fines on illegal dumping. Policing illegal dumping is, however, costly and labour intensive. Similarly, an environmental tax incentive may result in behaviour that causes more harm to the environment. For example, an incentive on electric vehicles may encourage excessive driving, further resulting in excessive use of electricity when the vehicles require shorter charging intervals.[75] In Europe, lower taxes on diesel resulted in an increase in atmospheric and noise pollution in towns.[76] Bazin, Ballet, and Touahri opine that some taxpayers may even argue "since I pay, I can consume and thus pollute".[77] In these cases, environmental taxes fail. Alternative measures must be implemented to realise the individual's environmental responsibility. Bontems and Bourgeon argue that an environmental tax design must also include an enforcement mechanism to deter non-compliance and tax evasion.[78] They posit that demand-and-control and environmental tax reform must be designed to operate together.

5.2.12 Inelastic Goods/Consumption: To Tax or Not to Tax?

Where no alternative environmentally beneficial goods or services are available, changing behaviour is unlikely to occur.[79] The general conception of taxpayers towards an environmental penalty will be affected negatively if taxpayers are penalised on behaviour over which they have no control. In these cases, behavioural reform is limited, especially where the behaviour being taxed is inelastic. Before an environmental levy on goods or behaviour is introduced, it must be determined if alternative goods and services are available, and if so, whether the cost of switching to alternatives would not hinder behavioural change. Where no alternative exists, earmarking of environmental taxes is essential to ensure public buy-in. Revenue must be dedicated to the research and innovation of alternatives or in other mitigating programmes.

In India, significant increases in taxes on fossil fuels together with a high cess on coal have resulted in electricity generated from fossil fuel to be among the most expensive in the world. While electricity consumption is inelastic, India's ambitious solar and wind power programme resulted in an overall reduction of carbon emissions year on year.[80]

Economic reform in the form of higher prices is likely to negatively influence the demand for certain products.[81] Pearson and Smith suggest that a carbon levy on the urban consumption of fuel will suppress the need for fuel and, ultimately, result in fewer carbon emissions.[82] In other words, motorists will drive less or make use of car pool systems or public transport if fuel is subject to a carbon tax levy.[83] Product taxes will only be effective if the consumer has the choice of either reducing his or her consumption or switching to an alternative product.[84]

5.3 Environmental Tax Incentives

Too much stick and no carrot make the donkey stubborn. Unless driven by a guilty conscience or passion for the environment, institutions and households are generally reluctant to invest in environmentally beneficial equipment.[85] Similarly, in the absence of financial incentives or gain, voluntary change in human behaviour – a change from environmentally detrimental behaviour to environmentally beneficial behaviour – is an unattainable expectation. Environmental tax incentives can be applied to influence and encourage institutions and households to practise more efficient resource use and limit (or even eliminate) the negative environmental externalities caused by their behaviour. To achieve this benefit on a sustainable level, environmental tax incentives must be developed carefully having regard to the requirements discussed below.

5.3.1 Adjoining Policy Objective

Environmental tax incentives must be structured to complement or promote existing adjoining government or private environmentally beneficial projects.[86] In some cases, environmental tax incentives cannot achieve the desired outcome on its own. In these cases, environmental tax incentives must be established to co-function with additional measures. For example, the environmental tax incentive can co-function with new or existing command-and-control measures.[87] Similarly, the environmental tax incentive can be joined to a concomitant environmental tax penalty to achieve the desired outcomes.[88] For example, the local authority in Delhi, to reduce urban congestion and reduce harmful gases in the city, exempts electric-operated public transport from taxes. While the lower cost of electric public transport appeals to many users, it does not make up for the convenience of a private vehicle. The implementation of a congestion tax, or an increased GST rate on fossil-fuel-driven public transport, will make the lower cost of electric-driven public transport more appealing, although considered less convenient or slow.

5.3.2 Not Overly Prescriptive

To gain the maximum environmental benefit, the environmental tax incentive must not be overly prescriptive. The objective is to achieve behavioural change of an entire community or industry. Where overly prescriptive rules prevent most taxpayers to benefit from the incentive, behavioural change is limited, and the environmental incentive fails to achieve the desired objective. The OECD recommends that the environmental tax incentive (and penalties) must be broad in scope and application, especially in cases where the impact of the environmental damage is not restricted to a specific area or industry.[89]

5.3.3 Spur Innovation

The Porter hypothesis claims that properly designed environmental policies can prompt innovation and production efficiency that may result in an absolute advantage over non-regulated establishments.[90] This hypothesis is based on the efficient environmental regulation, which translates to a complete integration of environmental fiscal reform through market-based instruments and command-and-control measures. Environmental taxes – absent any specific environmental tax incentive – encourage innovation because producers have the advantage of avoiding the environmental tax by finding alternative, more environmentally friendly means of production.[91] Similarly, environmental tax incentives must be structured in conjunction with the environmental tax penalties to spur environmental innovation.[92] Careful consideration is required to ensure that tax incentives do not subsidise environmentally beneficial behaviour that would have happened naturally or because of adjoining environmental command-and-control measures.[93] Similarly, the tax incentive benefits must not be too narrow that they do not stimulate any action.[94] To achieve balance, public comment, feedback from competent investigators, and comparative studies of environmental fiscal reform of other jurisdictions are necessary. Owens notes that where incentives are structured to counterbalance market distortions created by environmental levies, polluters will reduce pollution to limit the effect of environmental levies but will not invest in innovation to further curb pollution.[95] Placing a price on pollution and rewarding the implementation of measures to reduce pollution in all forms will encourage creative thinkers to develop innovative ideas to reduce pollution.[96]

In India, where water is considered a gift from God, water saving and the recycling of water have not achieved much progress. It is unlikely that a user charge or wastewater levy will be accepted by the larger community who can ill-afford to pay for water. Innovation is of utmost importance in securing sustainable development, and the interaction between environmental tax penalties and incentives to stimulate innovation must be considered carefully.[97] If designed creatively, existing property taxes, user charges, and environmental levies can be structured so as to provide a concomitant monetary incentive for environmentally beneficial practices and innovation in the field of environmental conservation.[98] However, this hypothesis is extrapolative, and the lack of empirical literature affects the integrity of the proposition negatively.[99] In this regard, the "Make India" campaign, together with carefully designed tax incentives, has the potential to promote Indian innovation that will boost the economy and have an environmentally beneficial effect.

5.3.4 Subscribe to the Double-Dividend Hypothesis

The term "double-dividend hypothesis" refers to the policy to tax environmentally detrimental behaviour and to reduce taxes (or incentivise) on environmentally beneficial behaviour.[100] This hypothesis aims to reach a win-win situation where the first dividend equates to positive changes in environmental reform and the second dividend equates to economic stimulation.[101] Bovenberg and de Mooij argue that the double-dividend hypothesis can be achieved if the "incentive" produces a less distortionary tax system.[102] For example, revenue raised from a pollution tax can be applied to lower taxes on labour. The increase in production cost is set off against the lower taxes on labour. Accordingly, the collaborative tax incentive need not be environmentally related. It is merely required that the collaborative tax incentive will result in some form of economic benefit.[103] The degree of success of this approach is highly speculative and can be illustrated as follows:

Scenario 1: Where a stern environmental levy is introduced on environmentally detrimental behaviour together with a concomitant relief on labour taxes, behavioural patterns could dramatically change to wholly eradicate the environmentally detrimental behaviour. The revenue that was earmarked to compensate for the loss in revenue (caused by reduced labour taxes) will be diminished, and the double-dividend hypothesis fails.

Scenario 2: Where an environmental levy is introduced on inelastic products/behaviour together with a concomitant relief on labour taxes, behavioural patterns will, as a result of the inelasticity of behaviour, not be altered significantly. In this scenario, the source of revenue is merely shifted from labour to an environmental levy. No environmental benefit will be achieved, and the double-dividend hypothesis fails.[104]

Fullerton and Metcalfe posit that a true double-dividend hypothesis requires both the tax and the concomitant tax incentive to be environmentally related.[105] Moreover, the tax on pollution must be accompanied by an environmental demand-and-control policy.[106] They argue that a mere reduction in labour taxes (as put forward by Bovenberg and de Mooij) creates a tax equilibrium, but that the environmental benefit is minimal.[107] For example, where energy from non-renewable resources is taxed, energy-efficient products such as LED light bulbs or solar energy products could be exempted from VAT/GST or custom and excise duties. Although energy consumption is inelastic, VAT/GST-exempted energy-efficient products will be more economical to a larger part of the community resulting in reduced energy consumption. The reduction in energy consumption will be significant enough to benefit the environment but would not cause a significant reduction in revenue that would lead to a loss to the *fiscus*. The economic cost is too insignificant for the double dividend to have failed.

Section 80JJA of the Indian Income Tax Act[108] provides for the full deduction of all the profits and gains deriving from the business of collecting, processing, and treating of biodegradable waste for generating electricity or producing bio-fertilisers, bio-pesticides, or other biological agents or to produce biogas or making pellets or briquettes for fuel or organic manure. Of importance is that there exists, apart from a levy on coal, no significant concomitant environmental penalty in the form of taxes, user charges, or levies to penalise the consumption of non-biological fertilisers, pesticides, energy, or heating. This ostensible environmental tax incentive does not subscribe to the double-dividend hypothesis. The success of achieving an environmentally beneficial outcome is speculative.

5.3.5 Counterbalance Market Distortions

In line with the double-dividend hypothesis, environmental tax incentives can be applied to counterbalance market distortions created by environmental tax penalties. Incentives can be applied to limit the impact of environmental levies on poor households that are dependent on inelastic products.[109] This can be achieved through VAT/GST exemptions on energy-efficient products or by issuing energy-efficient products to lower-income households free of charge.[110] Lower-income households are often reliant on landlords who are reluctant to invest in energy-efficient housing. Limited or no incentives exist for landlords to invest in energy-efficient products such as isolation, energy-efficient heating, and so on.[111] Command-and-control-type building regulations can be implemented requiring all new developments to comply with energy-efficient building practices.[112] Simultaneously, tax incentives in the form of capital allowances must be implemented together with the demand-and-control measures to reap maximum benefit.

An easy way out to balance market distortions – as some jurisdictions opted for – is to merely increase the social grants to lower-income groups. However, as these measures bear no environmentally beneficial outcome, the market balance may be restored, but the environmental benefit is not attained. Ultimately, it merely provides for the shifting of funds at a high administrative burden.

5.3.6 Not Burden to Fiscus

The use of subsidies in the form of tax incentives can overly burden the *fiscus* or negatively affect the market.[113] Where no concomitant environmental levy or penalty is charged to offset the loss of revenue, other revenue sources like labour taxes (income tax) must cross-subsidise the environmental incentive. In most cases, revenue from these sources is applied or earmarked for existing state expenses already. In the absence of a concomitant environmental levy or penalty, measures must be imposed to increase the revenue capacity from existing revenue sources. In developing countries that are dependent on income tax as primary source of revenue, adjustments in income tax rates or tax rebates are often used to subsidise revenue shortfall. This has a negative impact on the market. Furthermore, instead of achieving the desired environmentally beneficial outcome, the cross-subsidy principle indiscriminately diminishes taxpayers' income that would result in increased poverty. Under this system, the environmentally beneficial outcome cannot be achieved. As set out above, Section 80JJA of the Indian Income Tax Act results in a loss of revenue. No concomitant environmental levy, tax, or user charge exists to set off against this revenue loss.

5.3.7 Ensure Sustainable Environmental Benefit

Market reactions to tax incentives are often unpredictable, and it is difficult to "pick winners" to direct markets in a certain environmentally beneficial direction.[114] As a result, an environmental levy/penalty (as concomitant to an environmental incentive aimed at offsetting revenue losses) could potentially raise revenue for a short period of time only. Yet, the environmental tax incentive could potentially strain the *fiscus* for a significantly long period of time. Environmental tax incentives schemes should, therefore, include sunset clauses to evaluate the influence of the incentive on the reduction of harmful practices. Where it is evident that the environmental tax incentive is more beneficial to the environment than the negative impact the overall cost of its implementation has on the *fiscus*, the sunset period can be extended. The sunset clause will mitigate the cost to the *fiscus* where the environmental benefit of the incentive is minimal. The tax-free allowance in terms of Section 80JJA of the Indian Income Tax Act does not provide for a sunset clause. It is well known that environmental change remains a long-term goal, and results are often achieved in years far beyond the period in which the environmental incentive was implemented. Environmentally detrimental behaviour may reappear or persist where incentives or subsidies are revoked within a short period of implementation. Consequently, it is submitted that environmental tax incentives must be reviewed annually to ensure a sustainable environmental benefit or goal.

5.3.8 Not Create Other Social Dilemmas Like Food Shortages?

In non-oil-producing countries that are dependent on fossil fuels, an ever-increasing need to establish bio-fuels exists. It is trite that the cost of establishing bio-fuel-manufacturing plants and the cost of manufacturing bio-fuel exceed the cost of fossil fuel by far. Government incentives in the form of direct subsidies, tax reductions, tax exemptions, or other financial support are required to favour the production and use of bio-fuels over fossil fuels. However, Bugge warns that favourable conditions to manufacture bio-fuels could lead to food shortages if farmers convert traditional crop-producing farms into biofuel-manufacturing plants.[115] The increasing negative effect that climate change has on commercial farming, the increasing need for better (even super) quality fresh produce, and the significant input cost of commercial farming can convince commercial farmers to produce crops for the manufacture of bio-fuel or bio-fuel derivatives exclusively. To avoid food shortages, additional measures outside the realm of tax legislation may be required. For example, only crops not suitable for human consumption may be used in the production of bio-fuel, bio-fuel crop producers must be licenced, and the number of bio-fuel crop producers per geographical area must be limited.

5.4 Conclusion

If we want to save the planet from major degradation, environmental reform is unavoidable. Environmental reform starts with a change in human behaviour.[116] Rowell suggests that behavioural regulation in the form of "nudges" and choice architecture is necessary to change human behaviour.[117] Accurately understanding how humans behave is instrumental in developing these "nudges" to achieve the desired result. Without government intervention, no significant environmental change will take effect.[118] Environmental fiscal reform is but one method (or nudge) to change the way we live, we manufacture goods, and we consume natural resources and pollute our world. In India, environmental tax reform can be achieved by the imposition of environmental tax penalties and environmental incentives within the realm of the existing tax regimes. India has experienced the brunt of a complicated tax system. No one method of environmental tax reform is better than the other in achieving an environmental goal. However, an additional separate environmental tax system – like carbon tax – will further complicate the tax regime and create an additional administrative burden for the revenue authority and taxpayers. As environmental tax reform is based on speculation, it remains difficult to determine the market reaction and consumer behaviour. It is arguable if environmental tax penalties on inelastic goods will change behavioural patterns even if an (sometimes more expensive) alternative is available. The existence of die-hard consumer habits can negatively impact both environmental tax incentives and penalties.[119] Important is that tax penalties and tax incentives cannot be implemented willy-nilly. A definitive, well-structured, yet transformable environmental tax policy is essential. It remains clear that environmental tax reform can only be implemented successfully if the aim of the environmental tax reform is clearly defined, if there is a strong link between the tax and environmental reform, and if the revenue is earmarked for specific environmental reform or conservation.[120]

Notes

1 National Treasury of South Africa, A framework for considering market-based instruments to support environmental fiscal reform in South Africa i–ii (2006); Kasonen K, and Nicodème G, *The role of fiscal instruments in environmental policy* 9 (date last accessed April 5, 2018) http://ec.europa.eu/taxation_customs/resources/documents/taxation/gen_info/economic_analysis/tax_papers/taxation_paper_19.pdf.

2 Id.

3 Paterson AR, Pruning the money-tree to ensure sustainable growth: Facilitating sustainable development through market-based instruments, 9 *Potchefstroom Electronic Law Review* 88 (2006).

4 Id.; Klöck DP, The role of market based instruments to promote renewable energies-A critical legal comparison between South Africa's REBID and Germany's REFIT Scheme 7–8 (2013) (unpublished LLM dissertation, University of Cape Town) (on file with the University of Cape Town); See also Stavins RN, Experience with market-based environmental policy instruments, in *Handbook of Environmental Economics: Volume 1*, 358 (Mäler K & Vincent J eds., 2003); Stavins RN, Market-based environmental policies, in *Public Policies for Environmental Protection*, 31 (Portney PR, and Stavins RN. Eds., 2000).

5 Paterson, *supra* note 3, at 88–89.

6 Anon, *New levy: SA's Tyre recycling plan criticised as no plan at all*, The Witness, January 11, 2012.

Anon 2012 *The Witness*; Kasonen and Nicodème, *supra* note 1, at 9; Du Plessis A, Public participation, good environmental governance and fulfilment of environmental rights, 2 *Potchefstroom Electronic Law Review* 10–11 (2008).

7 See in general Stavins, *supra* note 4; Burns Y, and Kidd M, Administrative law & implementation of environmental law, in *Fuggle & Rabie's Environmental management in South Africa*, 259 (Strydom HA, and King ND, Eds., 2009).

8 Hanks J, Achieving industrial sustainable development is South Africa: What role for 'self-regulatory' and 'co-regulatory' instruments?, 5 *South African Journal of Environmental Law and Policy* 298 (1998).

9 Hahn R, and Stavins R, Economic incentives for environmental protection: Integrating theory and practice, 82(2) *American Economic Review* 464–468 (1992); Schöb R, *The double dividend hypothesis of environmental taxes: A survey*, Otto-von-Guericke-University Magdeburg and CESifo 3 (March 2003).

10 Baveye J, and Valenduc C, Are 'environmental' tax incentives efficient?, 71(2) *Documentatieblad* 144 (2011); Mandy K, as quoted in Dimmer K, *CO^2 Tax: The Dirty Tax*, April/May Professional Accountant 41 (2011).

11 Chaturvedi A, Saluja MS, Banerjee A, and Arora R, Environmental fiscal reform, 26 *IIMB Management Review* 193–194 (2014).

12 *See* Id. at 194–196; See also Eblen RA, and Eblen RW, The encyclopaedia of environment 177–178 (1994); Turpie JK, Environmental and resource economics, in

Fuggle & Rabie's Environmental management in South Africa, 63–66, 259 (Strydom HA, and King ND, Eds., 2009).

13 Fullerton D, Leicester A, and Smith A, *Environmental Taxes*, National Bureau of Economic Research 3 (2008) (date last accessed November 16, 2018) http://www.nber.org/papers/w14197.pdf. See also National Treasury *supra* note 1, at 59; OECD, Environmental Taxation: A guide for Policy Makers 6 (2011) (date last accessed March 14, 2018) http://www.oecd.org/dataoecd/17/7/48164926.pdf; Hudson V, and Roy-Chowdhury H, Green taxation in a recession, (date last accessed January 15, 2018) http://www2.accaglobal.com/pubs/about/public_affairs/unit/global_briefings/green_tax.pdf.

14 Oates W, Taxing pollution: An idea whose time has come?, in *The RFF Reader in Environmental and Resource Management*, 63–68 (1999).

15 Fullerton et al *supra* note 13, at 3–4; OECD *supra* note 13, at 6; Hudson and Roy-Chowdhury *supra* note 13; Schöb, *supra* note 9, at 4; Ekins P, European environmental taxes and charges: Recent experience, issues and trends, 31 *Ecological Economics* 39–62 (1999).

16 Fullerton et al., *supra* note 13, at 3; *Environmental Taxes* 3; National Treasury, *supra* note 1, at 40,60.

17 Fullerton et al., *supra* note 13, at 3,9,14,15.

18 National Treasury of South Africa, Discussion Paper for public Comment: Reducing Green House gas emissions: The carbon tax option, 8 (December 2010), (date last accessed on March 7, 2017) http://www.treasury.gov.za/public%20comments/Discussion%20Paper%20Carbon%20Taxes%2081210.pdf; OECD *The political economy of environmentally related Taxes*, February OECD Observer 4 (2007), (date last accessed on February 7, 2018) http://www.oecd.org/dataoecd/26/39/38046899.pdf; Kasonen and Nicodème, *supra* note 6, at 5; Barde J, and Owens J, The evolution of eco-taxes, 198 *The OECD Observer* 13 (1996).

19 Fullerton et al., *supra* note 13, at 3; National Treasury, *supra* note 18, at 8; OECD, *supra* note 13, at 9; Seymore R, The impact of environmental tax on electricity generation in South Africa, 32(2) *Journal for Studies in Economics and Econometrics* 5 (2002); Ekins, *supra* note 15, at 39–62; Barde and Owens, *supra* note 18, at 13.

20 OECD, *supra* note 18; OECD, *supra* note 13, at 2; Kasonen and Nicodème, *supra* note 6, at 7–8; Baveye and Valenduc, *supra* note 10, 145,148; Schöb, supra note 9, at 6.

21 Kasonen and Nicodème, *supra* note 6, at 11; OECD, *supra* note 6, at 2–3.

22 Baveye and Valenduc, *supra* note 10 148; Schöb, *supra* note 9, at 6.

23 National Treasury, *supra* note 18, at 64; OECD, *supra* note 18, at 4; OECD, *supra* note 13, at 9.

24 OECD, *supra* note 13 at 9; National Treasury, *supra* note 18, at 64; Bosquet B, Environmental tax reform: Does it work? A survey of the empirical evidence, 34 *Ecological Economics* 29–30 (2000).

25 Kasonen and Nicodème, *supra* note 6, at 5; Baveye and Valenduc, *supra* note 10, at148.

26 Kasonen and Nicodème, *supra* note 6, at 26.

27 Id, at 27.

28 Fullerton et al., *supra* note 13, at 5; National Treasury, *supra* note 18, at 62–63; OECD, *supra* note 18, at 3; Kasonen and Nicodème, *supra* note 6, at 8; Newman D, *Industry warns on carbon tax*, Business Day, February 9, 2011 (date last accessed on April 15, 2018), http://www.businessday.co.za/articles/Content.aspx?id=164475.

29 The Mahindra and TATA vehicle manufacturer companies have entered the international market since 2004. Mahindra entered the US market in 2019.

30 Ekins, *supra* note 15, at 39–62.

31 Fullerton et al., *supra* note 13 at 24–25.

32 OECD, *supra* note 13 at 10; See in general OECD, Renewable energy and Environmental taxes (date last accessed on March 13, 2012) http://client.viewontv.com/oecd/221106/index.htm.

33 Barker T, and Johnstone N, The impacts of environmental policy on competitiveness, in *International Competitiveness and Environmental Policies* (Barker T, Kohler J. (Eds.) 1998); See also OECD, Implementation Strategies for Environmental Taxes (1996).
34 Ekins, *supra* note 15, at 39–62.
35 Id.
36 Id.
37 Kasonen and Nicodème *supra* note 6, at 9.
38 OECD, *supra* note 13, at 10; National Treasury, *supra* note 18, at 8, 40–43. OECD, *supra* note 18, at 4; Hudson and Roy-Chowdhury, *supra* note 13.
39 Kasonen and Nicodème, *supra* note 6, at 9.
40 OECD, *supra* note 13, at 10; Fullerton et al., *supra* note 13, at 24.
41 OECD, *supra* note 13 at 9.
42 Id.
43 Id, at 4,8; National Treasury, *supra* note 18 at 41,46,49.
44 OECD, *supra* note 18, at 4–5; OECD, *supra* note 13, at 4.
45 Albrecht J, The use of consumption taxes to re-launch green tax reforms, 26(1) *International Review of Law and Economics* 94 (2006).
46 Id, at 94–95.
47 Patterson CD, Environmental taxes and subsidies: What is the appropriate fiscal policy for dealing with modern environmental problems?, 24 *William and Mary Environmental Law and Policy Review* 137 (2000).
48 McCoy D, Reflections on the double dividend debate, in *Ecotaxation*, 201 (O'Riordan T, ed., 1997); Smith S, Environmental tax design, in *Ecotaxation*, 27 (O'Riordan T, ed., 1997); Richards K, The instrument choice game: When do environmental taxes win?, in *Critical issues in environmental taxation: International and comparative perspectives* (vol 1) (Deketelaere K, Kreiser L, and Milne J, eds., 2008).
49 Patterson, *supra* note 47, at 137.
50 Smith, *supra* note 48, at 22–23, Marquez JJG, Constitutional constraints for environmental taxation in Mexico, in *Critical issues in environmental taxation: international and comparative perspectives* (vol 1), 138 (Deketelaere K, Kreiser L, and Milne J, eds., 2008); Hudson and Roy-Chowdhury, *supra* note13.
51 Fullerton, *supra* note 13, at 5,8,9; OECD, *supra* note 13, at 2.
52 Kasonen and Nicodème, *supra* note 6, at 11.
53 OECD, *supra* note 13, at 11.
54 Parvaiz A, *Despite state-level bans, plastic bags still suffocate India's cities* (date last accessed March 13, 2018) https://in.reuters.com/article/india-environment-plastic/despite-state-level-bans-plastic-bags-still-suffocate-indias-cities-idINKCN1GC0TE.
55 Sælen H, and Kallbekken S, A choice experiment on fuel taxation and earmarking in Norway, 70 *Ecological Economics*, 2181 (2011); Musgrave R and Musgrave P, *Public Finance in Theory and Practice* 231 (4th ed. 1984); Pirttilä J, Earmarking of environmental taxes and pareto-efficient taxation, 56 *Finanzarchiv N.F.*, Bd. 202 (1990).
56 Buchanan J, The economics of earmarked taxes, 71 *The Journal of Political Economy* 457–469 (1963); Goetz C, Earmarked taxes and majority rule budgetary processes, 58 *The American Economic Review* 128–136 (1968).
57 Sælen and Kallbekken, *supra* note 55, at 2182; Kallbekken S, Kroll S, and Cherry TL, Do you not like Pigou, or do you not understand him? Tax aversion and revenue recycling in the lab, 62 *Journal of Environmental Economics and Management* 53 (2011); Anesi V, Earmarked taxation and political competition, 90 *Journal of Public Economics* 680–691 (2001); Bös D, Earmarked taxation: Welfare versus political support, 75 *Journal of Public Economics* 439 (2000); Bluffstone RA, Environmental taxes in developing and transition economies, 3(1) *Public Finance and Management* 152 (2003); Parry IWH, Pollution taxes and revenue recycling, 29 *Journal of Environmental Economics and Management* 64–77 (1998); Palmer T and Riera A, Tourism and environmental taxes. With special reference to the "Balearic ecotax", 24 *Tourism Management* 674 (2003); Cherry TL, Kalbekken S, and Kroll S, The impact of trial runs on the

acceptability of environmental taxes: Experimental evidence, 38 *Resource and Energy Economics* 84–95 (2014).

58 GlobeScan P, *BBC World Service Poll: Most Would Pay Higher Energy Bills to Address Climate Change Says Global Poll*, www.worldpublicopinion.org/pipa/pdf/nov07/BBCClimate2_Nov07_pr.pdf (date last accessed May 15, 2018).

59 Rivlin A, The continuing search for a popular tax, 79 *The American Economic Review* 113–117 (1989); Kallbekken, Kroll and Cherry, *supra* note 57, at 53; Bös, *supra* note 57, at 439; Dresner S, Jackson T, and Gilbert N, History and social responses to environmental tax reform in the United Kingdom, 34 *Energy Policy* 930–939 (2006).

60 Dresner S, Dunne L, Clinch P, and Beuermann C, Social and political responses to ecological tax reform in Europe: An introduction to the special issue, 34 *Energy Policy* 895–904 (2006); Kallbekken, Kroll and Cherry, *supra* note 57 at 53; Harring Nh and Jager SC, Should we trust in values? Explaining public support for pro-environmental taxes, 5 *Sustainability* 214–215 (2013).

61 See in general the survey by Dresner, Jackson, and Gilbert, *supra* note 60; Cherry, Kalbekken, and Kroll, *supra* note 57, at 84–95.

62 Oates WE, Green taxes: Can we protect the environment and improve the tax system at the same time?, 61(4) *Southern Economic Journal* 921–922 (1995).

63 Id.

64 Id.

65 Sælen and Kallbekken, *supra* note 55, at 2182; Patterson, *supra* note 47, at 137.

66 Barde and Owens, *supra* note 18, at 13.

67 OECD, *supra* note 13, at 8.

68 Id, at 8–9.

69 Id, at 8.

70 See in general Rijo MJ, Rao MG, Deshpande RS, Selvaraj S, Rao RK, Moore J, Sengupta J, Chaloupka FJ, and Jha P, *The Economics of Tobacco and Tobacco Taxation in India* (Paris: International Union against Tuberculosis and Lung Disease, 2010) https://www.global.tobaccofreekids.org/assets/global/pdfs/en/India_tobacco_taxes_report_en.pdf (date last accessed March 13, 2018).

71 Hudson and Roy-Chowdhury, *supra* note 13.

72 Id; OECD, *supra* note 13, at 11–12.

73 Fullerton et al., *supra* note 13, at 5.

74 Id.

75 OECD, *supra* note 13, at 3; Baveye & Valenduc, *supra* note 10, at 145.

76 Barde and Owens, *supra* note 18, at 11.

77 Bazin D, Ballet J, and Touahri D, Environmental responsibility versus taxation, 49 *Ecological Economics* 129–134 (2004).

78 Bontems P and Bourgeon J, Optimal environmental taxation and enforcement policy, 49 *European Economic Review* 410 (2005).

79 Hudson and Roy-Chowdhury, *supra* note 13.

80 Gautam AK, *Chapter 9: From Carbon Subsidy to Carbon Tax: India's Green Actions*, Economic Survey (2015) https://abhijeetgautam.wordpress.com/2015/06/15/chapter-9-from-carbon-subsidy-to-carbon-tax-indias-green-actions/ (date last accessed March 13, 2018).

81 Pearson M, and Smith S, *Taxation and environmental policy: some initial evidence*, IFS Commentary no. 19 3,5–7 (1990); Driesen D, *Why pollution taxes cannot replace command and replace regulation (but should have a bright future nonetheless)*, in Critical issues in environmental taxation: international and comparative perspectives (vol 1) 51–52 (Deketelaere K, Kreiser L, and Milne J, eds., 2008).

82 Pearson and Smith, *supra* note 81, at 3,5–7.

83 Id.

84 Barde JP, *Environmental taxation: Experience in OECD countries*, in Ecotaxation (O'Riordan T, ed., 1997).

85 OECD, *supra* note 13 at 3–7.

86 Id, at 11; National Treasury, *supra* note 1, at 64.
87 OECD, *supra* note 18 at 6; Reichard M, *Green Taxes for South Africa*, ClimatechangeCorp (last updated June 17, 2009) http://www.climatechangecorp.com/content.asp?ContentID=6187; Kasonen and Nicodème *supra* note 6, at 9.
88 Id.
89 OECD, *supra* note 18, at 6.
90 Porter M, The Competitive Advantage of Nations (1990).
91 Patterson, *supra* note 47, at 121; See also Ekins, *supra* note 15, at 39–62; Albrecht, *supra* note 45, at 95–96.
92 Owens J, *Taxes for innovation*, 279 The OECD Observer (2010) (date last accessed January 15, 2018) http://www.oecdobserver.org/news/fullstory.php/aid/3271/Taxes_for_innovation.html, Owens J, *The OECD Observer* May 2010; OECD *Taxation, innovation and the environment* 3 (date last accessed January 15, 2018) http://www.oecd.org/dataoecd/24/25/48178034.pdf; Baveye & Valenduc, *supra* note 10, at 152.
93 Westin RA, Understanding environmental taxes, 2 *The Tax Lawyer* 360 (1993).
94 Id.
95 Owens, *supra* note 92, at 3–4.
96 OECD, *supra* note 92, at 4; Barnard M, Koolstofbelasting as voorgestelde ekologiese fiskalehervormingsmaatreël in Suid-Afrika, 13 *Litnet Akademies* 810 (2016) http://www.litnet.co.za/koolstofbelasting-voorgestelde-ekologiese-fiskalehervormings maatreel-suid-afrika/ (visited October 31, 2017) at 812.
97 Owens, *supra* note 92.
98 National Treasury, *supra* note 1, at 8, 79; OECD, *supra* note 92, at 5.
99 Baveye & Valenduc, *supra* note 10, at 153–154.
100 National Treasury, *supra* note 1, at 6; Fullerton et al, *supra* note 13, at 10; Schöb, *supra* note 9, at 1; Parry I & Oates W, Policy analysis in the presence of distorting taxes, in *Environmental Policy Making in Economies with Prior Tax Distortions* 5 (Goulder L (ed.), 2002).
101 National Treasury, *supra* note 1, at 7–8; Fullerton et al., *supra* note 13, at 10–14; Fullerton D and Metcalfe G, Environmental taxes and the double dividend hypothesis (date last accessed February 14, 2018), http://ase.tufts.edu/econ/papers/9706.pdf.
102 Bovenberg AL and De Mooij RA, Environmental levies and distortionary taxes, 84 *American Economic Review* 1085 (1994); See also Bovenberg AL, Environmental taxes and the double dividend, 25 *Empirica* 15–35 (1998); Bovenberg AL and De Mooij RA, Environmental taxes and labor-market distortions, 10 *European Journal of Political Economy* 655–683 (1994).
103 Id.
104 Fullerton & Metcalfe, *supra* note 101, at 14.
105 Id, at 24–26.
106 Id.
107 Id. See also Schöb, *supra* note 9, at 167–168.
108 1961.
109 National Treasury, *supra* note 1, at 50, 62; Fullerton et al., *supra* note 13, at 10–14.
110 Hudson & Roy-Chowdhury, *supra* note 13.
111 OECD, *supra* note 16, at 9.
112 Id, at 9–10.
113 Id. In Germany, the current subsidy for the production of renewable energy has led to extreme feed-in tariffs imposed on consumers. These surcharges negatively affected household spending, which, in turn, slows down the economy.
114 Id, at 3; Eckert V and Chambers M, *Merkel vows to rein in renewable subsidies*, Planet Ark (June 13, 2013) www.planetark.com/enviro-news/item/68930.

115 Bugge TD, *Food for Fuel-WTO consistency of export restrictions on certain agricultural crops*, Legal Discourse in Cyberlaw and Trade 473 (2009).
116 Rowell & Bilz, *The Psychology of Environmental Law* (2021, NYU Press).
117 Rowell A, Once and future nudges, 82 *MO.L Rev.* (2017).
118 Rowell & Bilz, *supra* note 116.
119 Baveye & Valenduc, *supra* note 10, at 148.
120 Barde, *supra* note 84, at 234–239; Vos H, Environmental taxation in the Netherlands, in *Ecotaxation* (O'Riardan T (1997)); Määtä K, Finnish energy taxation: How well has it worked?, in *Critical issues in environmental taxation: international and comparative perspectives* (vol 1) 178–179 (Deketelaere K, Kreiser L, and Milne J (eds.) (2002)); Soares CD, The earmarking of revenues within the environmental tax policy, in *Critical issues in environmental taxation: international and comparative perspectives* (vol 1) 249–263 (Deketelaere K, Kreiser L, and Milne J (eds.) (2002)).

Bibliography

Albrecht, J. (2006). The use of consumption taxes to re-launch green tax reforms, 26(1) *International Review of Law and Economics* 94.

Anesi, V. (2001). Earmarked taxation and political competition, 90 *Journal of Public Economics* 680–691.

Anon. (2002). New levy: SA's Tyre recycling plan criticised as no plan at all. *The Witness*, January 11, 2012.

Barde, J. and Owens, J. (1996). The evolution of eco-taxes, 198 *The OECD Observer* 13.

Barde, J. P. (1997). Environmental taxation: experience in OECD countries, in O'Riordan, T., ed., Ecotaxation, Earthscan (1st ed.). London: Routledge.

Barker, T. and Johnstone, N. (1998). The impacts of environmental policy on competitiveness, in Barker, T. and Kohler, J., eds., *International Competitiveness and Environmental Policies*. Cheltenham, UK: Edward Elgar,.

Barnard, M. (2016). Koolstofbelasting as voorgestelde ekologiese fiskalehervormingsmaatreël in Suid-Afrika, 13 *Litnet Akademies* http://www.litnet.co.za/koolstofbelasting-voorgestelde-ekologiese-fiskalehervormingsmaatreel-suid-afrika/ (visited October 31, 2017).

Baveye, J. and Valenduc, C. (2011). Are 'environmental' tax incentives efficient?. 71(2) *Documentatieblad* 144.

Bazin, D., Ballet, J., & Touahri, D. (2004). Environmental responsibility versus taxation, 49 *Ecological Economics* 129–134.

Bluffstone, R. A. (2003). Environmental taxes in developing and transition economies, 3(1) *Public Finance and Management* 152.

Bontems, P. & Bourgeon, J. (2005). Optimal environmental taxation and enforcement policy, *European Economic Review 49*(2), 409–435.

Bös, D. (2000). Earmarked taxation: welfare versus political support, 75 *Journal of Public Economics* 439.

Bosquet, B. (2000). Environmental tax reform: does it work? A survey of the empirical evidence, 34 *Ecological Economics* 29–30.

Bovenberg, A. L. (1998). Environmental Taxes and the double dividend, 25 *Empirica* 15.

Bovenberg, A. L. & De Mooij, R. A. (1994a). Environmental levies and distortionary taxes, 84 *American Economic Review* 1085.

Bovenberg, A. L. & De Mooij, R. A. (1994b). Environmental taxes and labor-market distortions, 10 *European Journal of Political Economy* 655.

Buchanan, J. (1963). The economics of earmarked taxes, 71 *The Journal of Political Economy* 457–469.

Bugge, T. D. (2009). Food for Fuel-WTO consistency of export restrictions on certain agricultural crops, In *Legal discourse in cyberlaw and trade* (pp. 473–489). International Association of IT Lawyers.

Burns, Y. & Kidd, M. (2009). Administrative law & implementation of environmental law, in Strydom, H.A., and King, N.D., (Eds), Fuggle & Rabie's Environmental management in South Africa 2nd ed (Vol. 259, pp. 243–257). Juta Cape Town.

Chaturvedi, A., Saluja, M. S., Banerjee, A., & Arora, R. (2014). Environmental Fiscal Reform, 26 *IIMB Management Review* 193.

Cherry, T. L., Kalbekken, S. & Kroll, S. (2014). The impact of trial runs on the acceptability of environmental taxes: Experimental evidence, 38 *Resource and Energy Economics* 84–95.

Dimmer, K. (2011). CO^2 Tax: The Dirty Tax, (April/May) *Professional Accountant* 41.

Dresner, S., Dunne, L., Clinch, P. & Beuermann, C. (2006). Social and political responses to ecological tax reform in Europe: An introduction to the special issue, 34 *Energy Policy* 895–904.

Dresner, S., Jackson, T. & Gilbert, N. (2006). History and social responses to environmental tax reform in the United Kingdom, 34 *Energy Policy* 930–939.

Driesen, D. (2004). Why pollution taxes cannot replace command and replace regulation (but should have a bright future nonetheless), in Deketelaere, K., Kreiser, L., & Milne, J. (eds.), *Critical Issues in Environmental Taxation: International and Comparative Perspectives* (Vol. 1, pp. 51–60). New York: Oxford.

Du Plessis, A. (2008). Public participation, good environmental governance and fulfilment of environmental rights, 2 *Potchefstroom Electronic Law Review* 10.

Eblen, R. A. & Eblen, R. W. (1994). *The Encyclopaedia of Environment*, Boston, MA: Houghton Mifflin Co.

Eckert, V. & Chambers, M. (2013). Merkel vows to rein in renewable subsidies, *Planet Ark* www.planetark.com/enviro-news/item/68930 (visited February 14, 2018).

Ekins, P. (1992). European environmental taxes and charges: Recent experience, issues and trends, 31 *Ecological Economics* 39–62.

Fullerton, D., Leicester, A., & Smith, A. (2008). Environmental Taxes, *National Bureau of Economic Research* http://www.nber.org/papers/w14197.pdf (visited November 16, 2018).

Fullerton, D. & Metcalfe, G. (2018). Environmental taxes and the double dividend hypothesis, http://ase.tufts.edu/econ/papers/9706.pdf (visited February 14, 2018).

Gautam, A. K. (2015). Chapter 9: From Carbon subsidy to carbon tax: India's Green Actions, *Economic Survey* https://abhijeetgautam.wordpress.com/2015/06/15/chapter-9-from-carbon-subsidy-to-carbon-tax-indias-green-actions/ (visited March 13, 2018).

GlobeScan (2007). *BBC World Service Poll: Most Would Pay Higher Energy Bills to Address Climate Change Says Global Poll*, www.worldpublicopinion.org/pipa/pdf/nov07/BBCClimate2_Nov07_pr.pdf (visited May 15, 2018).

Goetz, C. (1968). Earmarked taxes and majority rule budgetary processes, 58 *The American Economic Review* 128–136.

Hahn, R. & Stavins, R. (1992). Economic incentives for environmental protection: Integrating theory and practice, 82(2) *American Economic Review* 464–468.

Hanks, J. (1998). Achieving industrial sustainable development is South Africa: What role for 'self-regulatory' and 'co-regulatory' instruments? 5 *South African Journal of Environmental Law and Policy* 298.

Harring, N. H. & Jager, S. C. (2013). Should we trust in values? Explaining public support for pro-environmental taxes, 5 *Sustainability* 214–215.

Hudson, V. & Roy-Chowdhury, H. (2018). *Green taxation in a recession*, http://www2.accaglobal.com/pubs/about/public_affairs/unit/global_briefings/green_tax.pdf (visited January 15, 2018).

Kallbekken, S., Kroll, S., & Cherry, T. L. (2011). Do you not like Pigou, or do you not understand him? Tax aversion and revenue recycling in the lab, 62 *Journal of Environmental Economics and Management* 53.

Kasonen, K. & Nicodéme, G. *The role of fiscal instruments in environmental policy.* (visited April 5, 2018) http://ec.europa.eu/taxation_customs/resources/documents/taxation/gen_info/economic_analysis/tax_papers/taxation_paper_19.pdf

Klöck, D. P. (2013). *The role of market based instruments to promote renewable energies-A critical legal comparison between South Africa's REBID and Germany's REFIT Scheme.* (Unpublished LLM dissertation, University of Cape Town) (on file with the University of Cape Town).

Määtä, K. (2004). Finnish energy taxation: How well has it worked?, in Deketelaere, K., Kreiser, L., & Milne, J. eds., *Critical issues in environmental taxation: international and comparative perspectives* (Vol. 1, pp. 175–188). New York: Oxford.

Marquez, J. J. G. (2004). Constitutional constraints for environmental taxation in Mexico, in Deketelaere, K., Kreiser, L., & Milne, J. (eds.), *Critical issues in environmental taxation: International and comparative perspectives* (Vol 1. pp. 137–148). New York: Oxford.

McCoy, D. (1997). *Reflections on the Double Dividend Debate,* in O'Riordon, T., (ed.), *Ecotaxation.* McCoy, D. (1997). *Reflections on the Double Dividend Debate,* in in O'Riordan, T. (1997). Ecotaxation (1st ed.). London: Routledge.

Musgrave, R. & Musgrave, P. (1985). *Public Finance in Theory and Practice.* McGraw Hill Education; 5th edition (1 July 2017).National Treasury of South Africa. (2006). *A framework for considering market-based instruments to support environmental fiscal reform in South Africa.*

National Treasury of South Africa. (2010). *Discussion Paper for public Comment: Reducing Green House gas emissions: The carbon tax option,* http://www.treasury.gov.za/public%20 comments/Discussion%20Paper%20Carbon%20Taxes%2081210.pdf (visited on March 7, 2017).

Newman, D. (2018). Industry warns on carbon tax, *Business Day,* February 9, 2011, http://www.businessday.co.za/articles/Content.aspx?id=164475 (visited on April 15, 2018).

Oates, W. E. (1995). Green taxes: Can we protect the environment and improve the tax system at the same time?, *Southern Economic Journal, 61*(4), 921–922.

Oates, W. E. (1999). Taxing pollution: An idea whose time has come? in Oates, W. (ed.), *The RFF Reader in environmental and resource management* (pp. 63–68). Maryland: Resources for the future.

OECD. (1996). *Implementation strategies for environmental taxes.*

OECD. (2007). The political economy of environmentally related Taxes, February *OECD Observer,* http://www.oecd.org/dataoecd/26/39/38046899.pdf (visited on February 7, 2018).

OECD. (2011). *Environmental Taxation: A guide for Policy Makers,* http://www.oecd.org/dataoecd/17/7/48164926.pdf (visited March 14, 2018).

OECD. (2012). *Renewable energy and environmental taxes,* http://client.viewontv.com/oecd/221106/index.htm (visited on March 13, 2012).

OECD. (2018). *Taxation, innovation and the environment,* http://www.oecd.org/dataoecd/24/25/48178034.pdf (visited January 15, 2018).

Owens, J. (2010). Taxes for innovation, 279 *The OECD Observer*, http://www.oecdobserver.org/news/fullstory.php/aid/3271/Taxes_for_innovation.html (visited January 15, 2018).

Palmer, T. & Riera, A. (2003). Tourism and environmental taxes. With special reference to the "Balearic ecotax", 24 *Tourism Management* 674.

Parry, I. (1998). Pollution taxes and revenue recycling, 29 *Journal of Environmental Economics and Management* 64–77.

Parry, I. & Oates, W. (2002). Policy analysis in the presence of distorting taxes, in Goulder, L. (ed.), *Environmental policy making in economies with prior tax distortions* (p. 5). Edward Elgar.

Parvaiz, A. (2018). *Despite state-level bans, plastic bags still suffocate India's cities,* https://in.reuters.com/article/india-environment-plastic/despite-state-level-bans-plastic-bags-still-suffocate-indias-cities-idINKCN1GC0TE (visited March 13, 2018).

Paterson, A. R. (2006). Pruning the Money-tree to ensure sustainable growth: Facilitating sustainable development through market-based instruments, 9 *Potchefstroom Electronic Law Review* 88.

Patterson, C. D. (2000). Environmental taxes and subsidies: What is the appropriate fiscal policy for dealing with modern environmental problems?, 24 *William and Mary Environmental Law and Policy Review* 137.

Pearson, M. & Smith, S. (1990). Taxation and environmental policy: Some initial evidence, 19 *IFS Commentary* 3.

Pirttilä, J. (1990). Earmarking of Environmental Taxes and Pareto-Efficient Taxation, 56 *Finanzarchiv N.F., Bd.* 202

Porter, M. (1990). The competitive advantage of nations. *Harvard Business Review* (Vol. 73, p. 91).

Reichard, M. (2009). *Green taxes for South Africa*, ClimatechangeCorp http://www.climatechangecorp.com/content.asp?ContentID=6187 (visited March 13, 2018).

Richards, K. (2004). The instrument choice game: When do environmental taxes win?, in Deketelaere, K., Kreiser, L., & Milne, J. (eds.), *Critical issues in environmental taxation: International and comparative perspectives* (Vol 1, pp. 61–88). New York: Oxford.

Rijo, M. J., Rao, M. G., Deshpande, R. S., Selvaraj, S., Rao, R. K., Moore, J., Sengupta, J., Chaloupka, F. J., & Jha, P. (2010). *The economics of tobacco and tobacco taxation in India* https://www.global.tobaccofreekids.org/assets/global/pdfs/en/India_tobacco_taxes_report_en.pdf (visited March 13, 2018).

Rivlin, A. (1989). The continuing search for a popular tax, 79 *The American Economic Review* 113–117.

Rowell, A. (2017). Once and future nudges, 82 *MO.LRev.*

Rowell, A. & Bilz, K. (2021). *The psychology of Environmental Law.*

Sælen, H. & Kallbekken, S. (2011). A choice experiment on fuel taxation and earmarking in Norway, 70 *Ecological Economics* 2181.

Schöb, R. (2003). The double dividend hypothesis of environmental taxes: A survey, (March 2003), *Otto-von-Guericke-University Magdeburg and CESifo* 3.

Seymore, R. (2002). The impact of environmental tax on electricity generation in South Africa, 32(2) *Journal for Studies in Economics and Econometrics* 5.

Smith, S. (1997). Environmental tax design, in O'Riordon, T. (ed.), *Ecotaxation* (1st ed.). London: Routledge.

Soares, C. D. (2006). The earmarking of revenues within the environmental tax policy, in Deketelaere, K., Kreiser, L., & Milne, J. (eds.), *Critical issues in environmental taxation: international and comparative perspectives* (Vol. 3, pp. 249–265). New York: Oxford.

Stavins, R. N. (2010). Market-based environmental policies, in Portney, P.R., & Stavins, R.N. (eds.), *Public policies for environmental protection*. (pp. 41–86). London: Routledge.
Stavins, R. N. (2003). Experience with market-based environmental policy instruments, in Mäler, K. & Vincent, J. (eds.), *Handbook of environmental economics:* (Vol 1, pp. 355–422). Amsterdam: Elsevier.
Turpie, J. K. (2009). Environmental and resource economics, in Fuggle & Rabie's *Environmental management in South Africa,* 63–66 (Strydom HA, and King ND, Eds.) *(Juta Cape Town 2009).*
Vos, H. (1997). Environmental taxation in the Netherlands in O'Riordan, T. (1997). Ecotaxation (1st ed.). London: Routledge.
Westin, R. A. (1993). Understanding environmental taxes, 2 *The Tax Lawyer* 360.

6

IS THERE A CASE FOR BASIC INCOME SUPPORT IN INDIA? ASSESSMENT BASED ON VERIFIABLE CRITERIA

Ram Singh

6.1 Introduction

While designing a welfare scheme, the policymakers have to consider the following variables: the number of beneficiaries (the coverage), the quantum of benefit per beneficiary and the fiscal cost of the scheme. Invariably, there are trade-offs among these choices.

An increase in the benefit delivered per household and the coverage leads to higher total fiscal costs of the scheme, which is a serious concern in view of the fiscal constraints. Even for a given level of budget for the scheme, a larger coverage will come at the expense of the quantum of the benefits delivered per beneficiary and vice versa. Things become even more complex in the presence of the errors of exclusion and inclusion. A wider coverage can ensure that even those on the margin receive the benefits of the scheme, thereby reducing the error of exclusion. However, this will increase the errors of inclusion and will come at the expense of reduced quantum of the benefits delivered per household. Similarly, an increase in the quantum of benefits will reduce the number of beneficiaries, including the really needy ones, thereby increasing the errors of exclusion.

As a consequence of these trade-offs, several of the existing policies targeted at the poor end up being regressive. A case in point is the access to the subsidized institutional credit issued by the scheduled banks and cooperative societies.

According to the National Sample Survey Organisation's (NSSO) data from the 70th round, institutional credits account for less than 15% of borrowing needs of the landless agricultural workers; the similar figure for marginal and small farmers is only 30%. As a result, they do not benefit much from the interest rate subsidy for the agriculture sectors. Benefits of the subsidized fertilizers and power are also appropriated by the big farmers. The extended version of the Pradhan Mantri Kisan Samman Nidhi (PM-KISAN) promises annual payout

DOI: 10.4324/9781003150565-7

of Rs. 6,000 to every farming household. By treating all farmers equally, the scheme fails to target the really poor among the farmers.

In this chapter, we argue that the errors of inclusion and exclusion can be reduced by using verifiable criteria to identifying the poorest of the poor. Precise identification is crucial for the success of several schemes like Ujjawala and Ayushman Bharat. At present, these schemes rely on the Socio-Economic Caste Census (SECC) 2011, for identification of the poor households. As we will show below, categorization of the poor in the SECC misses out on some of the poor households and, at the same time, includes some of the non-poor households. Consequently, schemes based on the census end up missing out on some of the poor households while including some of the non-poor, even though they are aimed only at the poorest of the poor households.

As to the direct cash transfers, the idea of direct income support is gaining ground globally. It has supporters among the political left, the right, the proponents, as well as the opponents of the free-market economy advocate. Its execution entails guaranteed and regular income payments to all citizens. What has added to the appeal of the demand for direct income support is the fact that hundreds of millions people remain unemployed and extremely poor, despite the rapid economic growth witnessed during the past three decades.

In their latest book, *Good Economics for Hard Times*, Abhijit Banerjee and Esther Duflo have dedicated an entire chapter to the issue. According to them, 119 developing countries have implemented some sort of unconditional transfer programme, while 52 have conditional assistance for poor households. The listed benefits of these transfers are better nutrition, schooling and health outcomes. Some other positive evidence was also found, which motivates a case for Universal basic income (UBI) (SEWA Bharat and UNICEF, 2016). In view of the fiscal constraints, some researchers have argued for a Quasi-Basic Income Transfer (Felman et al., 2019). There also exist many studies that clearly show that identifying the poor with the precision suggested in the theoretical models involves extremely high administrative costs and an administrative superiority and capacity that may simply not exist in developing countries, thus posing a challenge (Mkandawire, 2005).

It must be kept in mind that for developed countries, the purpose of income transfers is different in the sense that it usually serves as unemployment compensation during rough times in the labour market. In contrast, in developing countries, the major concern is poverty alleviation.

Over the years, the states and the government of India have enacted several welfare schemes as part of their poverty alleviation programme. However, the effectiveness of these schemes in reaching the intended beneficiaries is not yet clear. Arguably, the most successful of them has been the National Rural Employment Guarantee Scheme (NREGS), which is universalistic in design and ensures employment for up to 100 days a year to those searching for work. In spite of its inclusive nature, the NREGS also suffers from the perils of misallocation of resources. Other welfare schemes include the Public Distribution System

(PDS: for food and kerosene), urea subsidy, LPG subsidy, the Sarva Shiksha Abhiyaan (SSA), the Mid-Day Meal (MDM) scheme and the Pradhan Mantri Awas Yojana (PMAY). Still, the most recent figures from the available data for rural households show that the average monthly consumption expenditure of households below the 30th decile class (when distributed according to the average monthly consumption expenditure) is greater than their average monthly income (NAFIS, 2016).

The PM-KISAN Yojana that has been effective from December 2018 under which an income support of Rs. 6,000 per year is provided to all farmer families across the country in three equal instalments of Rs. 2,000 every four months has been one of its kind, and the impact of the scheme is yet to be understood in its fullness.

The National Democratic Alliance government at the centre has already implemented a limited version of the direct income support in the form of the PM-KISAN Yojana, which promises Rs. 6,000 per annum to farmers who own less than 2 hectares of land. The Rythu Bandhu scheme, being implemented in Karnataka, and Krushak Assistance for Livelihood and Income Augmentation scheme, in Odisha, are examples of bringing that rationale and suggestion to life.[1] These schemes suffer from both types of errors of inclusion and exclusion of the poor. We argue that there is a case for a direct income support but only as an interim measure to help the households facing multi-dimensional poverty. The income support should be provided as a supplement of the universal basic services. We suggest a set of verifiable criteria that can be used to identify the poor. We also provide an estimate of the number of poor who should be helped with direct income transfers.

In Section 6.2, we estimate the number of poor households in rural India using two data sources that give information about income and expenditure for rural households. In Section 6.3, we propose some verifiable criteria that can be used to estimate the number of poor households. Given the limitation of data sources, we focus the enquiry on the rural poor. In Section 6.4, we discuss the pros and cons of direct income transfers as a tool to support the poor. In this section, we argue why there is a case for limited direct income support to the poor. In Section 6.5, we conclude by discussing the various trade-offs faced by any direct income support scheme.

6.2 Using Verifiable Criteria to Get a Sense of the Poor Households

To estimate the number of poor, we have to answer the following question: how many households have income that falls short of the amount needed to meet the basic consumption expenses? To assess the severity of poverty, we should ask: what is the quantum of difference between the poverty line and the actual income of the poor? A report of the National Bank for Agriculture and Rural

Development (NABARD) All India Rural Financial Inclusion Survey (NAFIS) 2017 helps answer this question.

Assuming average family size to be five, it shows that the rural households in the first three deciles do not earn enough to meet their monthly consumption expenses. See Figure 6.1. The average households in the fourth decile are barely able to cover their expenses. Even for the fourth decile class, the average monthly income and average monthly consumption expenditure of a household at Rs. 5,271 and Rs. 5,342, respectively, are both less than the inflation adjusted poverty line as defined by the Rangarajan committee.[2] In other words, about 45% of the rural households do not have income enough to meet their basic needs of food and essential non-food items. See Table 6.1.

Within rural households, the income and consumption levels differ across agricultural and non-agricultural households. For more than 30% of agricultural households, the income and consumption levels are below poverty line. In contrast, the non-agricultural households in even the fifth decile class have income less than the poverty line. As Figure 6.2 suggests, about 50% of non-agricultural households fall below the poverty line.

As Table 6.1 shows, for more than 40% of non-agricultural households, the shortfall between the actual monthly income and the poverty line is a large proportion of their income. Similarly, for 30% of agricultural households, the gap between the actual and required income is large.

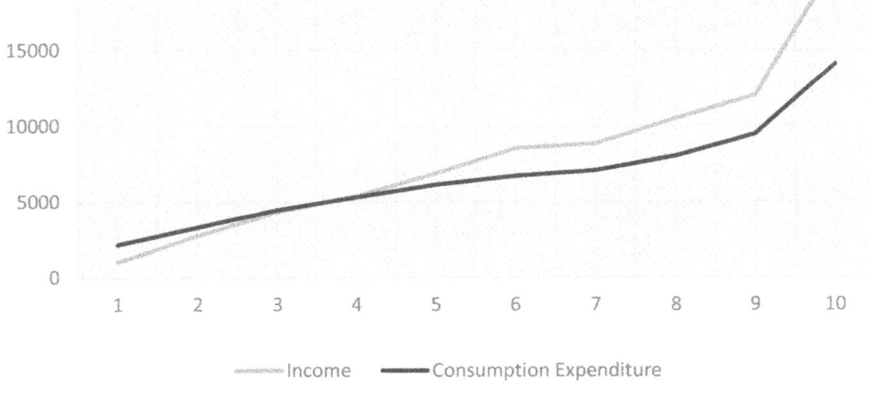

FIGURE 6.1 Average income-consumption expenditure according to decile classes (based on NAFIS 2016–2017).

In fact, in every decile class, income and consumption levels are lower for the non-agricultural households. See Table 6.1.

It stands to reason that the poorest among the non-agricultural households are the landless households deriving a major part of their income from manual casual labour. Many of these families have worked the Mahatma Gandhi National Rural Employment Guarantee Act (MNERGA),[3] a programme that serves as a very good screening device since only the poor households tend to work under the scheme.

TABLE 6.1 Average monthly income and consumption expenditure per household by decile class of monthly per capita expenditure (MPCE) (in rupees). NAFIS, 2016–2017

Decile class of MPCE	*Agricultural households*		*Non-agricultural households*		*All households*	
	Income	*Consumption expenditure*	*Income*	*Consumption expenditure*	*Income*	*Consumption expenditure*
1	1,293	2,465	793	1,899	1,019	2,156
2	3,033	3,591	2,498	3,008	2,753	3,286
3	4,963	4,793	3,800	4,173	4,330	4,456
4	5,970	5,711	4,728	4,841	5,342	5,271
5	7,475	6,596	6,231	5,558	6,881	6,101
6	9,856	7,118	7,011	6,246	8,484	6,697
7	9,781	7,584	7,836	6,500	8,817	7,047
8	12,012	8,847	9,169	7,305	10,449	7,999
9	13,702	10,333	10,633	8,716	11,981	9,426
10	22,269	15,134	19,175	13,149	20,548	14,030
Overall	8,931	7,152	7,269	6,187	8,059	6,646

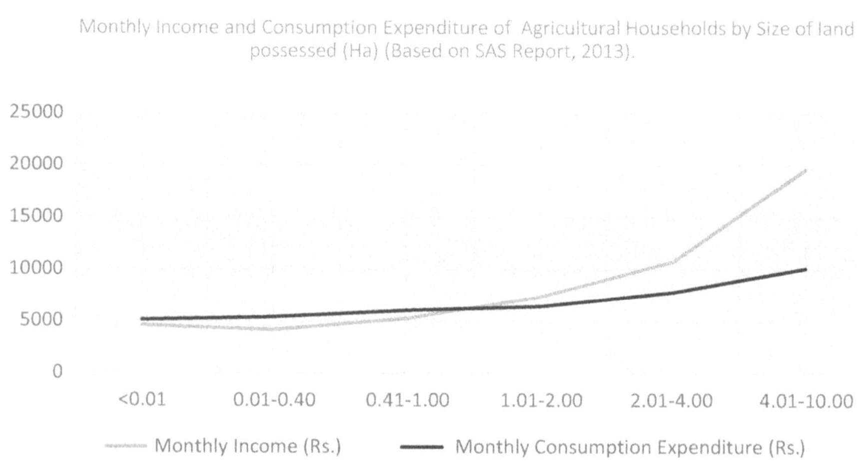

FIGURE 6.2 Monthly income and consumption expenditure of agricultural households by size of land possessed (Ha) (based on SAS Report, 2013).

Within agricultural households, plausibly the marginal farmers are at the lower end of the income and consumption spectrums. The Situation Assessment Survey (SAS) 2013, based on the data collected from NSS 70th Round, provides information on the income and consumption expenditure for agricultural households. It shows that average monthly income of most of the marginal farmers is less than or equal to the poverty line estimates at 2012 prices. See Figure 6.2.

That is, NAFIS 2016–2017 and SAS 2013 together suggest that the poverty in rural India is concentrated among the landless non-agricultural households and 'agricultural households' with marginal land holding. As is shown in the next section, about 9.5 crore families suffer from multi-dimensional poverty.

6.3 Identification Based on Verifiable Criteria

In this section, we derive estimates of the number of rural households facing multi-dimensional poverty. As is discussed above, the income and consumption levels are associated with the size of land holding. On average, the smaller the size of land holding, the lower the consumption and income levels, and vice versa. Besides, the poverty manifests itself in terms of the deprivations faced by the poor households. Several empirical studies show that poor households are characterized by a lack of asset ownership.[4] It makes imminent sense to consider the following households as deprived: households with one or less room, kuccha walls and kuccha roof; without an adult member in working age; female-headed household with no adult male member; and landless households deriving a major part of their income from manual labour. These deprivations are highly correlated to the low income. That is, the households with these deprivations generally are poor households. Besides, the deprivation criteria-based count of the poor would include the homeless, the destitute, those living on alms, the manual scavengers, etc.

These deprivation criteria are verifiable. That is, unlike income and consumption levels enjoyed by a household, it is possible to check whether a household actually suffers from these deprivations. Therefore, these deprivation criteria can help in grading of households along multiple dimensions of poverty, which allows for prioritization among the needy households. As is discussed in the first section, the land holding can be used as a proxy for income of the households. Therefore, the land holding along with the other attributes of multi-dimensional poverty discussed above can be used as the verifiable criteria to identify the poor households.

We use three complementary datasets to identify the households with multi-dimensional poverty; namely, the SECC-2011, the Agricultural Census 2010–2011 and the Agricultural Census 2015–2016. We take two different approaches for estimating the number of poor households. The relative merits of these approaches are presented towards the end of this section.

According to the SECC, the total number of rural households in 2011 was 17,97,87,454. Using SECC, we can divide the total number of rural households in the following mutually exclusive groups:

Total Rural Households excluded by at least one exclusion criteria: 7,07,54,003 (G1)
Total Rural Households that are automatically included: 15,95,469 (G2)
Total Rural Households with at least one deprivation: 8,73,03,948 (G3)
Total Rural Households that show no deprivation: 2,01,34,034 (G4)

The first group is the set of households that satisfies at least one of the 14 'exclusion criteria', such as ownership of motorized vehicles or a registered non-agricultural enterprise or a three-room house with pucca walls and roof, government employment, households with government, monthly income of more than Rs. 10,000 per month, income or professional tax payee and holding of more than 2.5 acres of irrigated land along with irrigation equipment.[5]

The second group (G2) satisfies at least one of the five 'inclusion criteria'; namely, households without shelter, poor, scavengers, primitive tribal groups and legally released bonded labour. The third group (G3) is the set of poor households that satisfy at least on the following seven 'deprivation criteria': households with one or less room, kuccha walls and kuccha roof; female-headed household and those without an able-bodied adult male member in working age; scheduled caste/scheduled tribe (SC/ST) households; households with no literate adult above age 25 years; and landless households deriving a major part of their income from manual labour.

The SECC count groups (G2) and (G3) towards the set of the poorest of the poor households. However, there are two issues with the above grouping in the SECC data.

The first issue pertains to the use of exclusion *criteria xii.* of SECC, for group (G1). As a consequence of this criterion, a substantial number of small farmers, i.e. the households owning more than 2.5 acres (~1 hectare) of irrigated land get included in the set (G1). That is, a significant number of small farmers are treated as non-poor simply because they possess more than more than 2.5 acres of irrigated land and irrigation equipment.

Agricultural census data shows that over 50% of the small-size holdings are irrigated. While the marginally sized irrigated holdings have been included by SECC, we need to carefully re-examine the exclusion of small-sized irrigated holdings. The SAS 2013 (NSS 70th Round) shows that compared to the agricultural households with unirrigated holdings, the average monthly expenditure is substantially higher for household owning irrigation equipment. According to the Report of 5th Census of Minor Irrigation Schemes,[6] the costs of maintenance of tube wells, the most commonly used irrigation equipment, can range till Rs. 10,000 per year. Therefore, exclusion of small agricultural households based on the possession of irrigation equipment does not appear to be plausible.

Further, the NABARD NAFIS data shows that the monthly income of the agricultural households with small holdings is less than Rs 10,000. Their income ranges from Rs. 8,136 to Rs. 9,990 per month, which is also dependent on the weather conditions. Therefore, there is a case for inclusion of all households, with small holdings included in the list of beneficiaries of income transfer. The number of small farming households excluded by (xii)th exclusion criteria

$$= 76,42,962$$

Alternatively, the set of small farmers who own an irrigation equipment can be arrived at by using two other datasets, namely the Agricultural Censuses 2010–2011 and 2015–2016.

From Agriculture Census 2010–2011, the total number of small holdings (1–2 ha) is 2,47,79,000. The number of these small holdings that are irrigated using an irrigation equipment is about 25%, i.e. 74,33,700 holdings in 2010. Using a decennial growth rate of 12.23, this number projected for 2011 is 75,19,967. Assuming a household is equivalent to holding the additional number of households that must be included is 75,19,967.[7] A similar exercise carried out with agricultural census 2015–2016 leads us to the number of small holdings that are irrigated using an irrigation equipment to be 74,70,006. That is, the figures arrived at using Agricultural Censuses 2010–2011 and 2015–2016 are not drastically different from those based on SECC 2011. To minimize the error of exclusion, we use the first number, i.e.

$$76,42,962. \qquad (X)$$

This means that these households should be taken out of the set (G1), the group of non-poor households. In the absence of the required information, we split this number equally between the groups (G3) and (G4).

The second issue with the SECC dataset pertains to the deprivation criteria (D5), which identifies the 'SC/ST Household'. So, the relatively well-off households get included in the set (G3) simply by virtue of being in SC/ST category household. Since our focus is on economic deprivation, it makes sense to exclude households with D5 as the sole deprivation criterion – a SC/ST household suffering from any of the economic deprivation would still be included in the set (G3), above.

The number of households facing D5 as the only deprivation criteria is:

$$76,72,263 \qquad (F)$$

These households should be dropped from the set of poor households facing multi-dimensional poverty, i.e. the set (G3).

To sum up, we rearrange the total rural population in the following mutually exclusive groups:

Non-poor (NP): The number of all non-poor households is given by:

$$(G1) - (X) = 7,07,54,003 - 76,42,962 = 7,83,96,965965 \qquad (NP)$$

Poor with multiple deprivation (PD): This group consists of households who are poor on income criterion and face at least one of the other deprivations D1–D4 or D6–D7. Total of these households is given by:

$$(G2)+(G3)-(F)+(X/2)=8,50,48,635 \qquad (PD)$$

Note that the set of poor with multiple deprivation includes all of the 5,40,00,648 landless households who rely on income from casual labour. It also includes 2,38,77,228 families without more than one pucca room house. Presumably, these are the families who mostly account of the 7.6 crore households enrolled under the Mahatma Gandhi National Rural Employment Guarantee Act (MGNREGA) programme. In view of discussion in Section 6.2, many of the marginal farmers (who possess less than 1 ha of land) earn much less than Rs. 10,000 per month. Therefore, most of them are included in this set, except those who get excluded on account of some other exclusion criteria. The number of households that do not satisfy any of the exclusion criteria and also do not suffer from any deprivations is 2,01,34,034.

The above estimates are for the year 2011. Decennial growth of population in 2011 was 12.23. Using this rate, we make the projections for the number of poor households for March 2019. For instance, for group PD, the estimated number of households in March 2019 is given by[8]

$$PD \star [1+(12.23/100)]^{(96/120)} \cong 9,32,72,693$$

This formula gives total number of rural households in 2019 to be 19,71,72,595, which is approximately the number of rural households. This suggests that our estimates are plausible.

The projected numbers are presented in Table 6.2.

Our estimate of the poor in the group PD satisfies some crucial conditions, which are required to identify and reach the poorest of the poor. First, the targeted set is identified using two comprehensive and consistent datasets: SECC data and Agricultural Census 2010–2011. This lends to it the distinct advantage of being the most consistent estimate. Second, it is based on observable individual characteristics and therefore minimizes the inclusion and exclusion errors.

However, our estimate is an upper bound on the number of poor households. First of all, it is greater than the number of poor households based on income criteria. Even if we assume that the real income of the poor has remained the

TABLE 6.2 Estimated number of poor and landless rural households

Category	*Poor with multiple deprivation (PD)*	*Landless poor (LLP)*	*All*
Estimated number of households	9,32,72,693	5,92,22,418	19,71,72,595
Percentage	47.3	27.3	100

same since 2015–2016, the estimated number of households (40% of the total) comes out to be 7,88,69,038. Moreover, during the past several years, some of the welfare schemes have targeted the poor. For example, a total of 1.37 crore houses have been built so far in the rural areas of the country since April 2014 under two housing schemes. Since lack of pucca house is one of the deprivations, it means that for a total of 1.37 crore households, there is improvement on this important count.[9]

6.4 Why Direct Income Support?

Is there a case for direct income support to the poor? A report of the NABARD All India Rural Financial Inclusion Survey (NAFIS) 2017, helps answer this question.

Assuming average family size to be five, it shows that the rural households in the first three deciles do not earn enough to meet their monthly consumption expenses. See Figure 6.1. The average households in the fourth decile are barely able to cover their expenses. Even for the fourth decile class, the average monthly income and average monthly consumption expenditure of a household at Rs. 5271 and Rs 5342, respectively, are both less than the inflation adjusted poverty line as defined by the Rangarajan committee.[10] In other words, about 45% of the rural households do not have income enough to meet their basic needs of food and essential non-food items. See Table 6.1.

Within rural households, the income and consumption levels differ across agricultural and non-agricultural households. For more than 30% of agricultural households the income and consumption levels are below poverty line. In contrast, the non-agricultural households in even the 5th decile class have income less than the poverty line. As Figures 6.1 and 6.2 above show, about 50% of non-agricultural households fall below the poverty line. As Table 6.1 shows, for more than 40% of non-agricultural households, the shortfall between the actual monthly income and the poverty line is a large proportion of their income. Similarly, 30% of agricultural households, the gap between the actual and required income is large. In fact in every decile class income and consumption levels are lower for the non-agricultural households. See Table 6.1.

Over the years, the government of India has enacted several welfare schemes as part of their poverty alleviation programme. However, the effectiveness of these schemes in reaching the intended beneficiaries is not yet clear. Arguably, the most successful of them has been the MGNREGA, which is universalistic in design and ensures employment for up to 100 days a year to those searching for work. In spite of its inclusive nature, the MGNREGA also suffers from the perils of misallocation of resources. Other welfare schemes that are more paternalistic in nature include the PDS (for food and kerosene), urea subsidy, LPG subsidy, SSA, MDM scheme and PMAY. It turns out that for schemes such as LPG subsidy and electricity subsidy, the rich benefit disproportionately more than the poor.[11] So, there seems to be an issue with targeting when it comes to providing subsidies. The food subsidy (PDS), which has the largest share of the government's budget for such schemes, also suffers from exclusion errors. Although the level of leakage has declined after the National Food Security Act was enacted in 2013, the leakages persist for poorer states such as Bihar and Uttar Pradesh.

However, as the above-cited data shows, despite the wide array of welfare schemes in effect, for a large number of rural households, the monthly expenditure exceeds their monthly income. Various welfare schemes have also failed to bring them out of destitution. For instance, the NSSO data from 70th round shows that for marginal and small farmers, the formal sector lending accounts for only about 30% of their total borrowing. The situation is worse for landless agricultural workers – institutional lending meets less than 15% of their total borrowing requirement. They do not benefit much from the interest rate subsidy for the agriculture sectors. As a result, these groups are forced to borrow from moneylenders and *adhatiyas* at usurious rates ranging from 24% to 60% per annum. Likewise, benefits of the subsidized fertilizers and power are enjoyed mostly by the big farmers.

As is shown in the previous section, crores of rural families suffer from multi-dimensional poverty. It stands to reason that the poorest among the non-agricultural households are the landless households deriving a major part of their income from manual casual labour. Many of these families have worked the MNERGA, a programme that serves as a very good screening device since only the poor households tend to work under the scheme. Within agricultural households, plausibly the marginal farmers are at the lower end of the income and consumption spectrums. The SAS 2013, based on the data collected from NSS 70th Round, provides information on the income and consumption expenditure for agricultural households. It shows that average monthly income of most of the marginal farmers is less than or equal to the poverty line estimates at 2012 prices. The NAFIS 2016–2017 and SAS 2013 together suggest that the poverty in rural India is concentrated among the landless non-agricultural households and 'agricultural households' with marginal land holding.

To sum up, the set of the most poor in rural India includes the homeless, the landless casual labours, agricultural workers and most of the marginal farmers. The benefits of the above high economic growth witnessed during past several decades have not percolated down to these groups. In spite of the above-cited schemes, they have remained the poorest of Indians.[12] Further, empirical evidence from India shows that the increase in income resulting from a food price subsidy has not had any significant impact on nutrition as measured by per capita calorie intake, protein intake and fat intake.[13]

True, the direct income support is neither an antidote to the vagaries of market forces nor a substitute for basic public services, especially the health and education. However, there is a strong case for direct income transfers to the poor facing the multi-dimensional poverty. This additional income can reduce indebtedness of landless labourers and marginal farmers, thereby helping them get by without falling into the clutches of the moneylender. This additional income can reduce incidence of indebtedness among marginal farmers, thereby helping them escape the clutches of the moneylenders and *adhatiyas*. Besides, it can go a long way in helping the poor to make the ends meet.

As several studies show, unconditional cash transfers do not lead to a decline in food security. They also do not find evidence suggesting that poor households use cash transfers in socially detrimental ways. In fact, at high levels of impoverishment, even a small income supplement can improve nutrient intake and increase enrolment and school attendance for students coming from poor strata.

6.5 The Trade-offs and the Way Forward

The main variables to be decided on when devising such a scheme are the number of beneficiaries (the coverage); the amount a household receives, i.e. transfer per household; and the fiscal cost to the central and the state governments. While we will examine how to arrive at an estimate of each of these in detail in the following sections, it is pertinent to note that we face a trade-off between each pair of the three components.

A larger transfer per household and the wide coverage lead to greater total fiscal costs of the scheme. A larger coverage will ensure that the exclusion errors are minimized, and even those on the margin, who are deserving but may have otherwise been excluded, receive the benefits of this transfer. However, keeping the transfer amount constant while increasing the coverage leads to an increase in the fiscal burden on the state and central treasury, keeping in mind the fiscal outlay on other welfare schemes. Along similar lines, a higher transfer amount for the same number of beneficiaries will result in greater fiscal costs.

In order for the scheme to be inclusive and be optimal from a fiscal point of view, it is important to strike the right balance between these three components, keeping in mind the trade-off faced. As an example, consider the following figures: if we fix the transfer amount at Rs. 30,000[14] a year, and the coverage at 10 crore rural households in 2019, then the fiscal cost of this scheme is calculated to be Rs. 3,00,000 crore per annum. For the same fiscal cost of Rs. 3,00,000 crore per annum, we can target 5 crore households such that each gets a transfer that is twice as much as the transfer considered before. However, this runs the risk of the scheme not being inclusive enough. Further, if the transfer amount were doubled to Rs. 60,000 a year per household, for a coverage of 10 crore households, the fiscal cost would also double to Rs. 6,00,000 crore per annum, keeping the coverage constant. This implicit trade-off which we call the Impossible Trinity of QUBRI (Quasi-Universal Basic Rural Income) is represented in Figure 6.3.

Given the trade-offs of offering such a scheme, we have identified that about 10 crore beneficiaries should be transferred an amount of Rs. 3,000 per month, which would cost up to Rs. 3.4 lakh crore, on average, which amounts to over 5% of gross domestic product. Ideally, other welfare schemes must be phased out, and the basic transfer under QUBRI must be increased to Rs. 4,500 per

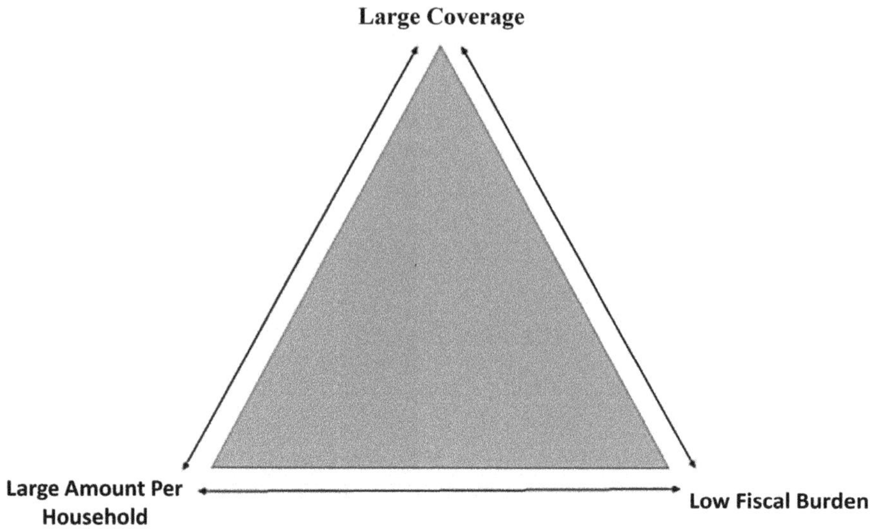

FIGURE 6.3 The impossible trinity of Quasi-Basic Income.

month per household gradually. The amount that is being transferred is very basic; what one should keep in mind is that handing out a sum of money to each household is not enough. We are trying to look at the issue of welfare from the demand side alone, i.e. we are trying to increase the purchasing power of the citizens. In a developing country like India, looking at the demand side is not enough. We have to take care of the supply side too; providing affordable and quality healthcare, education and infrastructure should not be side-lined. More importantly, the institutions that bind these demand and supply forces – markets and governments – have to work efficiently to minimize leakages and maintain competitiveness to help work such schemes out.

COVID-19 has shown that some aspects of UBI are quite doable than previously thought (Tyler, 2020). Multiple countries including the United States have announced a one-time transfer to the citizens in the wake of huge job losses. Even in India, we have our very own version of Quasi-Basic Income Transfer for farmers, women with Jan-Dhan Accounts, senior citizens, widows and the differently abled in the relief package announced by the government. All of this calls for enough empirical and theoretical evidence about the same especially in a developing country like ours.

Acknowledgements

This work has benefitted from valuable inputs by Alisha George, Aanchal Gupta and Meghna Kane. I thank the anonymous referee and Ranita Nagar, editor, for their valuable comments and suggestions on the first draft.

Notes

1 See Quasi-Universal Basic Rural Income (QUBRI): The Way Forward by Felman et al. Quasi-Universal Basic Income Transfers are called so because the beneficiaries will be a portion of the population. The word 'targeted' has been refrained from using because it might be so that the beneficiaries are grouped by excluding certain affluent categories as opposed to including the deserving ones. Felman et al. (2019) use Quasi-Universal Basic Rural Income or QUBRI in their paper.

2 According to the Rangarajan committee, any five-member family with monthly consumption expenditure below Rs. 4,860/month, at 2012 prices, is below the poverty line. As a rough approximation, the inflation-adjusted poverty line at 2016 prices is Rs. 6,380. Note that the poverty food basket used for determining poverty line and the Consumer Price Index (CPI) basket are not the same. The exact value would require revising the weights by appropriate re-scaling.

3 See NAFIS 2016–2017, p. 32.

4 See Factors Contributing to Income Inequalities among Agricultural Households in India by Bathla and Kumar (2019).

5 For more details, see https://secc.gov.in/reportlistContent.

6 Ministry of Water Resources, River Development and Ganga Rejuvenation Minor irrigation (Statistics) Wing, 2017. Link: http://www.indiaenvironmentportal.org.in/files/file/Report%20of%205th%20Census%20of%20Minor%20Irrigation%20Schemes.pdf

7 This assumption is justified by the number of beneficiaries claimed by the government under the PM-KISAN Yojana.

8 This population projection formula is the same as used in the Employment – Unemployment Survey 2015–2016 released by the Ministry of Labour and Employment Labour Bureau.

9 https://www.businesstoday.in/current/economy-politics/rural-housing-scheme-over-1-crore-houses-built-for-rural-poor-in-5-years/story/311418.html

10 According to the Rangarajan committee, any five-member family with monthly consumption expenditure below Rs. 4,860/month, at 2012 prices, is below the poverty line. As a rough approximation, the inflation-adjusted poverty line at 2016 prices is Rs. 6,380. Note that the poverty food basket used for determining poverty line and the CPI basket are not the same. The exact value would require revising the weights by appropriate re-scaling.

11 Economic Survey 2015–2016, Chapter 6, Volume 1.

12 Contract workers and employees in the informal sector in urban areas face a similar problem. Due to rapid mechanization of low-skill jobs in the construction and retail sector, employment prospects for these groups appear increasingly dismal.

13 Kaushal, Neeraj and Muchomba M. Felix. "How Consumer Price Subsidies affect Nutrition", *World Development* Vol. 74.

14 Given that the poverty line is estimated at Rs. 4,860 per month for a family of five (in 2011–2012), a transfer of Rs. 30,000 per annum would amount to Rs. 2,500 per month per household. This sum is greater than 50% of the 2011–2012 poverty line income and will cover at least 90% of the requisite food expenditure of a family at the margin.

References

Josh Felman, Paul, Boban, Sharan, M.R. and Arvind, Subramanian, "Quasi-Universal Basic Rural Income (QUBRI): The Way Forward", January, 2019.

Abhijit Banerjee and Esther Duflo, *"Cash and Care" in Good Economics for Hard Times* (New Delhi: Juggernaut Books, 2019), 288–289.

"A Little More, How Much It Is? Piloting Basic Income Transfers in Madhya Pradesh, India", SEWA Bharat and UNICEF report, January, 2014.
"Chapter 9: Universal Basic Income: A Conversation with and within the Mahatma", Economic Survey 2016–2017.
Government of India Ministry of Water Resources, River Development and Ganga Rejuvenation Minor Irrigation (Statistics) Wing, "Report of 5th Census of Minor Irrigation Schemes", November, 2017.
Socio Economic and Caste Census Data, 2011.
Agricultural Census Data, 2010–2011.
NAFIS Report, NABARD, 2016–2017.
Ministry of Labour and Employment Labour Bureau, "Report on Fifth Annual Employment – Unemployment Survey", Volume 1, 2015–2016.
Thandika Mkandawire, "Targeting and Universalism in Poverty Reduction", (United Nations Research Institute for Social Development: Geneva, 2005), p. 17.
Reetika Khera, "A Phased Approach Will Make a Basic Income Affordable for India," The Wire, December, 2016.
Tyler Cowen and Garry Kasparov, "Coronavirus Is Making Universal Basic Income Look Better," Bloomberg Opinion, May, 2020.
Seema Bathla and Anjani Kumar, "Factors Contributing to Income Inequalities among Agricultural Households in India", Economic and Political Weekly, 2019.
Neeraj Kaushal, Felix M. Muchomba, How Consumer Price Subsidies Affect Nutrition, *World Development*, 74 (2015), 25–42, ISSN 0305-750X, DOI: 10.1016/j.worlddev.2015.04.006. (https://www.sciencedirect.com/science/article/pii/S0305750X1500090X)
Shubhashis Gangopadhyay, Robert Lensink and Bhupesh Yadav, Cash or In-kind Transfers? Evidence from a Randomised Controlled Trial in Delhi, India, *The Journal of Development Studies*, 51:6 (2015), 660–673, DOI: 10.1080/00220388.2014.997219
"Over 1 Crore Houses Built for Rural Poor in 5 Years under Two Major Housing Schemes", Business Today, January, 2019. https://www.businesstoday.in/latest/economy-politics/story/rural-housing-scheme-over-1-crore-houses-built-for-rural-poor-in-5-years-159645-2019-01-18

7

'TO CENSOR OR NOT TO CENSOR' – IS IT A LEGAL OR SOCIAL CONUNDRUM?

Joshua Aston and Cecilia Anthony Das

> Art, morals and law's manacles on aesthetics are a sensitive subject where jurisprudence meets other social sciences and never goes alone to bark and bite because State-made strait-jacket is an inhibitive prescription for a free country unless enlightened society actively participates in the administration of justice to aesthetics.

What is obscene, immoral, or indecent? It is a question that bears no concrete answer. The English dictionary defines 'obscene' as *(the portrayal or description of sexual matters) offensive or disgusting by accepted standards of morality and decency* (Oxford). Interestingly, even the definition is elusive as it relies on accepted standards of morality and decency, suggesting it is ever evolving. Crossing the social era when a man and a woman cannot be found in proximity without chaperons, today, this notion rings absurdly. The moral vantage and advent of technology gnaw for this matter to be given serious consideration. Ease of circulation of materials and magnitude of reach ring alarm of concern. As the adage goes, information destroys as much as it empowers. When moral depravity is a form of destruction for a culturally and traditionally immersed society, the State is seen as the custodian of the moral gates of society.

Technological advancement invariably allows the media to circulate information easily to the masses. This reach and coverage overwhelmingly make the world a smaller place. It is this breadth and width of media reach that beget concern, as content management and/or restriction becomes nearly impossible. Further, the influence of *western media* is seen as undermining the Indian values, which are jealously guarded over the many decades. Given the gamut of cultural considerations, the censorship role of the State is deemed key to enforce and maintain the cultural limits (Mehta, 2012); this is often referred to as 'legal

DOI: 10.4324/9781003150565-8

paternalism'. Censorship aims to keep any untoward and tainting influence that may seamlessly reach the common man through the silver screen. The dangers of moral depravity through the silver screen becomes bigger than real life given its stupendous reach in India, where per capita screens stand at 1 screen per 96,300 residents (Mathai, 2016).

The authors in this chapter seek to review the various legal means that the State utilises to keep a check on the Indian cinema as the custodian of the moral gates of the society and highlight the debates surrounding rights and requirements of the society. Further, it seeks to analyse the socio-legal debates surrounding laws related to censorship and the entrenched constitutional right to freedom of speech and expression as guaranteed by Article 19(1)(a) of the Indian Constitution. The State intervention in a medium that has a huge impact on the population needs to be explored to elucidate its role in building a balance between freedom of speech and expression and cultural protectionism.

7.1 Obscenity versus Freedom of Speech and Expression?

The Indian Constitution guarantees every Indian citizen the fundamental right of freedom of speech and expression (Article 19(1)(a), Constitution of India). This fundamental right is almost always seen as being encroached when creative expression on celluloid is challenged as obscene and can corrupt the impressionable minds of the Indian fabric of society through the invoking of s292 Indian Penal Code, 1860 ('IPC'). This section has been punted to be going against the fundamental right that the Constitution has guaranteed.

> 292. Sale, etc., of obscene books, etc.
>
> (1) For the purposes of sub-section (2), [a book, pamphlet, paper, writing, drawing, painting, representation, figure or any other object, shall be deemed to be obscene if it is lascivious or appeals to the prurient interest or if its effect, or (where it comprises two or more distinct items) the effect of any one of its items, is, if taken as a whole, such as to tend to deprave and corrupt person, who are likely, having regard to all relevant circumstances, to read, see or hear the matter contained or embodied in it.]
>
> [(2)] Whoever –
>
> (a) sells, lets to hire, distributes, publicly exhibits or in any manner puts into circulation, or for purposes of sale, hire, distribution, public exhibition or circulation, makes, produces or has in his possession any obscene book, pamphlet, paper, drawing, painting, representation or figure or any other obscene object whatsoever, or
>
> (b) imports, exports or conveys any obscene object for any of the purposes aforesaid, or knowing or having reason to believe that such object will be sold, let to hire, distributed or publicly exhibited or in any manner put into circulation, or

(c) takes part in or receives profits from any business in the course of which he knows or has reason to believe that any such obscene objects are for any of the purposes aforesaid, made, produced, purchased, kept, imported, exported, conveyed, publicly exhibited or in any manner put into circulation, or

(d) advertises or makes known by any means whatsoever that any person is engaged or is ready to engage in any act which is an offence under this section, or that any such obscene object can be procured from or through any person, or

(e) offers or attempts to do any act which is an offence under this section, shall be punished[263] [on first conviction with imprisonment of either description for a term which may extend to two years, and with fine which may extend to two thousand rupees, and, in the event of a second or subsequent conviction, with imprisonment of either description for a term which may extend to five years, and also with fine which may extend to five thousand rupees].

[(Exception) – This section does not extend to –

(a) any book, pamphlet, paper, writing, drawing, painting, representation or figure – (i) the publication of which is proved to be justified as being for the public good on the ground that such book, pamphlet, paper, writing, drawing, painting, representation or figure is in the interest of science, literature, art or learning or other objects of general concern, or (ii) which is kept or used bona fide for religious purposes;

(b) any representation sculptured, engraved, painted or otherwise represented on or in – (i) any ancient monument within the meaning of the Ancient Monuments and Archaeological Sites and Remains Act, 1958 (24 of 1958), or (ii) any temple, or on any car used for the conveyance of idols, or kept or used for any religious purpose.]

A work would be deemed to be obscene if it could *deprave and corrupt person[s]*. This section has been attacked to be constitutionally invalid in *Ranjit Udeshi v. State of Maharashtra* (AIR 1965 SC 881). This case involved the prosecution of the partners of a book shop for selling a book authored by an English novelist D.H. Lawrence, titled *Lady Chatterley's Lovers*. One of the partners alleged that s292 infringed his fundamental right of speech and expression as provided by the Indian Constitution. However, the Supreme Court rejected the argument by stating that Article 19(1)(a) was subject to restrictions laid down in Article 19(2), which included public morality and decency (Chandra & Ramachandran, 2011). The Constitution, however, does not in any part define public morality and decency (Hariharan, 2014). The courts observed, 'The word obscenity is really not vague because it is a word which is well understood even if persons differ in their attitudes to what is obscenity and what is not'. Hence, the decision suggests that a definition is not required since it is clear what obscene is for the common man. Further, the call to declare the section unconstitutional was rejected on the basis that section which promotes public decency and morality cannot possibly be unconstitutional (Chandra & Ramachandran, 2011).

In deciding whether the work or material is considered obscene, on the one hand, the judge is to place himself or herself in the author's position to determine if the author of the work conveyed artistic or literary value. On the other hand, the judge also places himself or herself in the reader's position notwithstanding the age, in whose possession this material uncannily lands, to consider its effect on such a reader. In this exercise, the judge needs to be able to determine whether there is a genuine purpose of artistic value, or it is just a mere camouflage (Hariharan, 2014). This test, whilst being objective in nature, seems to ignore the subjective influence that the personal beliefs of the judge bring to the fore (Hariharan, 2014).

Some schools of thought seem to argue that the morality envisaged by the IPC is not related to the Indian religious beliefs, traditions, or culture since works like *Kamasutra* saw the light of day on Indian soil. In fact, the IPC allegedly pursued the Christian morality ideology (Hariharan, 2014), which was deemed to be a form of occupation by the British when the IPC was legislated in 1860.

The question that begs an answer is whether there is a correlation between the expression of obscenity and depravation of decency or morality (*Ranjit v. Maharashtra*, AIR 1965 SC 88 (885)). Key factors that may be deemed relevant to establish this correlation will be age, culture, and probable audience turnout (*Rajani v. State,* AIR 1958 All 360). However, the mere use of abusive language in the presence of persons towards whom the language is addressed or uttered will not come 'under the present ground' (*Kartar Singh v. State of Punjab*, AIR 1956 SC 541). In contrast, vulgarity should not be related to obscenity since anything vulgar, whether written, oral, pictorial, or a motion picture, is not necessarily obscene. Vulgarity stimulates a feeling of disgust but no degrading or shameful feeling and does not corrupt the morality of the readers/viewers, unlike obscenity (Basu, 1965).

Another issue that nags for attention is whether the policing by the State erodes the freedom of expression as alleged by many within the cinema sphere? Some authors argue that the State is progressing a conformist culture, and towards this end, censorship assists. They argue that cinema must conform to the prudery of sex and the hypocrisy in all possible things that are morally wanting, and this is an erosion of creative expression (Gupta, 1969). Others retort with disgust, as filmmakers are being presented as villains and pinned with the blame for rising violent crimes, sexual harassment, and degeneration of the Indian society (Bose, 2010). Arguments were also espoused that sex and female sexuality had no place in Indian cinema as it was clearly *unIndian* (Bose, 2010). Overall, there is a heated debate from the various quarters involved on what is permissible and what is deemed as erosion of morality. At this juncture, the real issue that needs serious consideration is whether freedom of expression takes the backpedal when it is against the issue of moral depravity. So far, Udeshi's case is a clear proponent that such monitoring is not eroding in any sense the limited freedom that has been entrenched in the Constitution.

A central theme in the debate in this area that justifies the State's interference with the freedom of expression is the *legal moralism concept* (Hariharan, 2014). This is where a State is warranted in preventing individuals from embarking on activities that potentially enrages the sentiments of the public (Hariharan, 2014). On the counter, justification for interference can only be tolerated if the said conduct will cause harm to others and nothing less. This is known as the *harm principle*, which takes precedence over personal freedom.

Accordingly, the decision in *Udeshi* clearly failed to demonstrate how private enjoyment of obscene materials correlated to violation of public decency and morality (Hariharan, 2014). Clearly, the *harm principle* card has been used successfully for the interference, but the courts have not pronounced this convincingly.

These debates are also amidst the Vaswani petition (6 SCC 705) (Arun, 2014), which sought a blanket ban on all phonographic and obscene (added by the authors) materials, as these materials allegedly led to increased sexual violence against women and children. The ease of access has potentially caused the creation of a group of people within the societal make-up to be 'pornography addicted' (Hariharan, 2014). The fragile sentiments of the public seem to be an argument that has been waywardly used to erode the personal freedom that has been guaranteed under the Constitution. Why should an individual not be given the liberty to decide on his or her moral compass when consuming these so-called despicable materials? What gives the State or a group of people in a confined room to decide whether those materials are suitable for the consumption of the greater public? These questions are in want of serious considerations and one that needs to be deliberated carefully. The balance between personal liberty and the protection of society needs to be seriously weighed.

However, the Bombay High Court in 2010 held that private viewing of obscene materials does not constitute an offence under s292 IPC (*Chandrakant Mansaram More v. State of Maharashtra*, WP (CrL) No. 1577 of 2010). This decision, however, did not refer to Article 21.[1] But it may be considered as the recognition of the right to privacy (this is not within the scope of the current discussion).

Hence, the discussions laid down above suggest that personal liberty is not generally deprived and remains very much so guaranteed. However, when it involves a media such as the cinema, where it no longer borders to an individual but rather extends to a society, the harm principle and legal moralism concepts emerge.

7.2 Indian Cinema and Obscenity

Indian cinema is ranked as one of the highest film producers in the world with a consumption of 3.6 billion tickets in 2002 (Fetscherin, 2010) per annum, pervasive in reach throughout the subcontinent. It is a social medium that potentially connects every common Indian and has the power to influence, control, and, to a certain extent, mould the populace with ideas, doctrines, and ideologies. It is indeed a powerful social tool and one that cannot go *un-hawked.*

According to a report published by Deloitte in 2016 titled *Indywood: The Indian Film Industry* (Deloitte, 2016), the movie world was reported to churn approximately 1,500–2,000 films per year in about 20 regional languages. This brings a box office revenue of $2.1 billion with a projected growth of $3.7 billion by 2020. Hence, it is clear that movie business in India has serious ramifications economically as well.

The common cocktail of success at the box office for most movies in the Indian context includes songs, dance sequences, fights, and some other entertainment *masala* (Sarkar, 2009). Of the most critical ingredient in the cocktail will be the show of flesh. This ingredient has been the cause of serious challenges, especially on the grounds of obscenity, sex, and sexuality (Sarkar, 2009), where the scissors of censorship[2] worked as the moral custodian of the public. The concept of obscenity/decency, however, is not one that is clear and cast in stone as have been readily witnessed in the development of the jurisprudence in this area. It carries different shades depending on factors such as culture, traditions, history, and social norms.

Cinema is normally a medium used to creatively portray the social reality with a link to returns. Sometimes the motivation on returns overturns the need to portray the reality accurately, and hence, censorship exists for sociocultural and political reasons (Pradhan, 2012). At various points in the history of cinema, the scissors of the censorship board have *snipped* severely to the dismay of the creators. The Central Board of Film Certification holds a very important role and one that is feared by the industry. Literature seems to suggest that the Central Board of Film Certification has not been consistent in its censorship and classification of movies in the past (Pradhan, 2012). The list of such censorship is just as prolific as the production of movies in India. The scissors have been quick with *kissing scenes, excessive violence, and even smoking* (Pradhan, 2012, pp. 164–167).

The dawn of the millennium brought a spate of changes to Indian cinema. More and more raunchy movies were beginning to be churned out of the Indian movie world. Concepts of kissing, live-in arrangements, premarital pregnancies, and extramarital affairs were becoming favoured themes (Rosenbaum, 2007). Is this a description of the current situation of the Indian population, or is this a nudge for society to consider such practices? These are some of the social conundrums plaguing the average middle-class families, who are the staunch advocates of monitoring the cinema. Does the divergent thinking of the average middle-class population denying the reality taking shape in the Indian society warrant consideration?

To date, there have not been any tests formulated to determine obscenity in films or media. The general test used to determine obscenity is equally applicable to the cinema. The Supreme Court initially favoured the 'Hicklin's test' or 'the most vulnerable constituency' test, but today, the 'Contemporary Standards

Test' is regarded as the more apt test to determine obscenity (Rajam, 2016). The development of these tests will be considered in the next section.

7.3 Hicklin's Test

Hicklin's test was established in the English case – *Regina v. Hicklin* (L.R., 3 Q.B. 360 (1868)). It is a legal test for obscenity, and the courts in India adopted it when seeking to identify or determine the meaning of obscenity in several cases. In Hicklin's case, Chief Justice Cockburn laid down the test and stated:

> I think the test of obscenity is this, whether the tendency of the matter charged as obscenity is to deprave and corrupt those whose minds are open to such immoral influences, and into whose hands a publication of this sort may fall ... it is quite certain that it would suggest to the minds of the young of either sex, or even to persons of more advanced years, thought of a most impure and libidinous character.

Hicklin's test was based on the notion of how a publication of obscene nature could affect vulnerable readers irrespective of whether they would read the material or not.

In the early 20th century, there were no defences available to literary work of merit. As such, some notable literary works fell prey to this test *inter alia* D.H. Lawrence's *Rainbow* (1915) and Radclyffe Hall's *The Well of Loneliness* (1928) (Gilmore, 1994, pp. 603–624). In the latter case, the magistrate opined that a mention of two women sleeping together in the book aroused impure thoughts and promoted and encouraged such conduct, which is sacrilegious to a puritan Victorian society in any count (Robertson & Nicol, 2002, p. 156). This test was dubbed to be the dead hand of *mid-Victorian morality* as it focused on the most sensitive person who needed protection (Hunt, 1978). Alternative approaches have been adopted in other jurisdictions, appreciating the inadequacy of the Hicklin test (*Roth v. United States,* 354 U.S. 476 (1957)).[3]

The English legislature partially modified this archaic and obscure test through the enactment of the Obscene Publications Act, 1959 (Motwani, 2013). The test was also rejected to some limited sense in the American jurisprudence and was thought to be *unconstitutionally restrictive of the freedoms of speech and press* (Stanley, 1971).

The American jurisprudence in the case of *Miller v. California* ((1973) 413 US1) enunciated the three-pronged test to determine obscenity:

a The average person, applying contemporary standards, should find that the work taken as a whole appeals to the prurient interest;

b The work must portray or describe, in a patently offensive way, sexual act, lewd exhibition of the genitals, excretory functions, and the like; and

c The work as a whole must lack serious literary, artistic, political, or scientific value (Motwani, 2013).

It can be seen that the focus when determining the issue of obscenity tinges towards the consideration of the substantive content of the material to determine whether it denotes sexual conduct that is evidently offensive in accordance with the norms of the community as it stood (Motwani, 2013).

Despite such development in the English and American jurisprudence, the Supreme Court of India persisted in applying the Hicklin test, six (6) years after the English legislature modified it in the case of *Ranjit D. Udeshi v. State of Maharashtra* (AIR 1965 SC 881). The Court opined that Hicklin's test need not be discarded merely on the view that 'it makes the Court the judge of obscenity in relation to an impugned book and lays emphasis on the potentiality of the impugned object to deprave and corrupt by immoral influences'. However, the definition or provisions under s292 (1) of the IPC is based on the effect of the publication on 'persons who are likely, having regard to all relevant circumstances, to read, see or hear the matter contained or embodied in it', and not on any person who would read the publication or may accidentally come across it.

The Supreme Court in 2006 was again called to consider what was meant by obscene in the case of *Director General of Doordarshan v. Anand Patwardhan* ((2006) 8 SCC 433). The Supreme Court took it upon itself to define obscenity since no legislative attempts were visible. In that case, the Court reaffirmed that the test for obscenity in India is the Hicklin test. However, it still ventured to explore the three-pronged test enunciated in *Miller* and stated that it could be used as a 'basic guideline' to determine what amounted to obscenity. The Court did not take a firm approach and marred the situation by referring to both the tests. The difference between these tests was wide, the former was wide and extensive, and the latter was very specific (Motwani, 2013). The Court favoured the Miller approach in *K.A. Abbas v. Union of India* (AIR 1971 SC481).

The situation was reviewed in *Aveek Sarkar v. State of West Bengal* (AIR 2014 SC 1495), where the Supreme Court rejected the Hicklin test. The Supreme Court introduced the 'community standards' test. The courts stated that nudity would not be deemed obscene unless it *aroused feelings or revealed overt sexual desire*. Hence, obscenity can only be gauged from the view of an average person through the lens of current community standards (Hariharan, 2014). This case was a death knell for Hicklin in the Indian jurisprudence.

7.4 Legal Aspects of Obscenity in India, the Censorship, and Media Law

Justice Krishna Iyer in *Raj Kapoor and others v. State and Others* (1980 AIR 258, 1980 SCR (1)1081) *(Delhi Administration)* stated:

> Art, morals and law's manacles on aesthetics are a sensitive subject where jurisprudence meets other social sciences and never goes alone to bark and bite because State-made strait-jacket is an inhibitive prescription for a free

country unless enlightened society actively participates in the administration of justice to aesthetics.

Article 39(b) of the Indian Constitution:

> 39. Certain principles of policy to be followed by the State: The State shall, in particular, direct its policy towards securing
>
> a that the citizens, men and women equally, have the right to an adequate means to livelihood;
> b that the ownership and control of the material resources of the community are so distributed as best to subserve the common good;
> c that the operation of the economic system does not result in the concentration of wealth and means of production to the common detriment;
> d that there is equal pay for equal work for both men and women;
> e that the health and strength of workers, men and women, and the tender age of children are not abused and that citizens are not forced by economic necessity to enter avocations unsuited to their age or strength;
> f that children are given opportunities and facilities to develop in a healthy manner and in conditions of freedom and dignity and that childhood and youth are protected against exploitation and against moral and material abandonment.

imposes a duty on the State to adopt policies that protect her people and serve their common good. Is common good served through restricted freedom of speech due to reliance on some obscure *standards* of obscenity? Should dated puritan Victorian considerations be permanently etched in the Indian jurisprudence? It would seem as though culture is cast in stone and remains constant. There seems to be a shift in the judicial bench; however, it may not be one that is fast enough to capture the change wave that is taking place amongst the vast population. The norm of society changes, but taking a cue from the conservative standards applied by the courts and the censorship scissors, this seems far from the truth. A protective measure may become counterproductive for a progressive society, which is aimed by the State given that India is an emerging economy.

India and its society cannot live in isolation without any foreign influence. In a globalised world, influences are inevitable. Economic, political, religious, and cultural differences are bound to transcend borders and reach the shores of India. Whilst the State has an obligation to sieve through these voluminous amounts of influence in shaping the mind of the impressionable youths of the country, there should be a balance. Some autonomy needs to be given to society to take responsibility for its moral vantage. A controlled media does not guarantee the ends that the State hopes to achieve.

In the Indian context, the Constitution refers to freedom of expression, thoughts, and beliefs in its Preamble. Apart from this, the Constitution of India in its Article 19(1)(a) guarantees the right to 'freedom of speech and expression' to all its citizens. This provision is where the media draws its fundamental right, which the Constitution has guaranteed to every citizen of the country. However, the film fraternity cannot exercise this right as some expressions of artistic works may be considered obscene or violate decency or morality.

Control is exerted through censorship and specific legislations to check on cinemas and other broadcasts to monitor the codes of decency (Article 19(2), Constitution of India). These laws *inter alia* are the IPC 1860, the Cinematograph Act 1952, and the Information and Technology Act 2000. Some of these legislations are dated, and the State has not attempted to update them according to the norms of time.

On many occasions, terms like 'obscenity', 'indecency', 'vulgarity', and 'nudity' have been used interchangeably. However, these terms differ in their meaning and need to be used consciously, judiciously, and according to the need and the purpose they serve.

The right to freedom of speech and expression, to say, comment, write, publish freely without any hindrance or fear of actions being taken, is the key to a successful and liberal society. Films generally play an important role in building the backbone of society. The Indian Constitution does not restrict the film industry or cinema as a medium of expression and discourse.

7.5 Provisions of the Indian Constitution for Censorship

Censorship generally means changing or suppressing any speech or written material that is condemned as subversive for the common good (Goetz, 1991). This idea was the norm in earlier times. However, increased awareness of rights has made the populace vocal and assertive over a period. Nevertheless, the government still has legislative provisions to curb or restrict the right of freedom of speech and expression, especially of the media and press.

Under the provisions of Article 19(1)(a), every Indian is guaranteed the right to receive and communicate any news or views as they deem appropriate. As the cornerstone of a democratic society, the media is guaranteed the right to disseminate information, news, and views on the government and other social ills generally to engage the society in serious contemplation, discourse, and debate.

In *Maneka Gandhi v. Union of India* (AIR 1978 SC 597), Justice Bhagwati had explained the importance of the freedom of speech and expression in a very well-crafted manner: "Democracy is based essentially on free debate and open discussion."

Article 19(1)(a) of the Constitution of India therefore includes the freedom of press and the right to receive and pass on information, news, and advertisements.

Thomas M. Cooley,[4] in his book *A Treatise on the Constitutional Limitations*, defined the freedom of speech and press in a very lucid manner, which is quoted below (Cooley, 1871, pp. 421–422):

> Freedom of speech and press is the constitutional liberty of speech and of the press, as we understand, it implies a right to freely utter and publish whatever the citizen may please, and to be protected against any responsibility for the publication, except so far as such publications, from their blasphemy, obscenity or scandalous character, may be a public offence, or as by their falsehood and malice and they may injuriously affect the private character of individuals.
>
> In other words, we understand liberty of speech and the press to imply not only liberty to publish but complete immunity for the publication, so long as it is not harmful in its character when tested by such standards as the law affords. For these standards, we must look to the common law rules which were in force when constitutional guarantees were established.

Some of the laws governing censorship in India are as follows:

7.5.1 The Cinematograph Act, 1952

This Act was passed to make provision for the certification of cinematograph films for exhibition and for regulating exhibitions by means of cinematographs (The Cinematograph Act, 1952). It came into force on 28 July 1952. Under the provisions of this Act, the central government made provisions for the Constitution of a Board called the Board of Film Certification (Section 3, The Cinematograph Act, 1952).

The function of the Board is to certify whether the films are fit for restricted or unrestricted public exhibition. The cinematographers apply to the Censor Board for a certificate for exhibition of their films, and the Board, along with a panel of advisors after the examination of the film, either certifies the film for unrestricted or restricted public exhibition or certifies the film as restricted to members of certain profession or class of persons. In some instances, the Board may refuse to certify the film for any public exhibition (Section 4, The Cinematograph Act, 1952).

7.5.2 Indecent Representation of Women (Prohibition) Act, 1986

The Indecent Representation of Women (Prohibition) Act 1986 came to force on 2 October 1986 to prohibit any kind of indecent representation of women through advertisements or publications, writings, paintings, figures, or in any other manner (The Indecent Representation of Women (Prohibition) Act, 1986). This legislation seeks to protect the dignity of women. Sections 3 and 4 of the

Act prohibit publishing any material with an indecent representation of women. Section 3 prohibits any person from publishing any advertisements, which contain any kind of indecent representation of women; Section 4 prohibits any person to publish, sell, hire, distribute, or circulate or sending by post any publications in the form of book, pamphlet, paper, slide, film, writing, drawing, painting, photograph, representation, or figure that contains indecent representation of women in any form.

7.5.3 Information Technology Act, 2000

The Information Technology Act 2000 (IT Act) came to effect on 17 October 2000 to deal with cybercrime and e-commerce. It adopted the UNCITRAL Model Law on Electronic Commerce of 30 January 1997. Apart from the provisions of preventing cybercrime or any kind of violations of rights in e-commerce, the Act also prevents transmission and publication of any kind of material that is obscene in electronic form through internet. S67 IT Act states that any person found in any kind of such act of publishing or transmitting obscene material on first conviction attracts a punishment of imprisonment, which may extend to three years and/or a fine up to Rs. 5 lakhs. For second or subsequent convictions, the imprisonment may extend to five years and a fine that may extend to Rs. 10 lakhs (Section 67, Information Technology Act, 2000).

7.5.4 The Press Council of India Act, 1978

The Press Council Act 1978 established a Press Council for preserving the freedom of the press and maintaining and improving the standards of newspapers and news agencies in India. Section 13 of the Act lists the objects and functions of the Press Council of India. Section 13(2)(a) guarantees newspapers and news agencies independence, whilst Section 13(2)(c) ensures newspapers, news agencies, and journalists maintain high standards of public taste and foster a due sense of both the rights and responsibilities of citizenship. Apart from this, Section 14(1) allows the Press Council, on receipt of any complaint against any newspaper or news agency or journalist/editor who may have offended the standards of journalistic ethics or public taste, to warn, admonish, or censure the newspaper, the news agency, or the journalist if a complaint is found true against him. However, the Council has to give newspaper or news agency or journalist/editor an opportunity of being heard (Press Council Act, 1978).

7.5.5 The Press (Objectionable Matters) Act, 1951

The Press (Objectionable Matter) Act, 1951, was enacted *to provide against the printing and publication of incitement to crime and other objectionable matter.* This Act makes provisions against the printing and publication of anything in the form of words, signs, or visible representations, which can incite or encourage any person to resort to violence or commit a crime or promote feelings of hatred or enmity or intend to blackmail matters that are indecent or obscene (The Press (Objectionable Matter) Act, 1951).

7.5.6 The Cable Television Networks (Regulation) Act, 1995

The Cable Television Networks (Regulation) Act 1995 was enacted to regulate the operation of cable television networks in the country. It was also aimed at controlling a perceived 'cultural invasion' by regulating the content of the programmes being telecast and further making cable operators accountable. Therefore, this Act does not permit any person to operate a cable television network without registration (Sections 3 and 4 of the Cable Television Network (Regulation) Act, 1995). The Cable Act also introduced a Programme Code and an Advertisement Code to regulate the transmission and re-transmission of any programme or advertisement unless it conforms to the prescribed code (Sections 5 and 6 of the Cable Television Network (Regulation) Act, 1995). Both these codes also comply with the restrictions provided under Article 19(2) of the Indian Constitution.

7.6 Conclusion

Indian cinema is and will play a significant role in the social fabric of Indian society. It will attempt to whittle the mind-set of the public to which it has pervasive access, much to the dismay of the middle-class-minded minority. The relentless attempt by the State through its censorship will continue to police the society as it has been tasked to do with the numerous legislations at its disposal. The humdrum life of a common individual will continue as he or she risks being tempted by the silver screen and begs the protection of the State to keep his or her moral vantage in check.

The academic debate will continue to challenge these provisions, which generally stifles the people's rights. Whilst the conclusion is that there is no erosion of the right of a private individual to consume materials that he or she pleases, this becomes a challenge when the media used to channel these materials has a vast reach. There is a thin line in balancing the freedom of speech and expression and attempting cultural protectionism. The authors opine that the State should not be blinded by the blinkers of cultural protectionism and the harm principle to the extent that the reality of the social mind-set of the present Indian populace is not appreciated. The Indian population has emancipated; it is a reality that the State and the judiciary need to grapple. The contemporary society is much liberal and should not be gauged through the lens of the society of the past. Although it is undeniable, there is still a need for moral standards and moral and cultural policing, and these must be based on the community's current standards. The authors opine that periodic surveys of the Indian public opinion on vulgarity, obscenity, and morality be undertaken to appreciate the prevailing community standards. These opinion polls are a better point of reference to determine the community standards when judges are deciding cases or censorship boards are lifting their scissors. Such an opinion poll was considered though not required in *United States v. Various Articles of Obscene Merchandise* (705 F.2d 41 (1983)); the Second Circuit alluded that whilst the prosecution did have the burden of proving obscenity, they did not have the burden to establish the community standards. However, the defendants were not stopped from introducing such evidence to assist the judge (Linz et al., 1995). However, the admissibility of such polls would depend on their reliability and validity based on how these opinions were collected and analysed (Linz et al., 1995, p. 131). Indeed, the mechanisms and the bodies to conduct such polls will need to be independent and free of biases, which is a proposition that the State should consider seriously, particularly when matters such as depravation of morality impinges on constitutional rights.

Hence, merely controlling access to materials that may potentially slight the *ultra*-sensitive just to maintain peace and appease the sentiments of a particular community group is not a long-term solution. The puritan Victorian laws need to be re-looked to reflect the reality of today's Indian society and draw a balance with entrenched constitutional rights.

Notes

1 'No person shall be deprived of his life or personal liberty except according to a procedure established by law'.
2 India's Central Board of Film Certification is the primary regulatory mechanism for film censorship.
3 Where the American courts substituted a functional definition 'whether to the average person, applying contemporary community standards, the dominant theme of the material taken as whole appeals prurient interest'.
4 25 th Justice and a Chief Justice of the Michigan Supreme Court, between 1864 and 1885.

References

Arun, C. (2014). Gatekeeper Liability and Article 19 (1)(a) of the Constitution of India. *NUJS Law Review, 7*, 73.

Basu, D. D. (1965). *Commentary on the Constitution of India.*

Bose, N. (2010). The Central Board of Film Certification Correspondence Files (1992–2002): A Discursive Rhetoric of Moral Panic, "Public" Protest, and Political Pressure. *Cinema Journal, 49*(3), 67–87.

The Central Board of Film Certification Correspondence Files (1992–2002): A Discursive Rhetoric of Moral Panic, "Public" Protest, and Political Pressure, March 2010, *Cinema Journal, 49*(3), 67–87.

Chandra, V., & Ramachandran, G. (2011). The Right to Pornography in India: An Analysis in Light of Individual Liberty and Public Morality. *NUJS Law Review, 4*, 323.

Cooley, T. M. (1871). *A treatise on the constitutional limitations which rest upon the legislative power of the states of the American union* (Second ed.). Little, Brown and Company.

https://repository.law.umich.edu/cgi/viewcontent.cgi?article=1009&context=books (accessed on November 28, 2021).

Deloitte. (2016). *Indywood: The Indian Film Industry.* file:///D:/CADAS/Downloads/in-tmt-indywood-film-festival-noexp.pdf

Fetscherin, M. (2010). The main determinants of Bollywood movie box office sales. *Journal of Global Marketing, 23*(5), 461–476.

Gilmore, L. (1994). Obscenity, Modernity, Identity: Legalizing "The Well of Loneliness" and "Nightwood." *Journal of the History of Sexuality, 4*(4), 603–624.

Goetz, P.W. (1991). *The new encyclopaedia Britannica.* Chicago, IL: Encyclopaedia Britannica Inc.

Gupta, C. D. (1969). Indian cinema today. *Film Quarterly, 22*(4), 27–35.

Hall, R. (1928). *The Well of Loneliness.* London: Virago.

Hariharan, G. (2014). Our Unchained Sexual Selves: A Case for the Liberty to Enjoy Pornography Privately. *NUJS Law Review,* 7, 89.

Hunt, C. (1978). Community Standards in Obscenity Adjudication. *California Law Review, 66,* 1277.

Linz, D., Land, K. C., Shafer, B. J., & Graesser, A. C. (1995). Discrepancies between the Legal Code and Community Standards for Sex and Violence: An Empirical Challenge to Traditional Assumptions in Obscenity Law. *Law & Society Review, 29,* 127.

Mathai, A. P. (2016). Indian Film Industry to Reach US$3.7 Billion by 2020. *IDEF Blog.* https://www.ibef.org/blogs/indian-film-industry-to-reach-us-3-7-billion-by-2020 (accessed on January 15, 2021).

Motwani, T. R. (2013). Obscenity as a Restriction in India. *International Journal of Legal Studies and Research, 2*(2), 160–171.

Oxford. Oxford English Dictionary. In *Lexico.* https://www.lexico.com/definition/obscene (accessed on November 28, 2021).

Pradhan, P. (2012). The Moral Basis of Censorship in Cinema in an Age of Digital Communication: A Study among Select University Communities of India. *Media Asia, 39*(3), 164–172.

[Record #398 is using a reference type undefined in this output style.]

Sarkar, S. (2009). Right to Free Speech in a Censored Democracy. *The University of Denver Sports & Entertainment Law Journal,* 7, 62.

Stanley, I. (1971). Still More Ado about Dirty Books (and Pictures): Stanley, Reidel, and Thirty-Seven Photographs. *The Yale Law Journal, 81*(2), 309–33. https://doi.org/10.2307/795138.

8

THE GOVERNANCE OF PROPERTY

The Gift Economy and the Sikh Gurdwaras Act, 1925

Jaivir Singh and Anmol Waraich

8.1 Introduction

Current television shows showcase India – whether they be travel or food shows, often enough land on *Guru ka Langar* in either the Golden Temple in Amritsar or some other Gurdwara, with the host being overwhelmed by the fact that food is available to any and every one.[1] The incredulous emotion of the hosts is indicative that something exceptional is being witnessed – it is a spectacle of large-scale consumption outside the exchange economy. This has been prominently manifest recently as the current Covid-19 pandemic has taken over the world; the *New York Times* took out a lead story documenting the Sikh delivery of food amidst disruption and turmoil in America.[2] This distribution of food is integral to the Sikh religion following from the notion of *seva* (service) – particularly visible in the prominent *Guru ka Langar* where food is provided to anyone and everyone. It is a giving or economic activity that does not look for a direct exchange or profit and is perhaps best described in terms of a gift economy.

To sustain such giving (gifting), those involved in the activity have to constantly be in touch with the exchange economy to provide inputs for the gift economy to run – thus raw food, fuel and labour have to be regularly exchanged to sustain the *Langar*. This is a continual and complex activity and clearly cannot be done without being embedded in an organisation – in fact, a complex organisation that is sustained by a set of property rights. This chapter, in particular, seeks to explore the nature of property law that supports religious activity. To phrase it otherwise, we are exploring the relationship between the economic activity (gift) that we see in the Sikh religion, as it is set around the Sikh Gurdwara, and the property rights that support it.

In comparison to other religions, the Sikh religion is quite young, and the system of governance of property associated with the religion has crystallised

DOI: 10.4324/9781003150565-9

comparatively recently. This is important for us because the Sikh community has worked out much of the contemporary governance of Sikh religious property by engineering the law to this end. Thus, in the second section of this chapter, we trace the historical events that led to the enactment of the Sikh Gurdwaras Act, 1925. In Section 8.3, we look at the notion of *seva* or selfless service as an essential component of the Sikh religion. In Section 8.4, we make a case that *seva* can be understood in terms of a moral economy of giving. In Section 8.5, we describe some of the key contents of the Sikh Gurdwaras Act, 1925, and proceed to make a series of analytical observations around emerging difficulties, springing from the governance of property and affecting the moral economy of giving or *seva*. We end with a conclusion that summarises the contents of the chapter.

8.2 Gurdwaras – A Brief History[3]

As the Sikh religion took root, Guru Nanak, the founder of the religion, pioneered small places of worship (*dharamsala*) where his disciplines would gather to listen to him and sing hymns. Apart from worship, these places were also locations where people came together for births, deaths and marriages, functioning also as places where children learnt to read and write and disputes settled. Prominently, there was a free kitchen – the *Guru ka Langar* where anyone could get free food. The scale of operation, of course, came to vary with the size of the shrine – the smaller shrines subsisting on contributions from the local community, while the larger shrines got support from the Sikh *Misls* and, of course, from Maharaja Ranjit Singh, when he came to rule the Punjab. The bigger Gurdwaras such as the Golden Temple and Nankana Sahib had large *jagirs* attached to them, and with the advent of the canal irrigation, they gained access to large resources. The rules of management of these shrines were very loose, largely administered by *mahants* who belonged to the *Udasi* sect[4] – a set of people who did not subscribe to the Khalsa creed and were therefore clean shaven. This attribute had allowed them to plead that they were not Sikhs over phases of Mughal oppression when Gurdwaras were attacked. However, even after Mughal rule, these *mahants* continued to look after Sikh shrines with the post of *granthi* (scripture reader) passing on from father to son.

While the British established their hegemony over Punjab, new settlement records were put into place, and in this process, lands attached to Gurdwaras came to be entered in the name of *mahants*. As pointed out by Khushwant Singh, using contemporary documentation (a speech by Mehtab Singh in the Punjab Legislative Council Debates), the notion of possession was put into place without distinguishing between possession as private ownership and possession for carrying on religious and charitable work.[5] The consequence of this was quite negative – to quote Mehtab Singh from a passage in Khushwant Singh's book – "The result was that the incumbents began to feel and exercise personal rights in the endowments which soon led, as it was bound to lead, to the deterioration of their characters."[6] This 'loss of character' not only included the increasing incorporation of Hindu idols by the *mahants* into the precincts of Gurdwaras but also gave rise to the fact that they started indulging in many forms of corruption, including debauchery.

Meanwhile, the Singh Sabha[7] movement gathered force to consolidate the Sikh faith after the defeat of the Sikh Empire armies in the two Anglo-Sikh wars in the middle of the 19th century, which had left the Sikhs in a state of disarray. Among the many concerns voiced by the prominent Sikhs who were involved in the movement was a deep distress regarding the activities of the *mahants.* Over a period of time, the Singh Sabha members tried to bring order to the Gurdwaras by making representations to officials and approaching the courts. The attitude of the courts, in particular, was frustrating because they took the position that the person in whose name a property was registered (namely the *mahant*) was the owner, and only a civil suit of possession could oust him.

Starting 1920, the Sikh community decided to take things in their own hands. The first activity was to form a committee of management from the Akal Takht, Amritsar – the Shiromani Gurdwara Parbandhak Committee (hereafter referred to as SGPC), alongside with the creation of the Akali Dal – a group that set out to take over Gurdwaras from obstinate *mahants.*[8] Soon after in 1921, large-scale violence erupted between the Akalis and the resident *mahant* at Nankana Sahib – the Gurdwara located in the birthplace of Guru Nanak. The Akalis had marched to Nankana Sahib to peacefully wrest control from the *mahant*, but the *mahant* mobilised local militia to attack them. As a result, hundreds of Akalis died, and their bodies were burnt in the Gurdwara. This led to a nationwide outcry with many nationalist leaders like Mahatma Gandhi visiting the site and expressing solidarity with the Akalis. Over the next four years, a series of agitations followed with the colonial government arresting Akali leaders. On occasion, the confrontation between the colonial powers and the Sikhs led to bloodshed, as in the case of the Jaito *Morcha.*[9] Finally, after a lot of political manoeuvring and sacrifice, in 1925, a law acceptable to the Sikhs was passed. The final Sikh Gurdwaras Act, 1925, was introduced by Sardar Tara Singh, a member of Punjab Legislative Council. The details of the law had been worked out through discussions with Akali leaders in Lahore Fort jail and government officials in Lahore and Delhi. The Act came into force on 1 November 1925 with a gazette notification from the Punjab government. With the promulgation of the Act, the colonial government withdrew a ban on SGPC, and the newly constituted Central Gurdwara Board in the Act was given the name of SGPC as per the wishes of the Sikh community. This brought the Akali movement to fructification to gain Sikh control over their places of worship.

To use the phrases of Khushwant Singh, the SGPC "became a sort of parliament of the Sikhs,"[10] whose decisions had a divine sanctity and was financially backed by the income of the Gurdwaras. In turn, the distribution of this income for the

> management of shrines, patronage in the appointment of hundreds of *granthis*, '*sevadars*' (temple servants), teachers and professionals for schools and colleges which were built, arrangements for the training of *granthis* and for missionary activity outside the Punjab, all made the S.G.P.C a government within the government.[11]

Among many activities the Sikh Gurdwara supports is the act of *seva* or selfless service – the Gurdwara is the backbone on which such *seva* becomes operational.

8.3 Seva

Seva is one of the key principles of Sikhism.[12] Ever since Sikhism was founded by Guru Nanak in the 15th century, the principles of this relatively new religion have emphasised selfless service to God as well as humanity. Much of this is reflected in what has come to be the supreme Guru of Sikhs – Sri Guru Granth Sahib, the holy book of the Sikhs, which is a compilation of hymns and teachings of Sikh Gurus as well as various Bhakti and Sufi saints. There are dozens of hymns in the Guru Granth Sahib, which encourage Sikhs to perform *Seva*. The daily morning and evening prayer ends with the chant of *Sarbat da Bhala* – which translates to the phrase 'common good for all.' Many hymns reiterate the point that selfless service is tantamount with the attainment of God – *Seva Karat Hove Nihkami Tis ko hot Prapat Swami*[13] (which translates to 'One who performs selfless service, without thought of reward, shall attain his Lord and Master'). The *Seva* performed is not done with the expectation of any quid pro quo or any immediate return or reward. Particular emphasis has been laid on the exhortation that *seva* should be done with devotion of mind and heart – *Satguru ki Seva Safal Hai Je ko Kare Chit Laye*[14] (which translates to 'Service to the True Guru is fruitful and rewarding, if one performs it with his mind focused on it').

The various forms of *seva* have also been described, according to the ways it can be performed, in Guru Granth Sahib. The *seva* can be broadly classified into three parts: *seva* done by *tan* (body), *mann* (mind) *and dhan* (material goods and money). This is not to suggest that material or monetary *seva* is essential for all the Sikhs. However, the principle of *dasvandh*, that is, donating one-tenth of your income for charitable purposes, is suggested for all Sikhs, though it is not mandatory and depends on the voluntary ability of a person to pay. In relation to the service offered by the body, the Sikh religion lays particular emphasis on *karseva* – the word *kar* means hands and *seva* means service; thus, service provided by the hands.

All seva is supposed to be *Nishkam* (without desire), *Nishkapat* (guiltless) and *Nimrata* (humble). The most popular example of *seva* in Sikhism is the practice of *Langar*. This practice of a free community kitchen serving food to all the people without any discrimination was established, as pointed out earlier, by Guru Nanak, and since then, the tradition has become well known all over the globe. This practice derives its meaning from the touchstone of Nanak's three pillars of philosophy – *Kirat Karo* (earn with labour), *Naam Japo* (contemplate on God's name) and *Vand Chako* (share with others). As is well known, caste and religious divides are well entrenched in Indian society and often characterise it. The sharing of meals by sitting together on the floor irrespective of their social background was a *one of its kind* taboo-breaking practice started in 15th-century India. It is reported that in the times of the third guru, Guru Amar Das, even the Mughal King Akbar sat down to have food with all the people when he came to visit the Guru.

The philosophy of *seva* is thus well embedded in the theoretical teachings and practices of Sikhism. It can, of course, be said that almost every religion of the world encourages charity and alms for the needy, and this is considered as service to humanity. What makes Sikhism different here is that the attainment of God is merged with the *seva*. The selfless service is seen as a ladder to get closer to God. The gifts to others, whether they be in the form of bodily, mental and material gestures, require a platform to become operational. This has generated institutions such as the round-the-clock *Langar*, which, in turn, can be sustained only with a material base, and such a material base is offered by the large amount of properties in the name of Gurdwaras, daily offerings in the form of money and other goods that are given in kind. The first of its kind material devotion in history of Sikhism can be traced to a donation of about 18,000 acres of land to Nanak by his Muslim family friend Rai Bular Bhatti in Nankana Sahib, the birthplace of Guru Nanak, a city in present-day Pakistan. The property continues to be in the name of Nanak and Gurdwara Janam Asthan, Nankana Sahib.[15] There are hundreds of more instances where large amount of properties and estates were gifted to Gurdwaras to keep running the charitable institutions of *Langar* and other forms of *seva*, particularly in the reign of Maharaja Ranjit Singh. The twenty-four-seven service of *Langar*, free accommodation and other charitable services in Gurdwaras revolve around this devotion of bodily, mental and material service, which give rise to a gift economy that makes this process smooth and continuous. While we have claimed Sikh *seva* as an important expression of the gift economy, it is important to interrogate the notion more closely so that it is understood in relation to received understandings of the gift economy.

8.4 The Gift Economy

The term *gift economy* is intimately associated with the anthropology classic authored by Marcel Mauss, whose work suggested the idea that gift giving is an expression of social connections in primitive societies, communicating power and status.[16] In this, he felt that the appearance of such behaviour in modern societies is but a remnant of the past. However, by continuing to privilege this interpretation of gift giving in contemporary times, we end up essentialising the observations of the early anthropologists for all times and contexts. Instead of following this course, it may be pertinent to think with David Cheal that apparently similar behaviour can end up having very different meanings in different social contexts.[17] While Cheal's own work attempts to study gift giving in contemporary urban Canada, his insight that gift giving is "institutionalisation of social ties within a moral economy" is of much wider relevance.[18] The term *moral economy* is in itself a very loaded term but is understood here very much in the manner in which Cheal wants us to think of the term – as "a system of transactions which are defined as socially desirable (i.e. moral) because through them social ties are recognised and balanced social relationships are maintained."[19] While the term *moral economy* is associated prominently with E.P Thompson's invocation of past ways of life to document the transition to a market way of life in 18th-century England,[20] as well as with James Scott's understanding of peasant relationships,[21] one can think of the term in wider contexts. In a recent discussion on the term *moral economy*, James Carrier points out that relationships are constantly being formed and reinforced; thus, when transactions and other relations create obligations – some of which truncate and therefore are in the mould of standard exchange (neoclassical economics), yet others that are sustained over time on some 'moral' principle can be thought of as a relationship where moral economic activity predominates.[22]

Indeed, the Sikh practice of *seva* does create a moral economy by creating a community in which the acts of giving without truncation of relations are definitional. As we have noted, the *seva* or giving in Sikhism is to give the body, mind and material self – *tan*, *man* and *dhan*. The rather insightful relationship between giving and the idea of community has been pointed out in the work of the Italian philosopher Roberto Esposito.[23] This reading of the community does not emphasise the common or the reciprocal (though these meanings are not necessarily denied). Rather Esposito draws on the Latin etymology of community and focuses on the constitutive *munus*, a term that means gift or giving but in a very specific sense – it "is the gift that one gives because one must give and because one cannot not give" and "indicates only the gift that one gives and not what one receives."[24] To quote him further – "All of the *munus* is projected onto the transitive act of giving ... The gratitude that demands new donations."[25] This account of the idea of community has led Arif to suggest that joining a community is to give up one's subjectivity.[26] Her interpretation is voiced in the context of making sense of suicides by widows (who express their subjectivity by exiting all communities) in the aftermath of anti-Sikh violence in 1984; however, the broad idea can be extended beyond this initial usage, as we seek to understand the property regime that underscores the system of Sikh *seva* or selfless service to God and humanity.

8.5 The Sikh Gurdwaras Act, 1925

To analytically approach the system of property governance, it is apposite to further invoke Esposito's understanding of community. At a point he says,

> If we linger a little and reflect on community without invoking contemporary models, the most paradoxical aspect of the question is that common is defined exactly through its most obvious antonym: what is common is that which unites the ethnic, territorial, and spiritual property of every one of its members. They have in common what is most properly their own; they are the owners of what is common to them all.[27]

This is precisely the point that helps us understand the relation of property resources in relation to the urge to give – the resources that sustain the moral economy of giving are a joint ownership in which the subjectivity of the constituent members is given away in various ways and in the governance of property that sustains the system of giving. To drive home this point further, let us note some considerations made in an important case in which the Indian Supreme Court was obliged to decide whether the Guru Granth Sahib is a juristic person.[28] We do not discuss the details of the case here, but broadly speaking, the case involved a contest of property between the SGPC and descendants of *mahants* because at some point, village functionaries had mutated the land in the name of the Guru Granth Sahib because they felt that the *mahants* were not managing the property correctly.

We invoke some of the observations made in the case in relation to our immediate concerns. Justice Mishra who has written out the judgement said that if the Guru Granth Sahib can indeed be treated as a juristic person

> then it can hold and use gifted properties given to it by its followers out of their love, in charity. This is by creation of an endowment like others for public good, for enhancing the religious fervour, including feeding the poor etc.

Over the judgement, particular emphasis is made, including making references to a lot of past judgements, that an endowment is a property that supports institutions that are active in giving to society, and a very important characteristic of such property is that "once an endowment, it never reverts even to the donor." The management of such property perforce has to be that of the community.

8.5.1 Some Salient Features of the Sikh Gurdwaras Act, 1925

Following up on this, one can showcase the basic components of the Sikh Gurdwaras Act, 1925. In this regard, let us recall some of the historical background to the Sikh Gurdwaras Act, 1925. The control of Sikh Gurdwaras was won by the Akalis after a long battle with the colonial government and the *mahants* who were not ready to cede control of the Gurdwaras even after many confrontations with Sikhs in Punjab. The Sikh Gurdwaras Act, 1925,[29] was passed after several deliberations between the Sikh bodies and the then Punjab government to provide a statutory basis to the management of the Sikh Gurdwaras. The Act placed the management of the Sikh shrines in the hands of the representatives of the Sikhs through a scheme of purely Sikh management, enabled by a statutory and legal sanction of Sikh places of worship.[30] The most important provision of the Act was to establish an elected board, which later came to be known as SGPC, to provide for better management of the Sikh shrines. Prior to passing of the Act in 1925, the SGPC had been in place since 1921 as a non-statutory body under the Societies Registration Act, 1860, with limited number of Gurdwaras under its control. The five years of Sikh struggle to gain control of the Gurdwaras finally got the British government to pass a law that the Sikhs had demanded for a long time. At the heart of this move to control the Gurdwaras was the question of ownership.[31] As we had noted earlier, the advent of British rule had changed the meaning of possession with the result that those in possession as servants of the community had become owners. The *mahants* who were appointed as the caretakers of the Gurdwara property, which, rightfully, belonged to whole Sikh community, had come to claim it as their private property.

Since one of the compelling reasons for the Gurdwara reform movement was to remove control by *mahants*, the Sikh Gurdwaras Act had to ensure that control was wrested away from the *mahants*. The Act does not define a Gurdwara as such – instead it lists the procedure to get a Gurdwara listed as a notified Sikh Gurdwara under the provisions of the Act. The Schedule I of the Act lists all such notified Sikh Gurdwaras. The provisions of the Act in Chapter II enable the procedure of getting a Gurdwara declared as a Sikh Gurdwara. With respect to this, Section 7 of the Act qualifies 50 or more worshipping Sikhs in a particular area to petition the state government to declare the Gurdwara as a notified Gurdwara so as to come under the jurisdiction of the Sikh Gurdwaras Act, 1925. The Act also facilitates the constitution of a Tribunal that can decide claims on a notified Sikh Gurdwara. The early decades after the passage of the Act saw enormous litigation as to whether the declaration of a Gurdwara as a notified Gurdwara was correct or not. The *mahants* claimed hereditary rights to certain properties and argued that mere installation of the Guru Granth Sahib in a place does not make that place a notified Sikh Gurdwara.

Once a Gurdwara comes under the Sikh Gurdwaras Act, 1925, it becomes subject to a regime of governance. To briefly describe the contents of the Act, it may be noted that the Act consists of three parts, 13 chapters and three schedules. The Act has been amended several times after Indian Independence, particularly after the inclusion of Patiala and East Punjab States in Punjab and finally after the Reorganisation Act, 1966. The jurisdiction of the Act extends to present-day Punjab, Haryana, Himachal Pradesh and Chandigarh. The Act provides for setting up a Board, Committees, a Tribunal and a Commission for administration and management of the Gurdwaras under its various sections. It is, of course, impossible to describe all details of the Act, and we only touch on some salient aspects of the Act.

As we have noted, with the passage of the Act, the SGPC got statutory basis and autonomy to manage the Sikh Gurdwaras. The SGPC is a body corporate with a perpetual succession and common seal under Part III, Chapter VI of the Sikh Gurdwaras Act, 1925. It has the right to sue and be sued. The present composition of the SGPC includes 170 elected members, the head ministers of the Darbar Sahib, Amritsar and five Sikh Takhts[32] (the five temporal seats of the Sikhs) and 25 co-opted members. The members of the board are elected from constituencies defined by the state where SGPC has its jurisdiction and the central government. The elections are held under the aegis of a Gurdwara Election Commission constituted by the central government on a date decided by the government. The Act lists down the qualification of the members who can contest the elections – the person has to be a practising Sikh with unshorn hair who can read and write Gurumukhi[33] and does not consume alcohol. The Act also provides the right to vote to all Sikhs registered on electoral rolls in any constituency subject to qualifications as per the Act. The Act gives the right to any Sikh above 21 years of age to vote in the elections provided he or she does not trim his or hair, does not smoke or consume alcohol.

The Sikh Gurdwaras Act, 1925, under Section 85(1) of the Act, confers vast powers on the SGPC to exercise direct managerial control over all major Gurdwaras in Punjab, Haryana, Himachal Pradesh and Union Territory of Chandigarh. The SGPC has the right to prepare a scheme for administration and management of the Gurdwaras described in Section 85(1) for their property, endowments, funds and income. Under the Act, the Gurdwaras that do not come under the purview of Section 85(1) have a provision to institute a local five-member committee, out of which at least one person should belong to a scheduled caste. These members whether elected or nominated are subject to similar qualifications as those of SGPC members.

Chapter IX of Part III of the Sikh Gurdwaras Act, 1925, concerns the finances of the notified Gurdwaras and lays down the road map for management of Gurdwara funds. Section 106(1) of the Act requires that

> all the properties and income of a notified Sikh Gurdwara shall be first used for the maintenance and improvement of the gurdwara; for the maintenance or religious worship and the performance and conduct of religious and charitable duties, ceremonies and observances; for the payment of allowances or salaries of dependents, officers and servants, for the maintenance of *langar* and for religious, charitable or educational purposes.

Further, it is stated in the Act under Section 106(2) that after providing for all these expenses, if there remains a surplus sum or income, the SGPC can allocate the sum to social welfare activities such as religious, educational and charitable purposes. The SGPC can also invest the surplus income in a bank or purchase government securities or National Savings Certificates or can purchase immovable property for the Gurdwaras under its management after due consultation.

Every committee of the Gurdwaras is also supposed to contribute to SGPC's funds annually. The Act establishes a General Board Fund, a research fund for carrying out research in Sikh history and publishing books and journals, a religious fund for matters dealing with the Sikh religion and also a General trust fund, all of which are linked to the SGPC. These funds are subject to internal audit as well as external audit by the government of Punjab. Section 119 of Chapter IX lays down the provision for presentation of annual budget by the executive committee of the SGPC. It estimates the income and expenditure for the ensuing financial year of the Board and each separate fund maintained by the Board. The annual budget of the SGPC has increased over time. In March 2019, it passed an annual budget of Rs. 1,205 crores, out of which Rs. 700 crores were earmarked for Gurdwara management, Rs. 37.40 crores for educational institutions and Rs. 84 crores for religious promotions.[34] As per the SGPC website, it currently runs a university, a medical and a dental college, various colleges and schools, hospitals and many charitable trusts in various cities.[35] At Golden Temple, Amritsar, alone, the SGPC spends Rs. 30 crores on twenty-four-seven *langar* from its annual budget. The SGPC no doubt is the conduit agency for making the Sikh principle of *seva* deliverable to those in need by utilising the Gurdwara funds composed of offerings. This is clearly recognised by contemporary jurisprudence. In the case decided by the Supreme Court (discussed earlier) as to whether the Guru Granth Sahib is a juristic person, it was observed that a Gurdwara is sacred because of the presence of the Guru Granth Sahib in it and goes on to further say:

> This reverential recognition of Guru Granth Sahib also opens the hearts of its followers to pour their money and wealth for it. It is not that it needs it, but when it is installed, it grows for its followers, who through their obeisance to it, sanctify themselves and also for running the *langar* which is an inherent part of a Gurudwara.[36]

The Gurdwara/s and its/their governance are clearly important conduits for the moral economy of *seva* or giving.

8.5.2 Some Emerging Difficulties

As we have seen that the enactment of the Sikh Gurdwaras Act was a conscious move to render the Gurdwara outside the realm of private property governance. To place the emergent regime of property governance in an analytical perspective, it is perhaps appropriate to turn to the property schematic suggested by the property theorist Michael Heller.[37] Heller uses degrees of exclusion to conceptually approach the idea of property – property, he says, can be thought of as covering a range of rights, starting with the absence of exclusion associated with the open access of the commons at one end, leading to the excessive exclusion of the anti-commons at the other end, while placing conventional private property with its standard formulations of exclusion, somewhere in the middle of the continuum. In this schema, the property regime engendered by the Sikh Gurdwaras

Act could perhaps be thought of as a *limited access commons* regime where a group of people representing the community govern the property – keeping those not following the community objectives out while using property resources to further the aspirations of the community. In so much so the internal governance rules are cohesive, and they do not allow selfish behaviour to go unpunished, and this clearly could be sustained by cooperative endeavour.

Indeed, the democratic nature of selecting the representatives to manage the affairs of Sikh Gurdwaras was hailed by many members at the time when the bill was passed in the Punjab Legislative Council in undivided India.[38] The then Governor of Punjab Sir Malcolm Hailey and a member of the Punjab Legislative Council Dr. Gokul Chand Narang, both, stated that the ultimate success of the Act lay in the spirit and temper with which Sikhs will implement this Act.[39]

Covering a much later period, Singh has comprehensively studied the interplay of religion and politics in Punjab and commented on the significant role played by the SGPC in the politics of Punjab due to the fact that it controls vast material resources that it has on hand.[40] The SGPC has been accused of playing into the hands of Shiromani Akali Dal, and on many occasions, its executive officers have been blamed for indulging into corrupt practices.[41] The issue of irregular elections[42] and disenfranchisement of *Sehajdhari* Sikhs makes the original democratic element diminish further. The question of whether *Sehajdhari* Sikhs, that is, those who practise Sikhism in their rituals and customs but do not keep an appearance with unshorn hair, can vote in the SGPC election has come to be a contentious issue of late between the SGPC and the Sikh population. A recent 2016 Amendment to the Act by the NDA-led Parliament stripped nearly 10 million *Sehajdhari* Sikhs of their voting rights in the Gurdwara election.[43] The question of Sikh identity and its different interpretations by different groups of Sikhs has made the true democratic functioning of SGPC land in a quagmire.[44] Furthermore, recently, Sikhs in Haryana have been demanding a separate Gurdwara Parbandhak Committee so as to take control of their Gurdwaras themselves.[45] The matter is in fact being considered in the court. The SGPC has tried in past to get an All India Gurdwara Bill passed in the Parliament so as to gain control of Gurdwaras in all parts of the country. However, such a move has been resisted by the Sikhs on account of excessive centralisation. Delhi, Jammu and Kashmir have their separate Gurdwaras Acts in place.

The Sikh Gurdwaras Act was one of its first kind of experiment in the pre-Independence era that gave a democratic right to the people who adhere to Sikh faith to choose their representatives to manage their own religious places. The working of the SGPC has been so far elicited a bag of mixed emotions from different sections of the Sikhs. Though it is sometimes lauded for its efficiency in managing the Gurdwaras, at the same time, it has been criticised severely for giving into political pressure and misuse of its position. Replacing the *mahant* by the member (of SGPC) surely transitioned the management of Gurdwaras. However, the element of integrity, honesty and truth, as defined by the Sacred

Sikh Scriptures like Guru Granth Sahib, is not very well entrenched when it comes to actual working of the SGPC in present times.

There are thus two problems that seem to be troubling the moral economy of Sikh giving or *seva*. One is that the representatives of the community who manage the property – those who manage the *limited access commons* – are suspected of (at least some) corruption. Clearly, sustaining the moral economy requires that resources indeed be channelled to the right ends. Unless corruption is particularly cataclysmic, this should be held in check but for a complete capture by factions. However, perhaps the bigger problem is that of the community itself – the demands of a centralised, conservative and increasingly essentialist faction imposing themselves on to a wide variety of Sikh congregations. To appeal to the ideas we have introduced, this is to suggest with greater loss of subjectivity, the Sikh congregation that bows to the current political dispensation may narrow down the community. Both of these can, in turn, unsettle the desired Sikh moral economy of giving and the property regime that sustains it.

8.6 Conclusion

The primary motivation behind this chapter was to explore the nature of property that supports religious economies of giving. In this we placed our focus on the Sikh religion where the Gurdwara and its governance are central to both the moral economy of giving and the property regime that supports this giving. We began with a brief historical prologue, which pointed to the fact that the colonial administration did not quite understand that the system of private property that they introduced would make the erstwhile managers of Gurdwaras – the *mahants* act like proprietors of property that they were meant to only manage. The Sikh agitations countered this and got the Sikh Gurdwaras Act, 1925, legislated. We then went on to describe a key Sikh religious activity, *seva* or selfless service, which the Sikh Gurdwara crucially supports in activities such as *langar* – the community kitchen that feeds anyone and everyone. We went on to describe how this can conceptually be thought of as a gift situated in a moral economy of giving. Using the work of the Italian philosopher Esposito, we underlined the fact that the act of giving is an integral constituent of the idea of a community. The property sustaining such communities, we go on to argue, must perforce be managed or governed by the community. We then go on to describe some of the salient features of the Sikh Gurdwaras Act trying to capture as to how it creates a community and outlining the rules (law) by which such a community governs the property that sustains it. It is perhaps possible to think of the governance of the property as a version what the property theorist Heller calls *limited access commons*. This allows us to view the nature of the current stress on the Sikhs. Such strain is largely on account two issues – first, the contested meanings of what aspects of one's subjectivity a person has to be given up to belong to the Sikh community, and, second, the corruption – real and/or perceived – in governing the resources of the *limited access commons*. Both these issues depend on how the community and its officers come to be constructed. These questions have been framed in relation to the Sikh religion here but need to be raised in relation to other religions as well.

Notes

1 See *John Torode's Asia*, series 1, episode 2, "Amritsar", aired on November 1, 2017, on UKTV's Good Food Channel.
2 Priya Krishna, 'How to Feed Crowds in a Protest or Pandemic?' The Sikhs Know *The New York Times*, June 8, 2020, https://www.nytimes.com/2020/06/08/dining/free-food-sikh-gundwara-langar.html. See also Jaivir Singh and Anmol Waraich, 'Seva in a pandemic: Guru ka Langar is an exemplary institution of the moral economy' The Indian Express, July 14, 2020, http://epaper.indianexpress.com/c/53444493.
3 The historical account presented here for a quick overview relies heavily on the magisterial work on Sikh history by Khushwant Singh. See Khushwant Singh, *A History of the Sikhs Vol II 1839–2004* (2004, 2nd edition) pp. 193–216.
4 A sect that developed parallel to Sikhism with elements of Hindu practices. The sect was started by Guru Nanak's son Baba Shri Chand.
5 Singh, op. cit., n. 3, p.195.
6 Singh, Id.
7 W. H. Mcleod, 'The contribution of the Singh Sabha movement to the interpretation of Sikh history and religion' in *Religious Studies in Dialogue: Essays in Honour of Albert. C. Moore*, eds. Maurice Andrew, Peter Matheson and Simon Rae (1991). Faculty of Theology, University of Otago, Dunedin.
8 Mohinder Singh, *The Akali Movement* (2015).
9 Singh, Id.
10 Singh, op. cit., n.3, p. 214.
11 Singh, Id p. 215.
12 This is not to suggest that *seva* in itself defines Sikhism; rather it is one of the prominent characteristics of the religion. Other aspects of the Sikh religion include the prominence of martyrdom. On Sikhism and martyrdom, see Louis E. Fenech, *Martyrdom in the Sikh Tradition* (2000).
13 Aad Guru Granth Sahib. 1983 CE (Reprint). 1430 p. Publishers: Shiromani Gurdwara Parbandhak Committee, Amritsar. Rag Gauri, Astpadi 18, p. 286.
14 Id. Rag Sorath, Mahala 3, p. 644.
15 Naveen S. Garewal, 'Guru Nanak's Estate Flourishes in Nankana', *The Tribune*, May 26, 2007. Accessed July 15, 2018, https://www.tribuneindia.com/2007/20070526/saturday/main1.htm
16 Marcel Mauss, *The Gift* Glencoe (1954).
17 David Cheal, *The Gift Economy* (1988).
18 Id., p. 15.
19 Id., p. 15.
20 E. P. Thompson, 'The Moral Economy of the English Crowd in the Eighteenth Century' (1971) 50 *Past and Present* 76.
21 J. C. Scott, *Moral Economy of the Peasant* (1976).
22 James G. Carrier, 'Moral Economy: What's in a Name' (2018) 18(1) *Anthropological Theory* 18.
23 Roberto Esposito (translated by Timothy Campbell), *Communitas: The Origin and Destiny of Community* (2010).
24 Esposito, Id., p. 5.
25 Esposito, Id.
26 Yasmeen Arif, *Life Emergent: The Social in the Afterlives of Violence* (2016).
27 Esposito, op. cit. n. 23, p. 3

28 *Shiromani Gurdwara Parbandhak Committee v. Shri Som Nath Dass & Ors* AIR 2000 SC 1421.
29 The Sikh Gurdwaras Act, 1925, https://mha.gov.in/sites/default/files/Sikh_Gurrdwara_Act1925_1.pdf.
30 For details see P. K. Riat, *A Historical and Theological Evaluation of the Sikh Gurdwaras Act, 1925* (2013) (Doctoral dissertation, University of Birmingham).
31 For details see M. L. Ahluwalia (ed.), *Gurdwara Reform Movement, 1919–1925, An Era of Congress-Akali Collaboration* (1985).
32 Takht literally translates to a throne or a seat. These five Takhts hold a special significance and are revered by the Sikhs. The five Takhts include the Sri Akal Takhat Sahib, Amritsar; the Sri Takhat Kesgarh Sahib, Anandpur; the Sri Takhat Patna Sahib, Patna; the Sri Takhat Hazur Sahib, Hyderabad Deccan; and the Sri Takhat Damdama Sahib, Tawlandi Sabo, Bathinda, Punjab.
33 The script in which the sacred text of Guru Granth Sahib is written. It was standardised by the second Sikh Guru, Guru Angad Dev.
34 'SGPC passes annual budget of Rs. 1205 crores', *The Tribune*, March 30, 2019, https://www.tribuneindia.com/news/punjab/sgpc-passes-annual-budget-of-rs-1-205-crore/750776.html
35 http://sgpc.net/
36 *Shiromani Gurdwara Parbandhak Committee v. Shri Som Nath Dass & Ors* AIR 2000 SC 1421.
37 Michael A. Heller, 'Boundaries of Private Property' (1999) 108(6) *Yale Law Journal* 1163.
38 G. R. Sethi, *Sikh Struggle for Gurdwara Reform. Including the Speeches Delivered by His Excellency Sir Malcolm Hailey, Governor of Punjab, in connection with the Gurdwara Reform Movement* (1927).
39 Ahluwalia op. cit., n 31.
40 Gobinder Singh, *Religion and Politics in the Punjab* (1986).
41 Yudhvir Rana, 'Reversal of power flow from Guru Ghars to government', *The Times of India*. April 19, 2019 https://timesofindia.indiatimes.com/city/amritsar/reversal-of-power-flow-from-guru-ghars-to-government/articleshow/68949824.cms
42 The last elections at SGPC were held in 2011. There is no maximum time limit for the continuance of the elected committee. The central government holds elections at its discretion.
43 Amandeep Sandhu, 'Nearly 10 million Sikhs have lost their religion because of this organization', *Scroll.in*, https://scroll.in/article/807847/nearly-10-million-sikhs-have-lost-their-religion-because-of-this-organisation
44 Amandeep Sandhu, 'The question of Sehajdhari rights is also a question of Sikh identity', *Caravanmagazine.in*, https://caravanmagazine.in/vantage/punjabs-sehajdhari-rights-question-sikh-identity.
45 'Supreme Court to hear plea on constitutional validity of Haryana Sikh Gurdwara Act', *The Economic Times*. August 6, 2014. https://economictimes.indiatimes.com/news/politics-and-nation/supreme-court-to-hear-plea-on-constitutional-validity-of-haryana-sikh-gurdwara-act/articleshow/39744602.cms

Bibliography

Aad Guru Granth Sahib. 1983 CE (Reprint). 1430 p. Publishers: Shiromani Gurdwara Parbandhak Committee, Amritsar (Religious Text citation).

Ahluwalia, M. L., ed. *Gurdwara Reform Movement, 1919–1925, an era of Congress-Akali collaboration: select documents*. New Delhi: Ashoka International Publishers, 1985.

Andrew, Maurice Edward, Peter Matheson, and Simon Rae, eds. *Religious studies in dialogue: Essays in honour of Albert C. Moore*. Faculty of Theology, University of Otago, 1991.

Arif, Yasmeen. *Life, emergent: The social in the afterlives of violence.* U of Minnesota Press, 2016.
Carrier, James G. "Moral economy: What's in a name." *Anthropological Theory* 18, no. 1 (2018): 18–35.
Cheal, David. *The gift economy.* London and New York: Routledge, 1988.
Esposito, Roberto. *Communitas: The origin and destiny of community.* Vol. 440. Stanford, CA: Stanford University Press, 2010.
Heller, Michael A. "The boundaries of private property." *The Yale Law Journal* 108, no. 6 (1999): 1163–1223.
Mauss, Marcel. *The gift.* Glencoe: Free Press, 1954.
Riat, Pritpal Kaur. "A historical and theological evaluation of the Sikh Gurdwaras Act, 1925." PhD diss., University of Birmingham, 2013.
Scott, James C. *The moral economy of the peasant: Rebellion and subsistence in Southeast Asia.* New Haven, CT: Yale University Press, 1976.
Sethi, G. R. *Sikh struggle for Gurdwara reform.* Amritsar: Union Press, 1927.
Singh, Gobinder. *Religion and politics in the Punjab.* New Delhi: South Asia Books, 1986.
Singh, Khushwant. *A history of the Sikhs (2nd Edition) 1839–2004.* Vol. 2. New Delhi: Oxford University Press, 2004.
Singh, Mohinder. *The Akali Movement.* Publication Bureau Punjabi University, 2015.
Thompson, Edward P. "The moral economy of the English crowd in the eighteenth century." *Past & Present* 50 (1971): 76–136.

9

USING CONTEMPORARY LITERATURE AND POPULAR CULTURE TO STUDY LAW

The Possibilities Inherent in Fantasy Fiction and Harry Potter

Shouvik Kumar Guha

The manner in which the concepts and images of law and literature have intermingled with each other is not a recent development; even if as an academic field of jurisprudence, it has been getting increasing attention only from the later part of the 20th century. There have been several instances of lawyers turning into celebrated authors,[1] just as there have been instances of authors effortlessly integrating legal settings in their narrative despite never having received any formal legal training.[2] Those who study law would testify to its many inherent theatrical components, just as they might acknowledge the fine nature of literary specimens that quite a few judicial pronouncements would make.[3] Similarly, legal aspects of intellectual property, plagiarism, defamation, obscenity and censorship are familiar bywords in the domain of literature.[4] Therefore, it is only natural that the boundary between these two fields would eventually begin to blur on occasions especially under any determined scholarly scrutiny carried out with inter-disciplinary motivations, which is what the law and literature movement is mostly about.

When one seeks to uncover the hidden nuggets of law in the myriad creations of literature and celluloid, one may get overwhelmed with the sheer variety of results on offer. They may range from the classic creations of Sophocles[5] or the exalted works of Anton Chekhov,[6] to the attention-gripping works such as the live broadcast documentary video of the sentencing hearing in *People v. Cahill*[7] or even more mainstream thriller movies such as *Solstorm*,[8] to the domain of satire and ridicule as apparent in Gilbert's works such as *Iolanthe*, *The Mikado* or *The Grand Duke*,[9] or veiled in the guise of science fiction as witnessed in popular television shows like *My Favourite Martian* or *3rd Rock from the Sun*,[10] to the domain of the deliberately shocking such as the movies of John Waters.[11]

Such range and variety involved in the field of law and literature mean that even when someone claims to be studying, teaching or conducting research in

DOI: 10.4324/9781003150565-10

this discipline, such activity may not always necessarily mean the same thing. For instance, it may be an attempt to look into the literary aspects of legal sources including judicial pronouncements, or it may be making an effort to examine how the author or poet or playwright might have perceived law and characters involved in the legal profession, or it may simply comprise exploring the concept of 'legal imagination' in the lines of James Boyd White's works involving styles and portrayal of images in literature.[12] When a law teacher is using literature in the confines of classroom, the focus may vary from seeking to highlight the notions of justice as expounded in such literature, or considering themes such as the interplay between law, freedom, authority, morality and punishment evidenced in the society as portrayed in literary creations; however, the objective may simply be to introduce the students to literature per excellence having a background steeped in law or to familiarize them with the usage of literature to bring forth socio-legal issues of contemporary relevance.[13]

There can indeed be multiple benefits that one may be able to glean by using literature and popular culture as background themes inside a classroom, especially one where discussions of law are taking place. Regardless of the diversity of the socio-cultural or geographical conditions that students may hail from, they are still likely to share a degree of common familiarity with certain 'pop-culture' characters and references – if hypothetical situations and analogies can be simulated based on images involving such references, it may turn out to be generating certain exciting visual cues for the students, which, in turn, can have a positive impact on the learning outcomes of any course that is being taught via said simulations.[14] Successful use of a recognizable fictional reality by a teacher as a background against which one may seek to examine new legal concepts can not only help the teacher forge a bond of common understanding with the students, but it also may provide invaluable assistance in testing out the limits of a standard legal doctrine applied in hypothetical possible scenarios borrowed from popular fiction.[15] One may, of course, try to explore the manner in which law and legal institutions have been portrayed in various media (including television, films and web series) in course of seeking to connect law with popular culture within the classroom[16] (and the author admits to having done exactly that with varying degrees of success over the years), but that does not form the subject matter of this chapter at this point. In the context of literature too, portrayal of law and the legal system is more common than one may think, yet the author is of the opinion that while using such works to discuss legal principles, the teacher's job may become more challenging inasmuch as they would need to emphasize upon the possible absurdities of such portrayal without compromising the literary value or attraction in the process.[17]

There are other planes also where literature engages with law, and some of them are quite commonly explored in the classrooms of a law university in classes of Media Law, Intellectual Property Law, Constitutional Law and so on. These range from censorship of famous literary creations, on charges of obscenity, heresy, seditious or inflammatory nature,[18] to the various facets of copyright law that allow the author of such creations to exercise varying degrees of control over them. There are various interesting arguments extended by both sides of the censorship debate; for instance, if one argues that a literary work should not be censored because it really does not have much of an impact in shaping the readers' psyche or that it does not enjoy a wide enough readership to begin with, then such an argument might, in turn, be used to argue the lack of necessity for according special protection to such literary work from state action or censorship to begin with.[19] Similarly, the instances of authors facing protracted legal challenges on the ground of plagiarism and copyright violation are manifold.

However, despite all the aforesaid possibilities surrounding law (specifically the teaching of law), literature and popular culture, the author would specifically like to focus his attention for the rest of this chapter on certain personal experiences faced in the course of attempting to connect fantasy fiction literature with law. Fantasy, speculative fiction and science fiction (often popularly depicted collectively as SFF) represent a genre that, in the opinion of the author, has been oft-neglected even its due share of literary analysis – it is, therefore, perhaps unsurprising that when it comes to the increasingly frequent discussions about law and literature as a popular subset of jurisprudence or a possible methodological tool for imparting legal education, this genre has scarcely been looked at, aforementioned instances of the utility of popular culture in its use inside classroom notwithstanding. While the creators of such literature have always enjoyed an interactive proximity to the readers who have been denied to many a brethren of theirs who engage in more 'serious' and 'realistic' versions of literature, the genre has not always attracted the kindest of literary critiques. Yet in course of the past few years, this barrier has displayed signs of wearing down, a debt that the genre perhaps owes to some of the most renowned creators of its kind, including the likes of J.K. Rowling, George R.R. Martin, Terry Pratchett, Kazuo Ishiguro, Ursula Le Guin and Neil Gaiman. The sheer levels of creativity involved in the 'fantastic' world-building, character formation and development, cultural and linguistic innovation that form the hallmark of fantasy fiction of the best quality have to be seen to be believed, and, indeed, in that aspect, this genre is in no manner whatsoever inferior to any other – an even cursory glance at the works of one of its most famous exemplars, viz. J.R.R. Tolkein, or even the more contemporary works of Robert Jordan, Brandon Sanderson, Glen Cook, Robin Hobb, Margaret Atwood and others would be sufficient to establish that both beyond any reasonable doubt or via preponderance of all ascertainable probabilities. Not only does the immense popularity of these works ensure that even any passing reference to them within classroom would resonate far more deeply within the minds of the students, but many of these worlds also have their own sets of laws and legal systems bearing more than a passing resemblance with those prevailing in the real world, and the number of potential hypothetical scenarios as has been mentioned earlier in this chapter that are at the disposal of the skilled teacher for use as background of discussions on various legal doctrines is nearly endless.

This was perhaps one of the key motivations that gave birth to the idea of an experimental elective course offered to senior students on the verge of graduating from a national law university, a course that might not only, by marrying law with fantasy fiction literature, help them think beyond what the law is and where it is to be found to actually what purpose the law serves but also, by introducing them to a fantastic world with extraneous conditions and set of rules, can actually help them try to observe the interplay of law and society from the outside and eventually be fascinated enough to attempt doing so by venturing inside too. The author chose to focus on the works of J.K. Rowling for this exercise involving her teenage protagonist, Harry Potter. The underlying assumption was a common familiarity of the students with such work, be it through Rowling's literary creation or its celluloid version.

The very outline of the course began with the following:[20]

> "Are you planning to follow a career in Magical Law, Miss Granger?" asked Scrimgeour.
>
> "No, I'm not," retorted Hermione. "I'm hoping to do some good in the world!"[21]

This is merely one of the several instances of Rowling expressing her thoughts about law and legal institutions being merely redundant at best and posing impediments at worst in the archetypical struggle between good and evil, justice and injustice, freedom and oppression in her creation of the magical world of Potterverse. Millions of readers have joyfully immersed themselves till date in the cultural phenomenon that the Harry Potter novels represent. Some have grown up reading them and later introduced them to the next generation, while others have discovered to their astonishment that adulthood does not really pose a barrier to enjoy the experience that Potterverse promises, despite having been introduced as fantasy fiction literature meant for the consumption of children and young adults. The engrossing narrative built by Rowling in course of the seven main books has been further enriched by supplementary books providing additional glimpses into the Potterverse, be it a discussion of the fascinating magical game of Quidditch,[22] or an effort to trace the origins of the magical world in the annals of history,[23] or an introduction to the various mythological creatures that have made one or more appearances in Potterverse[24] or even a brief look into what has been referred to as 'fantasy-within-fantasy', the popular folktales prevalent in Potterverse.[25] It is true that fantasy fiction literature and children's literature, in particular, have often been neglected by several law and literature scholars as well as literature critics for lacking in socio-cultural significance. However, there are others who believe that children are not simply spellbound by the plot-twists and inherent excitement that are the hallmark of fantasy fiction; in addition, they represent the very future, and they are the ones who are going to lead humanity into that future, provide the thinking that is going to serve as the guiding force in that journey and bring forth the change that is going to make survival and growth possible. Therefore, the fact that the wealth of social values and cultural mores intrinsically posited within the literature that they are exposed has the potential to mold their minds and hearts is of the utmost importance, and it is therein that the significance of fantasy fiction resides.

The author would indeed be one of the first to admit that none of the books penned by Rowling is directly about any legal themes, which gives rise to the question of their efficacy when it comes to the teaching of law. Nonetheless, the entirety of Potterverse is fraught with laws and legal institutions, and from time to time, Rowling has drawn images that vividly expose beyond any doubt that neither such laws nor such institutions are immune to fallibility. It is in Rowling's creation that one finds a government that has its officials torture children for what they perceive to be a lie even when they are aware in their hearts that it is nothing but the truth; the same government is shown to subject its citizens to imprisonment or even capital punishment without ever allowing them the benefit of due process of law. Rowling conceives of a society that designs its prisons in a way meant to drive the inmates to despair and suicidal tendencies without ever sparing a thought for their reformation, a legislature that seldom displays its desire to go through the steps of a democratic legislative procedure, a sociopolitical economy that enables the wealthy to bend government policy at their will, a Press that operates under curtailment of freedom and a pawn in the hands of the authority to serve its propaganda and a citizenry that often has little choice other than to accept government surveillance.[26] It is by no means a wholesome picture of the law, the organs of the state or the system in place, yet it is by using several shades of such a picture that Rowling intends to critique its various shortcomings on levels more than one, ranging from the functions of the government to its nature and the bureaucracy busy in running it. The degree to which such an attempt on her part often resonates with the readers in comparison to their own governments in the real world is evident from the global popularity of her creation. That is where the boundary between reality and magic begins to blur, and that is perhaps one of the strongest appeals that Potterverse holds. Illustratively, imagine the stark difference between the plain, even somewhat boring Dursley household obsessed with 'normalcy' and the seemingly invisible, wilder, unpredictable magical world as introduced in *Harry Potter and the Philosopher's Stone*, and the way in which these two worlds tend to crash into each other with the appearance of the Dementors in Private Drive and Voldemort's destruction of the Brockdale Bridge in *Harry Potter and the Order of the Phoenix* and *Harry Potter and the Half-Blood Prince*, respectively. Similarly, the secure, protective boundaries of Hogwarts tend to weaken with Dumbledore's death (as Ronald Weasley said once, "Everywhere's the same now!"), revealing the ways in which the borders between safe and unsafe, public and private, home and away may be eradicated at a moment's notice, as may the ones between childhood and adulthood (Harry's rite of passage and assumption of adult responsibilities as witnessed throughout the series), between student and teacher (while still a student at Hogwarts, Harry ends up playing the role of a teacher for the rest of Dumbledore's Army), between multiple identities and consciousness (the Harry–Voldemort connection and periodic possession and also the Horcruxes) as well as between life and death (Harry's experience in the limbo-like state resembling Platform 9¾). One may even get a glimpse of the radical manner in which the various social and political barriers get weakened, reorganized and outright demolished with Rowling's blessings in the aftermath of the final battle in *Harry Potter and the Deathly Hallows* ("Nobody was sitting according to House anymore: All were jumbled together, teachers and pupils, ghosts and parents, centaurs and house-elves".), or even in the Gargoyle standing guard before the Headmaster's Study not requiring any password when the trio seeks to enter (It merely groans, "Feel free!"). Perhaps readers can imbibe this reorganization by breaking down the social hierarchies they themselves face in the form of socioeconomic conditions, gender, race, ethnicity or religion, making law an ally instead of an enemy in their struggle, or perhaps some of them will still be filled with doubt just like Albus Severus Potter leaving for Hogwarts at the end of the seventh book.

It is true that lawyers may not feature as prominent characters in the *dramatis personae* itself, unlike say, journalists or bureaucrats do, yet one may argue that the implicit presence of what James Boyd White refers to as the 'legal imagination'[27] in the thematic language and context of the Potterverse novels makes lawyers one of the privileged 'implied reader' groups when it comes to the novels. Take, for instance, the graphic representation of the trial scenes through the vision of the Pensieve; or the multiple references to rights including gender rights and class rights, which cumulatively form one of the most dominant idioms of jurisprudence; or the very controlling value of jurisprudence that is arguably the underlying theme of the entire narrative, justice. Be it by delivering a satirical critique of the Left (consider Hermione Granger's advocacy of house-elf rights) or the Right (as MacNeil illustrates in the form of "apologia for the status quo as voiced by the Weasley twins"[28]), Rowling has proceeded to paint Hogwarts, the 'ideal sanctuary' in Potterverse, as a place that needs protection from external threats (Voldemort) as well as internal reforms (freedom from the various status inequities). Potterverse is often a depiction of the limitations rather than the utility of law, but at the same time, its creator often urges the readers, the potential future lawmakers, to proceed 'beyond the popular notions of law' in pursuit of justice.

On a lighter note, surely one can notice the similarities between law school and Hogwarts. Law students end up reading about Hogwarts (and other make-believe worlds) either in between reading commentaries and statutes or often even instead of reading commentaries and statutes. Both places can and ought to teach students about power, how to acquire it and how to use it, whether explicitly or otherwise, using education as a tool that, when used properly by students, makes one expect of those students things great and terrible (or hopefully, not-so-terrible). With questions about grades, internships and jobs looming in the horizon, how much consideration is given to the question about what sort of a lawyer the law student should become? Choice is, after all, the central tenet of Potterverse, one would say – between Dumbledore and Voldemort, between Draco and Ron, between Umbridge and McGonagall, between Lupin and Snape, between Sirius and Bellatrix, between Dobby and Kreacher or any of multiple other options.

The course eventually involved a wide range of discussions about similarities between law school experience and Harry's days at Hogwarts – some of the more obvious ones can perhaps be mentioned here.[29] An elite institution where a minority are selected to join, a process-oriented place where the grueling curriculum often makes students face self-doubts and anxieties in their initial years (and for some, in their later years too), only for them to eventually realize that not all knowledge or answers can be had from books and to gain the self-confidence needed to think like wizards and to make the right choice, with the admission committee (or the Sorting Hat) wondering how to segregate (whether on the basis of the scores in the competitive entrance examination or moot/debating achievements/publications or something else) an already competitive bunch without giving rise to even more intensive rivalries. There would be intense and difficult courses like Potions that students would have to face in their very first semester (Contracts, perhaps?), as well as easy courses such as Muggle Studies (for students in a law school, maybe a course like this very one?). There would be students who would display remarkable diligence and exceptional caliber with their color-coded notes and study schedule (and those who might ask the teacher questions in class such as the nuances of the 48th paragraph of Lord Denning's dissenting judgment in a case involving chalk and how it might have an impact on the price of cheese fixed 20 years hence); at the same time, there would be those who would not wish to go through examination papers afterward (because "it would make them feel ill"). There will be long-lasting bonds forged in the university in the camaraderie of late-night study sessions and memorial preparations (challenging tasks, despite perhaps lacking the flair of knocking out together a 12-feet-tall Mountain Troll). There would be teachers who are the nightmarish personifications of the Socratic methodology, those whose routine and lectures are so dull that their presence would hardly be felt even by themselves, those who have the gift of keeping a class silent without effort and those who would wish at some point of time or another to turn at least a few students into ferrets and bounce them around the classroom and, when asked about what they thought they had been doing, would give the monosyllabic reply, "teaching". Practical applications and clinical courses would usually be deemed more interesting than theoretical concepts, to the extent that the mystique of the real-life practitioner-teacher will never lose its charm (because, "He *knows* ... what it's like to be out there *doing* it ... he's seen it all."). Part of the education process would involve identifying the words of power in the books, while another part would involve learning the limitation of the books themselves (because "books can take you only so far in this field"). Used textbooks left behind by seniors might at times be preferred because not only are they cheaper, but they also might be marked up with invaluable notations left behind by the previous owners. There would be examinations, assignments and grades, more often than not integral to the career path (while some would believe they deserve the elusive E because they have exceeded all expectations by simply turning up for the examinations, yet others would learn the meaning of T is for Troll). While Recruitment Day Zero for law school students might not offer much of a variety, yet the truth remains that legal education can prepare students for a wider range of careers than most other disciplines can (though such careers may not be as colorful as the ones asking, "Have you got what it takes to train Security Trolls?").

The author takes considerable pleasure in admitting that the course, despite its experimental nature, has witnessed considerable success till date while, at the same time, emphasizing that a course of this nature is meant to be a supplement to and *not* a replacement of the fundamental courses meant to be taught to a student of law. The classroom experience has been an enriching one for both the teacher and the students alike (if one goes by student reviews), and the directions that the discussion within and beyond the classroom has taken show great promise so far. The sheer variety of the topics discussed perhaps matches any other law course in terms of diversity. From discussing the role that rule of law plays in a society governed by magic like the one in Potterverse[30] to exploring the notions of crime and punishment as explained through the concepts of Memory Charms, Unforgivable Curses, the Kiss of the Dementor and the Prison of Azkaban,[31] from analyzing the familial relationships and the contractual nature of transactions taking place in Potterverse (including Unbreakable Vows[32]) to understanding the peculiar nature of the wizarding economy[33] and the roles played by money and banks in it,[34] from considering the exclusionary, discriminatory and disenfranchising aspects of the relationship between wizards and witches, on the one hand, and ordinary non-magic Muggles, on the other, and other non-human/part-human species in Potterverse such as the Goblins, House-Elves, Giants, Centaurs and Werewolves and associated human and non-human rights concerns to analyzing gender roles by viewing the narratives from the eyes of Hermione Granger rather than Harry Potter himself[35] – each class ended up yielding lively discussions and engaging debates with vociferous participation on behalf of the students and the teacher. Some classes saw the form of bureaucracy as witnessed in Rowling's works being dissected from the perspectives of efficiency and accountability,[36] while others were about learning to identify false narratives built through propaganda (such as the entire narrative being told from the standpoint of a supporter of the villainous Lord Voldemort in the House of Slytherin, with the protagonists like Harry and Dumbledore being portrayed in a negative light[37]). In true spirit of clinical exercises, a class had even been spent recreating an exercise of mediation between Harry and the Dursleys with real-life laws instead of magic serving as tools for resolution of existing disputes. Concepts like terrorism and counterterrorism, civic rights, militant literacy, power inherent in racial identities and politics related thereto[38] were some of those sought to be explored and commented upon, whereas ideas such as profiling, limitations of criminal law and prosecution, with analogies such as the

Innocence Project from the United States,[39] were also put forward and debated upon. Some of the literature produced by the students as part of the course also turned out to be rather fascinating, be it a commentary on the susceptibility of the Potterverse economy to multi-jurisdictional trade and liberalization or an innovative take on a piece of legislation applicable to governing courtroom procedures inside the Wizengamot.

From a rich academic culture to obsessing about rankings and competitions, from formalities of dress to formalities of address, from wondering about life after (law) school to learning the wisdom of where to act and where not to and from knowing how to apply old rules to new cases to perhaps even envisioning a reshaping of the law by leaving formal education behind before its completion, the journeys through Hogwarts and law school both often turn out to be the veritable 'Bildungsroman'[40] for young minds. Perhaps that is what this course too was meant to be all about, as was this entire chapter and the exercise in connecting legal education with fantasy fiction literature and popular culture, along with reminding people that studying and learning law need not be devoid of sheer, unadulterated fun!

Notes

1 Mention may be made in this instance of the likes of Franz Kafka, Gustave Flaubert, Wallace Stevens, James Fenimore Cooper, Honoré de Balzac and several others.

2 William Shakespeare and Fyodor Dostoevsky's works, in particular, deserve mention in this category.

3 *See* Richard A. Posner, Relations between Law and Literature, 34 *Irish Jurist (N.S.)* 18 (1998).

4 Id.

5 For an experimental analysis of the parallels between the portrayal of democracy and law in Sophocles' *Antigone* and the modern U.S. justice system, *see* Ruthann Robson, Demokratia and Antigone: Before and after Sappho, 39 *Stetson Law Review* 3 (2009).

6 In particular, Chekhov's two stories, *Home* and *A Visit to Friends*, are of particular interest here, given the way they portray two different lawyers seeking to achieve a delicate balance between their professional and personal lives but choosing different means for the same. For further details, *see* James D. Redwood, Anton Chekhov's Home and a Visit to Friends: The Dichotomy between the Personal and the Professional, or the Lawyer Subjectified and Objectified, 39 *Stetson Law Review* 47 (2009).

7 809 N.E. 2d 561 (N.Y. 2003); for a detailed discussion of the usage of the said documentary video in the context of classroom teaching in law school, *see* Kate N. Day & Russell G. Murphy, Just Trying To Be Human in This Place: Storytelling and Film in the First-Year Law School Classroom, 39 *Stetson Law Review* 247 (2009).

8 For references to the usage of this movie of Swedish origin with the objective of looking at how law has been portrayed in films, *see* Steve Greenfield, Solstorm: Developing a Semantic/Syntactic Approach to Law Films, 39 *Stetson Law Review* 119 (2009).

9 For a detailed analysis of how Gilbert has sought to perceive law and its limitations through the twin lenses of illogic and irrationality, *see* Michael L. Richmond, Sir William Schwenck Gilbert and the Illogic of the Law, 39 *Stetson Law Review* 85 (2009).

10 To read about the manner in which such science fiction 'pop culture' television shows have been used to explore legal issues involving human rights and civil rights, *see* Christine A. Corcos, Visits to a Small Planet: Rights Talk in Some Science Fiction Film and Television Series from the 1950s to the 1990s, 39 *Stetson Law Review* 183 (2009).
11 For an engaging discussion on how Waters used his films such as *Pink Flamingoes, Hairspray, Serial Mom, Crybaby* and *Female Trouble* to showcase law and trial scenes as well as discuss issues relating to racism via narratives involving the marginalized so-called white trash, *see* Taunya Lovell Banks, Troubled Waters: Mid-Twentieth Century American Society on Trial in the Films of John Waters, 39 *Stetson Law Review* 153 (2009).
12 For a detailed analysis of the multiple shapes that studies in law and literature may assume, *see* Elizabeth Villiers Gernmette, Law and Literature: An Unnecessarily Suspect Class in the Liberal Arts Component of the Law School Curriculum, 23 *Valparaiso University Law Review* 267 (1989).
13 Id. *See also* William Domnarski, Law and Literature, 27 *Legal Studies Forum* 109 (2003).
14 *See* Thomas E. Simmons, What Zombies Can Teach Law Students: Popular Text Inclusion in Law and Literature, 66 *Mercer Law Review* 729 (2015).
15 *See generally* Victoria Salzmann, Here's Hulu: How Popular Culture Helps Teach the New Generation of Lawyers, 42 *McGeorge Law Review* 297 (2011) and Lenora Ledwon, Understanding Visual Metaphors: What Graphic Novels Can Teach Lawyers about Visual Storytelling, 63 *Drake Law Review* 193 (2015).
16 Exercises like that have been attempted by those who sought to trace specific legal themes across multiple audiovisual media, as well as those who have identified one or more legal themes as having been portrayed in certain media, and those who have sought to highlight the differences between different media by way of comparing their portrayals of the same legal theme. For further details, *see* Mark Niles & Naomi Mezey, Screening the Law: Ideology and Law in American Popular Culture, 28 *Columbian Journal of Law & Arts* 91 (2005).
17 *See*, for instance, the incongruities existing in the trial scene and procedures of interpretation depicted in Shakespeare's *The Merchant of Venice*, the use of rhetoric to further a claim as portrayed in Shakespeare's *Julius Caesar* and similar other works.
18 A classic case would involve the celebrated work of James Joyce, *Ulysses*, having been banned in most of Britain and Ireland back in the 1930s. For a look into Paul Vanderham's powerful critique of the judgment that led to such a ban, involving discussions about what constitutes obscenity, artistic intent, aesthetic impression and dominant nature of the literary creation as a whole, *see* Posner, *supra* note 3. *A Clockwork Orange* by Anthony Burgess, *Fahrenheit 451* by Ray Bradbury, *The Jungle* by Upton Sinclair, *Naked Lunch* by William S. Burroughs, *Sleeveless Errand* by Norah C. James, *Howl, and Other Poems* by Allen Ginsberg, *The Catcher in the Rye* by J.D. Salinger, *A Farewell to Arms* by Ernest Hemingway, *Anandamath* by Bankim Chandra Chattopadhyay, *Nil Darpan* by Dinabandhu Mitra, *Hindu Heaven* by Max Wylie, *Rangila Rasul* by Pandit M.A. Chamupati, *Captive Kashmir: Story of a Betrayed and Enslaved People* by Aziz Beg, and many other books belong to the list of literary works facing governmental censorship or complete ban from time to time.
19 *See* Posner, *supra* note 3.
20 The following part of the chapter closely follows the course outline of the elective paper 'An Interface between Fantasy Fiction Literature & Law: Special Focus on Rowling's Potterverse', offered to the students of the undergraduate B.A., LL.B. (Hons.) Programme at the West Bengal National University of Juridical Sciences, Kolkata, in the Winter Semester, 2019–2020.
21 J.K. Rowling, *Harry Potter and the Deathly Hallows*, Arthur A. Levine Books (2007).

22 *See* J.K. Rowling, *Quidditch through the Ages: From the World of Harry Potter*, Bloomsbury Press (2001).
23 *See* British Library, *Harry Potter – A History of Magic: The Book of the Exhibition*, Bloomsbury Childrens (2017).
24 *See* J.K. Rowling, *Fantastic Beasts and Where to Find Them*, Bloomsbury Childrens (2017).
25 *See* J.K. Rowling, *The Tales of Beedle the Bard*, The Children's High Level Group (2007).
26 For a more detailed discussion on this matter, *see* Paul R. Joseph & Lynn E. Wolf, The Law in Harry Potter: A System Not Even a Muggle Could Love, 34 *University of Toledo Law Review* 193 (2003).
27 James Boyd White, *The Legal Imagination*, Little, Brown (1973).
28 William P. MacNeil, Kidlit as Law-and-Lit: Harry Potter and the Scales of Justice, 14 *Law & Literature* 545, 547 (2002).
29 For a more detailed discussion about this matter, *see generally* Lenora Ledwon, Harry Potter Goes to Law School, in Jeffrey E. Thomas & Franklin G. Snyder (eds.), *The Law and Harry Potter*, 275, Carolina Academic Press (2010).
30 *See* Susan Hall, Harry Potter and the Rule of Law: The Central Weakness of Legal Concepts in the Wizard World, in Giselle Liza Anatol (ed.), *Reading Harry Potter: Critical Essays* 147, Westport, CT: Praeger Publishers (2003).
31 *See* Joel Fishman, Punishment in the Harry Potter Novels, 12(1) *Texas Wesleyan Law Review* 452 (2005).
32 *See* Timothy S. Hall, Magic and Contract: The Role of Intent, 12(1) *Texas Wesleyan Law Review* 427 (2005).
33 *See* Avichai Snir & Daniel Levy, Economic Growth in the Potterian Economy, in Jeffrey E. Thomas & Franklin G. Snyder (eds.), *The Law and Harry Potter*, 211, Carolina Academic Press (2010).
34 *See* Eric J. Gouvin, The Magic of Money and Banking, in Jeffrey E. Thomas & Franklin G. Snyder (eds.), *The Law and Harry Potter*, 237, Carolina Academic Press (2010). *See also* Heidi M. Schooner, Gringotts: The Role of Banks in Harry Potter's Wizarding World, in Jeffrey E. Thomas & Franklin G. Snyder (eds.), *The Law and Harry Potter*, 261, Carolina Academic Press (2010).
35 *See* Eliza T. Dresang, Hermione Granger and the Heritage of Gender, in Lana A. Whited (ed.), *The Ivory Tower and Harry Potter: Perspectives on a Literary Phenomenon*, 211, University of Missouri Press (2004).
36 *See* Benjamin H. Barton, Harry Potter and the Half-Crazed Bureaucracy, 104 *Michigan Law Review* 1523 (2006).
37 *See* Geoffrey R. Watson, The Persecution of Tom Riddle: A Study in Human Rights Law, in Jeffrey E. Thomas & Franklin G. Snyder (eds.), *The Law and Harry Potter*, 103, Carolina Academic Press (2010).
38 *See generally* B. Barratt, *The Politics of Harry Potter*, Palgrave Macmillan US (2012).
39 *See* Geoffrey Christopher Rapp, Sirius Black: A Case Study in Actual Innocence, in Jeffrey E. Thomas & Franklin G. Snyder (eds.), *The Law and Harry Potter*, 91, Carolina Academic Press (2010).
40 A novel of development, a story tracing the formation of a hero or heroine through childhood to adolescence to young adulthood, such as Charles Dickens' *David Copperfield* or Thomas Hughes' *Tom Brown*. *See* Jerome Buckley, *Season of Youth: The Bildungsroman from Dickens to Golding*, Harvard University Press (1974).

Bibliography

B. Barratt, *The Politics of Harry Potter*, Palgrave Macmillan US (2012).

Benjamin H. Barton, Harry Potter and the Half-Crazed Bureaucracy, 104 *Michigan Law Review* 1523 (2006).

British Library, *Harry Potter – A History of Magic: The Book of the Exhibition*, Bloomsbury Childrens (2017).
Christine A. Corcos, Visits to a Small Planet: Rights Talk in Some Science Fiction Film and Television Series from the 1950s to the 1990s, 39 *Stetson Law Review* 183 (2009).
Eliza T. Dresang, Hermione Granger and the Heritage of Gender, in Lana A. Whited (ed.), *The Ivory Tower and Harry Potter: Perspectives on a Literary Phenomenon*, 211, University of Missouri Press (2004).
Elizabeth Villiers Gernmette, Law and Literature: An Unnecessarily Suspect Class in the Liberal Arts Component of the Law School Curriculum, 23 *Valparaiso University Law Review* 267 (1989).
Giselle Liza Anatol (ed.), *Reading Harry Potter: Critical Essays*, Praeger Publishers Inc. (2003).
James Boyd White, *The Legal Imagination*, Little, Brown (1973).
James D. Redwood, Anton Chekhov's Home and A Visit to Friends: The Dichotomy between the Personal and the Professional, or the Lawyer Subjectified and Objectified, 39 *Stetson Law Review* 47 (2009).
Jeffrey E. Thomas & Franklin G. Snyder (eds.), *The Law and Harry Potter*, Carolina Academic Press (2010).
Jerome Buckley, *Season of Youth: The Bildungsroman from Dickens to Golding*, Harvard University Press (1974).
J.K. Rowling, *Fantastic Beasts and Where to Find Them*, Bloomsbury Childrens (2017).
J.K. Rowling, *Harry Potter and the Deathly Hallows*, Arthur A. Levine Books (2007).
J.K. Rowling, *Quidditch through the Ages: From the World of Harry Potter*, Bloomsbury Press (2001).
J.K. Rowling, *The Tales of Beedle the Bard*, The Children's High Level Group (2007).
Joel Fishman, Punishment in the Harry Potter Novels, 12(1) *Texas Wesleyan Law Review* 452 (2005).
Kate N. Day & Russell G. Murphy, Just Trying to Be Human in This Place: Storytelling and Film in the First-Year Law School Classroom, 39 *Stetson Law Review* 247 (2009).
Lenora Ledwon, Understanding Visual Metaphors: What Graphic Novels Can Teach Lawyers about Visual Storytelling, 63 *Drake Law Review* 193 (2015).
Mark Niles & Naomi Mezey, Screening the Law: Ideology and Law in American Popular Culture, 28 *Columbian Journal of Law & Arts* 91 (2005).
Michael L. Richmond, Sir William Schwenck Gilbert and the Illogic of the Law, 39 *Stetson Law Review* 85 (2009).
Paul R. Joseph & Lynn E. Wolf, The Law in Harry Potter: A System Not Even a Muggle Could Love, 34 *University of Toledo Law Review* 193 (2003).
Richard A. Posner, Relations between Law and Literature, 34 *Irish Jurist (N.S.)* 18 (1998).
Ruthann Robson, Demokratia and Antigone: Before and after Sappho, 39 *Stetson Law Review* 3 (2009).
Steve Greenfield, Solstorm: Developing a Semantic/Syntactic Approach to Law Films, 39 *Stetson Law Review* 119 (2009).
Taunya Lovell Banks, Troubled Waters: Mid-Twentieth Century American Society on Trial in the Films of John Waters, 39 *Stetson Law Review* 153 (2009).
Thomas E. Simmons, What Zombies Can Teach Law Students: Popular Text Inclusion in Law and Literature, 66 *Mercer Law Review* 729 (2015).
Timothy S. Hall, Magic and Contract: The Role of Intent, 12(1) *Texas Wesleyan Law Review* 427 (2005).

Victoria Salzmann, Here's Hulu: How Popular Culture Helps Teach the New Generation of Lawyers, 42 *McGeorge Law Review* 297 (2011).
William Domnarski, Law and Literature, 27 *Legal Stud. F.* 109 (2003).
William P. MacNeil, Kidlit as Law-and-Lit: Harry Potter and the Scales of Justice, 14 *Law & Literature* 545 (2002).

10

THE NECESSITY OF TEACHING HISTORY TO LAW STUDENTS

V.S. Elizabeth

10.1 Introduction

Law cannot be separated from the study of other social sciences and the humanities. Since law is as old as human society, studying the history of the law/s, the legal system etc., cannot be neglected. Human society has grown from the simpler tribal communities to the more complex urban societies. The purpose of law and the legal system/s have changed over time just as the theories of punishment, and therefore the kind of punishments given, have. In order to understand the reasons for the changes and the nature of the changes, the study of history of the contemporary societies is inevitable.

If we don't study the history of law and the legal system in the Indian subcontinent over time, we end up assuming nothing has changed and therefore not realising how much injustice is meted out as a consequence or that everything has changed and become nostalgic without reason, harking back to time periods when there was no idea of equality between all human beings and seeking to revive laws and systems that were inherently unjust and unfair to people of different genders, castes etc.

Given that today we have a constitution that sets out the values that we as Indians should adhere to, values that are rooted in human rights, of equality, justice, liberty, dignity of the individual, it is important to understand the context that led the constitution makers to set these values as the driving force of change in India that was brought into existence in 1947. Many of the contemporary problems of discrimination based on caste, gender and religious identity stem from a lack of understanding of the factors that led to the foundation of this constitution and therefore the efforts to overturn it.

The call for retributive justice instead of restorative justice or the demands for punishment instead of seeking reform all arise from a similar lack of understanding

DOI: 10.4324/9781003150565-11

of how communities and societies have evolved over time and how as the nature of the economy and society changes the nature of law and the understanding of what is justice will also have to change. Failure to do that is to take our society back by several hundreds of years leaving large numbers of the citizens frustrated at the lack of change and justice.

In India, the idea of teaching history, economics, sociology and political science to students of law as an integrated part of the study of the law programme began with the establishment of the National Law School of India University (NLSIU) in 1988, in Bangalore. For the first time, students were to enter the study of law right after their high school through an all-India entrance exam and were to be awarded a B.A., LL.B. (Hons.) degree at the end of the five-year programme. This was to be an integrated degree. This experiment worked so well that today we have nearly 25 National Law Universities (NLUs) in different parts of India; in addition, the five-year law programme is taught in many private universities and government law colleges. Unfortunately, over time we see either a complete lack of appreciation of the need to study history by law students or an undermining of the study of history in many of these institutions due to the ignorance of the importance of the study of the research methods and perspectives that the study of history can bring to understanding law. In fact, learning the tools for the study of the past and acquiring an understanding of the discipline of history can ensure better appreciation of the legal processes, the legal system itself and the legal institutions. When the purpose of the law is to ensure that justice is delivered, how can that be done without understanding the society that the legal system seeks to serve? Understanding the society does not mean only the current society but also the society of the past in which the laws and the legal systems took birth. Only a thorough appreciation of the discipline of history can facilitate this.

Having one course in Legal History for students pursuing the study of law was more or less a practice prior to 1988, but not taken seriously enough. In the Indian context, however, post-independence, this course largely involved studying in chronological order the judicial reforms and the various legislations, particularly the Indian Councils Acts and their provisions in an effort to understand the judicial, legislative and administrative history of the institutions that survived independence. In some instances, it also included a history of the "Hindu" and "Muslim" legal history. This was mostly studying what the Brahmanical texts prescribed in terms of law and justice and the description of the judicial system that prevailed under the Mughals. This was the understanding of what should be the content of the history courses to be taught to law students even when NLSIU was set up. During the first three years of its existence, the three courses that were taught as History were focused on chronological development of laws, legal and judicial institutions etc. History I was the administrative and judicial history during the colonial period, while History II was legislative developments in the colonial period and History III was the history of Roman and English law and legal institutions. Thus, the idea of legal history was restricted to a study of the chronological development of the legal and judicial systems.

The first Indian Legal History Congress was held only in February 2020, on the premises of the Gujarat National Law University bringing together some of the faculty teaching history or using historical methods in the law universities and other institutions teaching law as an undergraduate programme. Papers were presented on various aspects of legal history by faculty and students from different parts of India. The organisation of such an event in itself reflects the progress made in legal education in India since the 1980s. It demonstrated the fact that the interdisciplinary approach to the study of law has now been institutionalised and that after over three decades, its place in the law universities has been duly recognised.

During last year, we saw some important Supreme Court decisions that involved an understanding of the historical methods and an appreciation of the discipline of history. If legal education from the time of independence had incorporated the interdisciplinary approach to the study of law, there might have been a more nuanced understanding of the issues that were before the courts, which I felt went missing and therefore left many disappointed with the reasoning provided and the judgements that were delivered.

In this chapter, I hope to provide, with the help of examples, the difference that studying history of the societies makes to our grasp of the problems that beset India, the solution for which lies in contextualising the development of law. What I seek to do through this chapter is first present the purpose of legal education, followed by the use of studying history, an overview of how law schools in the United States approached the teaching of history to law students and then provide a brief account of the teaching of history at NLSIU. I will conclude with why I think the study of history is mandatory for every student of law, what kind of history should be taught, how it enriches the understanding of the laws and the legal systems in India and, more importantly, that it is one of the important ways to ensure that the purpose of law is served, viz., to see that justice is done.

10.2 The Purpose of Legal Education

Let me begin by asking first what is the purpose of a university education. This is a question that has been answered by different universities, in different parts of the world, differently over the ages. Bologna and Salerno said it was "to train students for certain professions," while Oxford and Cambridge said that universities were to "function as a nursery for gentlemen, statesmen and administrators." On the contrary, universities in Charlottenburg, Zurich and Massachusetts said it was to function as "a staff college for technological experts and specialists."[1] Prof. Edward Shils in 1983 said, "Universities have a distinctive task. It is the methodical discovery and the teaching of truths about serious and important things."[2] This diversity of thinking regarding the objective of a university education besets the law universities as well since the very inception of the reforms in legal education in India.

Prof. Madhav Menon, the founder and first vice chancellor of the NLSIU, asserted that the purpose of the Law School was to produce social engineers; however, since the success of the National Law School model, the law firms, the legal fraternity and many students who enter these law universities believe that the latter exist "as a service institution for the profession (the professional school model)," i.e. to provide only the knowledge and skills needed for practice. There are others who belong to the group that believes that a law school should function "as an academic institution devoted to the advancement of learning about law (the academic model)."[3] The questions that have arisen in this context are whether history should be taught in these law universities or not. If history is to be taught to law students, then what kind of history should it be? How many courses in history should be taught? These questions arise due to these diverse ideas about the purpose of legal education and the role of the law universities. So, if we can agree about the purpose of legal education, then there can be consensus regarding the place of teaching history in these institutions.

The International Legal Centre in its report, *Legal Education in a Changing World*, stated:

> Law schools, perceived as multipurpose centers, can develop human resources and idealism needed to strengthen legal systems; they can develop research and intellectual direction; they can address problems in fields ranging from land reform to criminal justice; they can foster the development of indigenous languages as vehicles for the administration of law; they can assist institutions involved in training paraprofessionals; they can help to provide materials and encouragement for civic education about law in schools and more intelligent treatment of law in the media; they can organise, or help organize, advanced specialized legal education for professionals who must acquire particular kinds of skills and expertise.[4]

This vision of a law school is what motivated Prof. Menon and the founding faculty of NLSIU. However, what happened in fact was that NLSIU, and I think all the NLUs, inadvertently pursued the model which is essentially that of an undergraduate teaching institution with a little commitment to research. The consequence has been that these universities treat undergraduate teaching as their main function and these universities are therefore perceived as factories producing people for the law firms or the profession in general. The NLUs ostensibly have a broader objective, see themselves as having a more diversified role with emphasis on advanced and interdisciplinary studies. In reality they have functioned, to a great extent, as nothing more than undergraduate teaching institutions preparing students for the profession, and with a very restricted idea of what the legal profession means. The result has been the failure to pursue an interdisciplinary approach in the study of law and the marginalisation of the teaching of history, economics, political science and sociology in spite of the professed objective.

The importance of an interdisciplinary approach to the study of law will be appreciated when we realise that law graduates often adopt a career in public life, either politics or civil service. Besides every aspect of our lives is impacted by law and legal education therefore can be a good means for acquiring knowledge of society, legal education has a number of characteristics that combine to make it an excellent vehicle for general education. Besides when we refer to "development" it implies both material and cultural change, involving issues of social justice; "law and the legal system are important features of these processes, especially when guided by basic values of fairness, justice and equity; and finally, legal education can be a particularly good vehicle for developing important human skills."[5]

Legal Education in a Changing World brings out the point that the discipline of law is considered to be a part of the humanities because of the fact that it covers so many human activities and relationships and deals with more or less the same phenomena as the social sciences and is increasingly informed by them. It also states that the discipline of law has a rich heritage of literature, philosophy and historical experience. The failure or inability to recognise this aspect of the discipline of law is the reason why despite the objective of teaching law from an interdisciplinary approach the NLUs have failed to do so and teach law from a strictly liberal positivist approach, treating the discipline of law as an island, as having developed in a vacuum without any history behind it or a context in which it became what it has. This has resulted in a very narrow and false understanding of what the law can do. Without analysing the impact that laws have had in the past on different sections of society and without examining whether the people for whose welfare presumably various enactments were made benefited from them or not there is no point to agitating for more laws, or more stringent laws. It is the failure to do so which has caused the frustration with the law and legal system and a lack of faith in the justice system itself.

The study of law ought to be exciting and inspiring, broadening the mind and widening the understanding of society even as it deepens the appreciation of the law and society interface. I think that *Legal Education in a Changing World* has very succinctly put this;

"The study of law can be (a) as intellectually exacting as philosophy, but more down to earth; (b) as concerned with contemporary, real-life problems as medicine or engineering, but with a greater diversity of concerns and with closer links to the humanities;"

"The strength of law as a discipline lies in the fact that it is so multidimensional. The teacher is called upon (a) to strike a balance between the

> elements which make up law; (b) to be informed about and deal adequately in today's world, with the closely related subjects from which law must draw most of its wisdom; (c) to provide both 'academic' and 'practical' insights; and (d) to use methods which motivate, stimulate and engage students in issues of theory, doctrinal learning, skill-development and engagement with concrete problems."[6]

If legal education in India were to realise these elements, then it is essential that the interdisciplinary approach has to be more seriously pursued.

10.3 Relevance of Studying History

Having laid down what I believe should be the role of law schools in legal education, I wish to now proceed to present the importance of the study of history for law students. At the end of 1892, the Committee of Ten's Subcommittee on history (including Woodrow Wilson) said that all high school students should study history of America and the outside world for four years, and the reason they gave for the same was that the study of history best prepared the student to exert "a salutary influence upon the affairs of his country," because it best promoted "the invaluable mental power which we call judgment."[7] "Judgement implies nothing less than wisdom – an even bigger word – about human nature and society." The Bradley Commission on History in Schools spelled out how this judgement is developed. They said that studying history

> helps students to develop a sense of "shared humanity"; to understand themselves and "otherness" by learning how they resemble and how they differ from other people, over time and space; to question stereotypes of others and of themselves; to discern the difference between fact and conjecture; to grasp the complexity of historical cause; to distrust the simple answer and the dismissive explanation; to respect particularity and avoid false analogy; to recognise the abuse of historical "lessons," and to weigh the possible consequences of such abuse; to consider that ignorance of the past may make us prisoners of it; to realise that not all problems have solutions; to be prepared for the irrational, the accidental, in human affairs; and to grasp the power of ideas and character in history.[8]

Clearly these are qualities that are greatly desired in a student of law too, and when a study of history can instil them in the law students, it is obvious that study of history is crucial to legal education. It is essential for the student of law to understand that the struggles for realising the objectives of our constitution are always ongoing; it is as we go about our daily business of how we do what needs to be done and how we treat one another and the rest of humanity that we realise those goals. An essential part of any well-rounded education is learning where we have come from and where we are headed. History is the discipline through which this understanding can be gained.

This is even more important for a student of law even though many students, law teachers and lawyers often "discuss the legal system as if it was a monolith standing independent of space and time, as a phenomenon on its own." The result of such an attitude is the short-sightedness with which we approach problems of law and justice. For example, in response to the hue and cry raised over the increasing instances of sexual violence against women and children in India was asking for the death sentence for the perpetrators without examining why this was not thought of or included in the Indian Penal Code (IPC) in the first instance. A perusal of the documents relating to the drafting of the IPC in the 19th century would have revealed the far-sightedness of Macaulay who argued that if the death sentence was awarded for such crimes, then the perpetrator will kill the victims so as to avoid being prosecuted at all. This is one of the reasons that women activists and lawyers give even today as they argue against the death sentence for sexual violence. Ignoring history results, on the one hand, is the arrogance on the part of the legal fraternity that law is the solution for all problems, and on the other hand, it results in reinventing the wheel, over and over again.

An eminent Sri Lankan jurist, the late Judge C.G. Weeramantry, in his book, *An Invitation to the Law*, states,

> Not merely specific rules of law but even, more importantly, the basic attitudes and spirit of a legal system will be completely missed by a student who ignores its historical aspects. The English legal system, like all others, is incapable of being understood apart from the events of English history: The Norman Conquest, superimposing alien rules upon an ancient Saxon legal system; the struggles for supremacy between the nobility and the Crown resulting in Magna Carta; … the World Wars which spawned the concept of the welfare state. All these are the warp and woof whereof English law is made.[9]
>
> Nor was the impact of history on law confined to political history. The social, economic and cultural history of England provided important strands contributing to both the spirit and the content of the modern English law. The analysis of any other system would show similar results. All people, lawyers and judges included, are the creatures of their times and circumstances, and the legal systems they evolve are not purely logical exercises but practical compromises and suggestions, prompted by contemporary events. Even the rare jurist or judge who is able to rise above the currents of his times and to point magisterially to basic improvements, is to a large extent conditioned in thought and action by his milieu.[10]

This is exactly what E.H. Carr has said in his book *What Is History?* regarding historians.

10.4 A Brief Overview of the Research and Teaching of Legal History Outside India till the 1980s

Henry Sumner Maine and Frederic W. Maitland were two of the early legal historians. While the latter together with Pollock carried out a very detailed history of the development of Common Law, Maine is known for his contribution to "insights with practical knowledge of the history of the legal systems." He had studied both Hindu and Roman laws besides others and saw some patterns from his studies of these legal systems leading to the famous statement, "the movement of progressive societies is from status to contract." This statement, of course, stands challenged today, but it brought attention to the importance of the study of legal development over the years and the fact there is a great deal of similarities in the way in which legal systems have developed in various societies. Nevertheless, not too many legal academicians at that time were convinced about the importance or even the relevance of teaching legal history to law students, nor were they convinced that it should be anything more than tracing the chronological development of the various laws and institutions. More recently, we have scholars like Anthony Musson who have taken the study of legal history very seriously, and realising the need for treating it as an independent discipline has contributed greatly to the methodologies to be used for pursuing the same.[11]

In India, there was no debate because of the poor understanding of the discipline of history and even poorer understanding of the relevance of the study of history for law students and therefore the content of such a course. Almost all contributions to legal history of India have been by foreign scholars, beginning with Henry Maine, followed by Mensky, Rudolph and Rudolph, Alen Gledhill, Elizabeth Kolsky, David Skuy etc. The two oft-referred-to textbooks on legal history have been by two retired judges, Rama Jois and M.P. Jain. Dr. H.V. Sreenivasa Murthy's book was probably the first foray into Indian legal history by a practising historian, for Indian historians have rarely, if ever, shown any interest in this field. That this attitude to the study of history by historians and law teachers was not unique to the Indian context is best brought out by what Daniel Boorstin, noted historian and librarian of Congress Emeritus, said about legal history in the United States. He said it was as a "Dark Continent," stating that, "we are ignoramuses about America's legal past." However, legal history gained a little popularity in the United States after that and so was taught as a course or seminar, and many people wrote articles on various aspects of the history of law. However, even then the legal fraternity was not fully convinced about the utility of teaching legal history in the law schools. In the 1980s, legal history became popular according to David W. Raack who in his article "Some Reflections on the Role of Legal History in Legal Education" discussed the utility of the study of legal history in legal education by surveying the history of the teaching of legal history in the United States.[12]

The debate regarding what should be the content of legal history is quite old so far as even the United States is concerned as the very titles of two articles on the subject demonstrate Presser, "Legal History or the History of Law: A Primer on Bringing Law's Past into the Present," and Hoeflich, "A Renaissance in Legal History?"[13] In the said article, Raack first examined the changes made to the teaching of legal history since the 1950s both as an independent discipline and as a part of the "law school curriculum," followed by discussing the benefit of teaching legal history and concluding with a section on the timing of teaching of legal history, its content and as a separate course of study.

Early legal history in the United States was categorised as doctrinal history,[14] meaning thereby a study of the legal doctrines and rules, especially their origins and growth. This approach essentially treated law as an isolated discipline, as not being impacted by the socio-economic and political changes and therefore without even the need to refer to them in order to understand the developments and changes in the legal doctrines and rules. Morton Horwitz characterised most of the research and writing in legal history before the 1970s as "lawyers' legal history."[15] Such a study excluded the interaction between law and broader social trends. They did not explore the social context of law or the social effects of law.

Later came the Wisconsin School followed by the Critical School. Friedman says that the critical legal historians tried to show how the law was manipulated for economic interests. While the earlier American legal history concentrated on legal concepts and institutions to the exclusion of developments in society that affected the law or were affected by it, "[t]he new Legal History insists that the evolution of American law cannot be studied in isolation from attending social, political and especially economic circumstances."[16] In other words, law or legal events are studied in their social context, with special emphasis laid on the effects of economic forces. It was during that phase that a shift from the history of constitutional law was made, focusing on one county or state and linking legal behaviour with social change. Alongside this developed a "cultural" approach, one that studied the effect of social context and broader social trends and patterns on the law.[17]

When we examine why despite these developments teaching and study of legal history have not progressed very much, even though there is must research and writing in this area, one of the important factors is that law students whether in India or the United States do not believe it to be an indispensable course of study, partly because there is an anti-historical bias among students in general.

> The naivete of my American students sometimes suggested to me that they thought ... the history of the law (started) on the day they entered law school. They seemed to be blissfully oblivious of the power established patterns of thought and behaviour of the formative influence of traditional ideologies, in the law more than anywhere else.[18]

This was stated in 1957 but is so true of law students even today, at least in many of the NLUs. The second reason that law students consider the study of history to be irrelevant to their course of study is because of their obsession with the training they think will be useful to them as practitioners, which they obviously don't think comes from a study of history.[19] I would say that this is largely due to the content and the way that history is taught in the law schools. Not only that it is, as Halpern argues, also due to the fact that law students treat their law schools practically as a place for training and for acquiring credentials required to be practitioners, and therefore, all intellectual enquiry of a broader character takes second place to their concern for the nuts and bolts preparation required to pass the bar, obtain a good job and become a successful practitioner. With such an understanding as this with regard to the purpose of legal education, the pursuit of legal history was set aside as irrelevant to this goal.

Another argument already discussed above derived from the idea that a law school's business is to train students for legal practice sees no place for the study of history in law schools as it lacks any practical or professional value both in its content and in its method of analysis. The latter, of course, is based on the understanding that historians pursue an empiricist approach to the study of the past from a liberal positivist perspective. Maitland noted that historians look for evidence that will allow them to understand the past on its own terms, while lawyers look to the past for authorities that can be used, or adapted to be used, to solve present legal problems and cases. Clearly Maitland was not familiar with Croce and Collingwood's approach to the study of history or that of Carr. His idea of history arose from a positivist understanding of the nature of history. While the three philosophers mentioned above make it very clear that "[a]ll history is contemporary history," that history is the interaction between the historian and his facts and an unending dialogue between the present and the past.[20] This is precisely I believe why I believe that it is necessary to teach not just legal history but also the philosophy of history and the historical methods in the law universities. There has been so much progress in the study and practice of history that is of direct relevance and will be of immense use to the students and the discipline of law of which even now most law teachers and law students are ignorant of. The idea that law is concerned with analysis regardless of time while history focuses on a narrative style and is limited by time is clearly a problem. A little bit of study of history as a discipline in the 20th century alone will demonstrate the error of this belief as will a study of historiography.

The progress in the study and teaching of legal history in the United States, however, has progressed to the extent where now scholars are examining more intricate relations between law and history. In the book *The Oxford Handbook of Legal History*, the authors examine whether law is free from the impact of the changes and developments in the economy and show the early responses made by scholars like Friedman and Horwitz, discussed earlier in this chapter, and the more recent research in this field that goes beyond some of the early suppositions. Such developments are yet to take place in the study of Indian legal history. History and law are concerned with facts and the pursuit of truth. Thus, analysis of facts is at the heart of both the disciplines as Carr, Collingwood and Bloch have demonstrated in their respective works.[21]

10.5 The Teaching of History at NLSIU

At NLSIU till 2003, all the students studied three courses in history. While for the first three years the curriculum, syllabi and reading material had been identified and prepared by the faculty of law, from 1992, I completely transformed the first two courses in history. With the one year of teaching history to law students I saw the huge gap in the understanding of the forces that had changed our society, economy and polity on the part of the students. At the same time, I saw the immense value in exposing the students to the developments in the discipline of history per se in terms of the debates on objectivity and truth, the analytical tools and research methods that historians employed in the pursuit of their discipline – the variety of methods that were available besides the basic and common methods for all historians of external and internal criticism of sources. I knew that a study of the philosophy of history will transform the way that these young minds engaged with the world of not only knowledge but also the world they lived in, that it will sharpen their skills of analysis and awaken them to the existence of bias in themselves and in all that they read and the need to be aware, to be conscious of that if they wanted to be objective, to arrive at the truth. I also wanted to sensitise them to the issues that affected contemporary India – poverty, communalism, caste and gender-based discrimination; in other words, the inequalities and injustice perpetrated in the name of pursuit of law and order. I believed that a critical approach to the past will, in turn, enable a more critical approach to what they saw before them in the contemporary world.

With these objectives in mind, I developed the course content and syllabi and prepared the reading list for the first two courses initially and later for the History III course as well. So the first course was designed to introduce the law student to the discipline of history – its philosophy, the methods, the concepts. The second part of the History I course was designed, as per the then Bar Council regulations regarding legal education, to introduce the students to the history and culture of India. I used that direction to lead the students to a study of some of the problems in Indian history that continued to affect the contemporary Indian society – origin and development of caste and untouchability, gender-based discrimination, communalism, the interest in a civilisation that existed more than 5,000 years ago and the irrational interpretations of the origin, authors and end of that civilisation, among other problems. The first part of History I involved not only studying the philosophy of history as propounded by Collingwood, Carr and others but also a survey of the historiography of the definition and nature of history and also the methods of history.

This was done with the intention that the students will learn that the very idea of what is history, its nature and the methods used to study the past have undergone changes, with the changes in the different societies over time. It is important to appreciate the fact that no idea, no concept, no methods are static, that each society conceptualises these in accordance with the nature of that society and what it prioritises. At the same time, this enabled students to develop sharp analytical skills and ability to question every preconceived idea or knowledge and knowledge formation. Nothing could be sacrosanct after that. They learnt that nothing is constant and everything changes all the time everywhere. As Lyotard said, the postmodern world is characterised by the collapse of centres and incredulity towards meta-narratives, which makes it impossible to continue gender- and caste-based discrimination or the perpetuation of institutions that facilitate such injustice in the name of tradition and precedents.[22] This was followed by a study of the different schools of Indian Historiography to make the students aware that historians choose facts from the myriad traces of the past that are available even as it is impossible to recover all of the past, that historians select the methods for interpreting such facts and therefore what one consumes through the history textbooks are not much more than what the historian or rather the society considered to be important at that time. For many of my students, History I was a life-changing experience, as a result. It shattered their long-held beliefs about objectivity, about truth and, more importantly, about history and therefore about law itself.

On the contrary, for many others, it was History II that shaped their thinking and impacted their understanding of history and law. Given the autonomy that I enjoyed, as a teacher at the NLSIU, I never taught the same course twice. Every time the course was offered, I had changed the content, the readings or the very method and perspective itself. Till around 2016, I taught this course using the materialist conception of history. It was focused on the colonial period in Indian history, largely from mid-18th century to mid-20th century. I considered it important for students to understand the nature of colonialism, its impact on the economy, society, polity of the Indian subcontinent and the development of law and the legal system. For so much is presented as unchanged – the "personal laws," the religious identities of communities, inequality and, of course, poverty – but I wanted the students to learn that the very nature of colonialism underwent change according to the interest of the metropolis and that colonialism was a specific stage in the history of the subcontinent. There are no benefits from colonisation or advantages that came from being colonised. Colonialism drastically altered not just the nature of the economy, polity and society, but it also transformed the very identities of the various peoples in the subcontinent. It was important to see that the very perception of our past itself is a product of the colonial period. From 2016, I decided to adopt a radical feminist approach to the study of the same period – only this time the focus was on women. It became necessary to appreciate the fact that history like law is gendered that what is passed off as a neutral approach is really a male perspective of the past and of law, that women and men, of different castes, communities and regions were impacted differently by colonialism. For example, hailing industrialisation and modernisation as benefits that came about due to colonisation actually resulted in marginalising women and pushing them into poverty. Similarly, the so-called social reform legislations actually had an adverse impact on women, for example, the Hindu Widow Remarriage Act, instead of enabling upper-caste

Hindu widows to remarry took away the rights of inheritance of Sudra women and that over time the castes that practised widow remarriage began to abandon the practice in favour of Brahmanisation.

For many years since 1992, History II was focused on impact of colonialism and rise and growth of nationalism. Due to the suggestions from students who shared some of the more interesting articles on legal history of India, I began to slowly change the content of History II so as to include gradually more and more of legal history – not just the socio-religious reform legislations and their impact but also the background leading to the enactment of the IPC, the Companies Act etc. and the consequences or problems with them. At the same time, some topics that were a constant were Indian Historiography for the colonial period, understanding what is colonialism and its impact. I also thought it useful to include topics that shed light on some of the changes in society that resulted from colonial policies and through the law and courts – the status of the *devadasis*, women's property rights, formation of identities based on the textbook understanding of religion etc.

History III was taught till the batch of 2003 and was briefly back for the batch of 2007 but discontinued after one of the vice chancellors, without consultation and on the advice and recommendation of a bunch of undergraduate students, decided that there was no need for three courses in history. It was a bad decision, but it liberated me to explore the teaching of feminist legal theory in various ways – as feminist jurisprudence, as violence against women, as sexual violence against women and the state's response to it etc. This is another dimension of interdisciplinary teaching that I ventured into – history, feminism and law coming together at a law university. But returning to History III, it was designed, as I have mentioned earlier, as a course to teach the history of Roman and English aw and the legal developments in the European Union. It was taught in that form for the first few years; thereafter, to be precise from 1994, I decided to make it more directly relevant to the law students of the postmodern period by exploring the history of the development of rights. So, through the course I placed before the students the way in which words like "liberty" and "liberties" meant since the medieval period in Europe, why and how such concepts developed, who were the people and why they got to exercise these liberties. The history of Magna Carta, the Civil War in England to the French and American Revolutions and the evolving understanding and meaning of rights through all of this was a major part of History III. The 19th century was an era of rapid social and economic changes, which were reflected in the developments in the concepts of law and political ideas and the women's movement, and the working-class movements impacted these ideas, and these were used to understand how the Universal Declaration of Human Rights came to be. From rights to man to human rights was a journey that was the product of the changes in the society and economy of countries world over. Thus, this course gave an overview of the history of rights so as to enable the student of law to understand the new demands to include the rights of sexual minorities, transgenders, children's rights etc. History III then came to be offered as an elective after further reforms in the undergraduate programme a few years ago.

Much of what I was able to do at NLSIU was because of the fact that over the years, the teachers came to have total autonomy to design the course outline and determine the content of the curriculum for their course with little to no interference. Prof. Menon's vision to give teachers such autonomy even as they had to present the syllabus to the faculty ensured that the courses could evolve even as I learnt over the years what should be and should not be the content of the courses I taught. If I didn't have such freedom and if there had been too much scrutiny by the law teachers, I am quite sure that it would have been more difficult to have achieved what I did in the realms of teaching history to law students.

At least two alumni of the NLSIU have begun to research and write on legal history of the colonial period in South Asia as have other Indian historians studying and teaching abroad, like Rohit De and Kalyani Ramnath[23] and Mithi Mukherjee. This is a welcome development as in the past, legal history of India was mostly the work of foreign scholars. However, not all the NLUs use their works for teaching history in the NLUs. For the interdisciplinary approach to the study of the past to be a meaningful engagement in the NLUs, it is important that the content of the courses, the methods used for teaching as well as for study of the past and the readings recommended are updated and of high quality. Not only will the teaching of history in the law schools be seen as necessary, but it will actually provide students with the much-coveted skills of research, writing and analysis, and history will come to be seen as a dynamic discipline that it is.

Justice Weeramantry concluded the section on law and history in his chapter on "Interrelationships between Law and Other Fields of Human Knowledge" by stating that "[t]he intimate connection between law and history is clear enough, despite these varying views, to require legal instruction to include an exposure to history, without which laws may be learnt but never completely understood."[24]

10.6 Conclusion

I strongly believe that interdisciplinary teaching in the NLUs cannot be limited to the role of history, political science, economics and sociology as handmaidens of law. In order to fulfil the much-acclaimed idea of interdisciplinary approach to the study of law, it is important that students of law are taught the research methods of these disciplines in addition to the legal methods that they are taught. It is important that the teachers of the different faculties in the NLUs learn from each other's disciplines and incorporate the recent tools of analysis into their own. No discipline has developed in a vacuum; the richest disciplines are those that have borrowed from the methods and developments of the sister disciplines.

In order to do this, it is important that at least through one course, the philosophy and methods of history are taught and students are introduced to the most recent developments in the study of some of the problems of Indian history so that they learn to delve a little deeper into the study of the past at the undergraduate level. What they learn at the high school through textbooks is several decades behind the most recent findings and developments in the development of history, so it is important that there is a course through which they learn these things so as to not become bigoted and narrow-minded in their perception of their fellow citizens and other human beings. In the name of legal history, students should not be led to a meaningless veneration of the past, which has long gone by, a past that cannot be recalled and reawakened in a society far different from the one in which it took birth.

It is important for every citizen of India to be taught the lessons that the past has to teach so that we do not repeat the mistakes of the past. Though, one of the truths that every historian knows is no one learns from the past. A study of history by law students not only adds to their knowledge, but, more importantly, it also opens their mind, deepens their understanding of not only law but also the society as a whole and provides them the skills of research, writing and analysis that will stand them in good stead in all walks of life, whatever be their choice of vocation. It will make them more understanding of their fellow beings, more sensitive to the needs of their society and enable them appreciate the need for substantive equality and justice.

Notes

1 Eric Ashby, Technology and the Academics 68 (1963) as cited in William Twining, Blackstone's Tower the English Law School, 49 (1994).
2 Edward Shils, The Academic Ethic 3 (1983) as cited in William Twining, Blackstone's Tower the English Law School 49 (1994).
3 William Twining, Blackstones's Tower the English Law School 52 (1994).
4 International Legal Centre, Legal Education in a Changing World 39 (1975) as cited in William Twining, Blackstone's Tower the English Law School 54 (1994).
5 William Twining, Blackstone's Tower the English Law School 58 (1994).
6 International Legal Centre, Legal Education in a Changing World 36 (paras. 90–92 (1975) as cited in William Twining, Blackstone's Tower the English Law School 60 (1994).
7 Paul Gagnon, *Why Study History? The Atlantic Monthly* 43, 43–66 (November 1988).
8 Id., at p. 44.
9 C.G. Weeramantry, An Invitation to the Law 68 (1982).
10 Id.
11 Making Legal History, Approaches and Methodologies, Anthony Musson, Chantal Stebbings eds. (2013).
12 David W. Raack, Some Reflections on the Role of Legal History in Legal Education, 26(4) *Duquesne Law Review* 893, 893–923 (1987–1988).
13 Stephen B. Presser, "Legal History" or the History of Law: A Primer on Bringing Law's Past into the Present, 35 *Valparaiso University Law Review* 849, 850 (1972) & Michael H. Hoeflich, *A Renaissance in Legal History?* (1984) *University of Illinois Law Review* 507, 508 or in the very titles of the journals that deal with the subject, *The American Journal of Legal History, Law and History Review* etc.
14 Lawrence Friedman, American Legal History: Past and Present, 34 *Journal of Legal Education* 563 (1984). An interesting book by him on the subject matter under discussion, *A History of American Law* (1973).

15 Morton Horwitz, The Transformation of American Law 1780–1860 (1977).
16 Astorino, History and Legal Discourse: The Language of the New Legal History, 23 *Duquesne Law Review* 363, 364–365 (1985).
17 White, Some Observations on a Course in Legal History, 23 *Journal of Legal Education* 440, 445 (1971).
18 Murphy, *Legal History as a course,* 10 *Journal of Legal Education* 79, 79 (1957), where the author refers to a foreign scholars experience with regard to American students at Yale.
19 Stephen C. Halpern, On the Politics and Pathology of Legal Education, 32 *Journal of Legal Education* 383 (1982).
20 E.H. Carr, What Is History?
21 E.H. Carr, What Is History? R.G. Collingwood, The Idea of History, Marc Bloch, The Historian's Craft.
22 Keith Jenkins, Rethinking History.
23 Both are alumni of NLSIU who went to complete their LL.M. from the Yale Law School, followed by a Ph.D. in History from Princeton University. While Rohit De is currently Assistant Professor of History at Yale University; Kalyani Ramnath is a Fellow at the Centre for History and Economics, Harvard University. Rohit De's most recent work is *A People's Constitution*.
24 C.G. Weeramantry, An Invitation to the Law 69 (1982).

11

WOMEN AND EMPOWERMENT

Pay Disparity in Organised and Unorganised Sectors

Hiteshkumar Thakkar and Anant Agarwal

11.1 Introduction

Labour market discrimination has been a perennial feature of the Indian economy.[1] Many economists post-independence focused on the labour market discrimination, such as Wadhawa (1975)[2] and Berreman (1979).[3] However, these studies were usually through the lens of caste discrimination and did not offer a concrete analysis of the labour markets i.e. the unorganised and organised sectors per se. Further, since the mid-1990s, interest regarding the gender wage gap arose due to the apparent divide prevalent between males and females in India (Bhaumik and Chaudhary, 2008[4]; Sengupta and Das, 2014[5]). The 1991 economic reforms increased labour market flexibility, which, in turn, led to rising informalisation of the work.

The concept of women empowerment has been held to hold the key for India's economic development; however, there still exists a gap between males and females in most spheres of life. Gender remains a primary factor for pay disparity across sectors in the Indian market. At the same time, there also exists a disparity between the employees in the organised sectors and the employees in the unorganised sectors, which exacerbates the already present disparity due to gender.

Presently, about 75% (324 million) of Indian women of economically active age are not engaged in formal and paid work today (Report by Google and Bain & Company – Powering the Economy with Her: Women Entrepreneurship in India, 2019). The main reason for this, among other things, can be attributed to the fact that the working women are often deprived of the similar income/wage given to their male counterparts. The Monster Salary Index, 2019, reported women in India earn 19% less than men. According to the International Labour Organization's data, India's female labour force participation (FLFP) rate has

DOI: 10.4324/9781003150565-12

remained consistently low, ranking 121 out of 131 countries, making it one of the lowest in the world. With the exception of Pakistan, India had the lowest FLFP rate in South Asia (World Bank, 2016).[6]

Additionally, the majority of India's female workforce is currently employed in unorganised sectors. With limited policies and laws to protect them, they are routinely paid out lesser wages and salaries. Undeniably, the role of women to boost the economy cannot be discredited. According to a joint report by Google and Bain & Company (Powering the Economy with Her: Women Entrepreneurship in India, 2019), women in entrepreneurship can create 150–170 million job opportunities in India, accounting for more than 25% of the new jobs required for the entire working-age population by 2030.[7]

Therefore, increased FLFP can significantly contribute to the growth and development of the economy. Women's labour market participation must be increased by providing decent and productive employment opportunities and closing the wage gap. To accomplish this, appropriate policy interventions addressing gender discrimination in the labour market must be implemented (Joshi and Kumra, Women and Wage Gaps: A Critical Analysis of the Indian Scenario, 2018).[8]

The present study aims to provide the understanding regarding disparity on the basis of gender and organised/unorganised sectors in the form of a thematic chapter. It is significant to note that while there is sufficient literature separately on gender disparity and wage disparity on the basis of organised/unorganised sectors, there still exists a research gap on the overlap of the topics. This thematic chapter intends to fill this research gap through a qualitative understanding regarding the law and economics concept of a trade-off between the efficiency and equity i.e. when the productive efficiency increases, it may lead to less equitable outcomes. Section 11.1 of this chapter gives the introduction. Section 11.2 presents an extensive literature review and outlines the research questions involved. Section 11.3 provides a thematic understanding of the law and economics perspective of the aspect of gender pay disparity and organised/unorganised sectors in light of legislation in India. Finally, in Section 11.4, the authors put forward the suggestion that both efficiency and equity can be balanced in the present scenario to produce effective outcomes to reduce pay disparity.

11.2 Literature Review and Forming the Research Questions

Even after existence of constitutional rights that consider men and women equal, there still exists discrimination between them. Women are considered as second gender in the organised sector, and there still exists a pay disparity between them. Boro and Mazumder (2019) aim to study women's status in the working sector. For this, the study analyses women's status in the Oil and Natural Gas Corporation of Sivasagar district.[9] Descriptive research design was used. Twenty-nine women were selected for the purpose of data collection using purposive sampling technique. Data was collected using questionnaire, interview, and observation. Secondary data was also referred for this study using journals, books, and websites. The results suggest that there are much less women workers than men. Though women are more burdened than men, they get much less paid than men. Also, hierarchical rule is seen in the organisation where generally men are in the upper position. Therefore, to enhance women's status in the organisation, there is a need to give more recognition to women's work.[10]

Gender equality is a precondition for sustainable growth, employment competitiveness, and social cohesion (Obadic, 2016).[11] However, women are being paid less than men and receive less education and training as compared to men. This study focuses on tourism industry's role in employment generation and gender discrimination's impact on tourism industry. The chapter focuses on selected European countries and uses published articles and analyses statistical databases. The results indicate that women are overrepresented in lower-status jobs. Also, there is much less chance for their career progression. The results also indicated that discrimination still exists even in advanced European countries and that women are paid less than men. To improve this, it is recommended to increase women's participation in the tertiary sector and also improve their education and training. Also, more proactive gender equality policies can help improve this situation.

For high performance of organisations, inclusion and diversity are one of the focus areas. Different gender, ethnicity, age group, etc. are indicators of diversity, and despite efforts to bring diversity, these indicators are not encouraging. Online labour marketplaces, also known as freelancing marketplaces, are growing rapidly. Freelancers get paid based on complexity of work, and because of this, it is interesting to study if online marketplaces demonstrate positive diversity indicators. Dubey, Abhinav, Hamilton and Kass (2017) aim to study the labour marketplace and pay gap and career progression gap between males and females.[12] Data was collected from a freelancing platform on five different job categories. Data of around 37,599 freelancers was collected. The results suggested that even after having similar profiles, there existed a pay gap between males and females. It has also been observed that women often undervalue themselves. Also, the career progression of men freelancers is more than women. This data also showed that the pay gap is decreasing in the organised sector due to various initiatives by the organisation. Thus, there is a need for similar initiatives in the unorganised freelancing sector as well.[13]

According to studies, otolaryngology, among medicine fields, has the highest gender pay gap. Even though both male and female otolaryngologists have the same qualifications, there still exists a difference in their pay. Lindsay (2020) aims to investigate the reason for existence of gender pay gap and discrimination and how it can be resolved. The study presents reports of gender pay inequity in the US and compares it with other professions both inside and outside of healthcare.[14] The results suggest that unequal distribution of resources, organisational culture and maintenance of status quo, lack of transparent pay and equity review processes, etc. are some of the reasons for the gender pay gap. There is a need for proper resource allocation, and changes are required in organisational culture. Salary equity should also be made an institutional strategy by the organisation's leadership.[15]

Researchers, since many years, have being trying to investigate forms of workplace discrimination and have pay gap and access to promotion as the most common forms of discrimination. Bishu and Alkadry (2016) analyse past studies to study the themes associated with gender pay gap and also analyse how different sectors work on closing this gap. For the purpose of this, previous studies have been reviewed.[16] The study reveals three recurring predictors of gender pay gap: difference in access to workplace authority, difference in access to hiring and promotion, and gender representation. The results also suggest that the public sector performs better in many aspects of the gender pay gap. Still there exists certain limitations like there is lack of data indicating factors responsible for gender pay gap across all sectors. Also, this study is based on previous studies and relies on their findings and rigour and lacks empirical data.

Organised and unorganised sectors both have their own advantages and disadvantages, but they both contribute to the development of a nation. Generally unskilled workers are more in the unorganised sector, and the organised sector has more skilled workers. For the effective utilisation of the workforce, it is important to study about their conditions in both the sectors. Satpathy, Patnaik and Tripathy (2017) aim to study and compare various dynamics of working and living conditions of both the sectors. Secondary research is undertaken, and existing literature is analysed.[17] The results suggest that there exists a wage difference in the organised and unorganised sectors. Also, the unorganised sector's workforce suffers from many problems like improper working environment, low earning, temporary job, and harassment at workplace, among many other problems. There also exists inadequate and unequal wage structure in the unorganised sector. Thus, there is a need to address these problems in the unorganised sector.[18]

11.2.1 Identifying the Research Gap and Forming Research Questions

The above studies show the trend that while studies have focused on gender-based wage gap and organised/unorganised sectors separately, there exists a research gap in the current social science research regarding study on pay disparity as a comparison between organised and unorganised sectors. The present research project would aim to fill this research gap existing at the overlap of unorganised and organised sectors and the gender wage gap.

The following research themes are formulated in light of the preceding discussion:

1 Analyse the overlap of gender pay gap and disparity between organised and unorganised workers through Indian legislations.
2 Seek to identify the equity–efficiency trade-off in the present aspects.

3 Why a balanced approach to the equity–efficiency trade-off would be the suitable path to ensure that the gender wage gap and the organised and unorganised sector wage gap are bridged?

11.3 Law and Economics of Gender Pay Gap and Disparity between Unorganised and Organised Sectors

11.3.1 Gender Pay Gap: Highlighting the Loopholes

The gender pay gap is expressed in terms of the difference between the earnings of females and males. A trend of the gap in favour of males has been observed across nations and professions, with females being paid a fraction of the payment to their male counterparts.

Sengupta and Puri (2021) show through quantile regression technique in their study that for females, characteristics such as age may be taken for fixing their wages, whereas for males, industry characteristics are given more weightage.[19] Though certain studies show that the gender wage gap has now closed (Blau and Kahn, 2006),[20] such studies are more focused on international jurisdictions, where the formal employment policy has been greatly aligned through the use of standard form contracts and fixed remuneration clauses, which have been mandated through labour codes.[21]

There is a clear indication through the National Sample Survey (NSS) Employment-Unemployment Survey conducted by the National Sample Survey Organisation (NSSO) that the gender wage gap has sustained in India for a period of time.[22] The most recent data is from the 68th round of the NSS, conducted in 2011–2012, under which the *average gender wage differential (AGWD)* was 37.86. This is extremely crucial as there was an increase of 13.01 percentage points (1301 basis points) as compared to the previous figure of the same variable for the year 2009–2010. The variable of the AGWD is calculated with the below formula:

$$\text{AGWD} = [\text{Daily Average Wage (Male)} - \text{Daily Average Wage (Female)}] \\ / \text{ Daily Average Wage(Female)}$$

In the above formula, both variables of Daily Average Wage (Male) and Daily Average Wage (Female) are in the terms of 'Rupees/day'. The numerator signifies the absolute difference between the daily average wages between males and females, with a positive value signifying a higher wage of males, and vice versa. In a similar manner, the denominator is taken as the daily average wage of females in order to bring the effect of the variable into the calculation of the average, and further to present a percentage value regarding the fraction of the absolute wage difference between males and females, presented as a percentage of the average daily wage of females. Hence, a higher AGWD would signify a higher wage disparity between males and females.[23]

We observe that there is a clear trend from the below table, adapted from the NSS and the analysis by Sengupta and Puri (2021), that though the AGWD declined in the period from 2004–2005 to 2009–2010, a stark increase was observed from 2009–2010 to 2011–2012. See Table 11.1.

This would render many of the employment-related initiatives and measures enacted since the period of 2004–2005 as inefficient. Such measures included the National Rural Employment Guarantee Act (NREGA). It is to be noted that a large percentage of such schemes were enacted for the unorganised sector. Hence, we can draw the inference that the policy of formulating schemes for unorganised employment would need to employ a certain degree of economic and legal formality in order to bridge the gender wage disparity. This is also due to the efficiency in the usage of standard form contracts, which would reduce the transaction costs. The parties here are the unorganised labour with incomplete information and the government/authority. We also recognise that even within the sample of unorganised labour, the division between males and females, Saussier (2000) defines this as a position of contractual completeness.[24]

TABLE 11.1 Gender Wage Gap: India 1999–2012

Year	*1999–2000*	*2004–2005*	*2009–2010*	*2011–2012*
Daily wage for males (Rupees/day)	151.42	176.9	325	342.12
Daily wage for females (Rupees/day)	116.93	131.89	260.31	248.16
Average gender wage differential	29.5	34.13	24.85	37.86

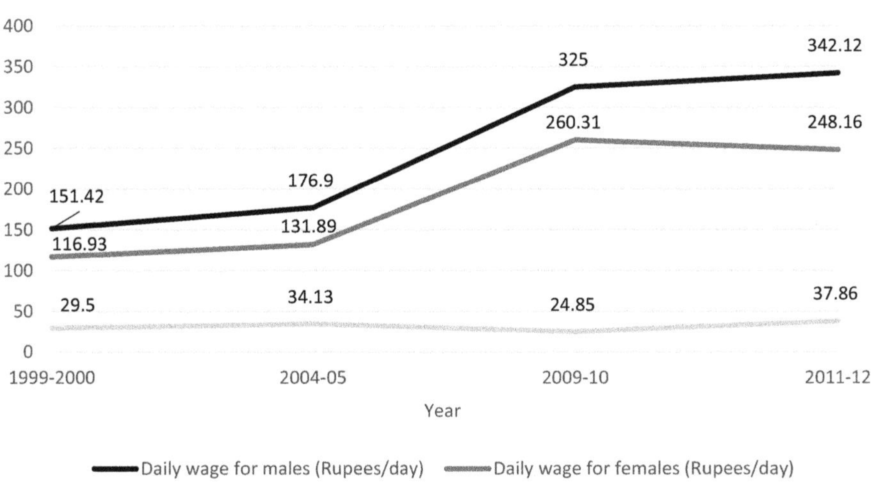

FIGURE 11.1 Gender wage gap: India 1999–2012. Data from the NSS; analysis by the author.

The level of contractual completeness can be defined as reflecting the desire and intention of the parties through the legal instrument of a contract to save transaction costs (Figure 11.1).

We observe from the above graph that there is a significant difference between the daily wage levels of males when compared to females for the time period between 1999 and 2012, as measured by the NSSO. This is to be crucially observed, as we draw an assumption based on the NSS, that the males would be better informed in comparison to the females. Hence, males in the unorganised sector would be able to better negotiate the contract and bring their contract to a graphical point where marginal cost (MC) would equal marginal benefit (MB) (Figure 11.2).

The above figure is based on the framework advanced by Saussier (2000) and the authors' analysis. We observe that the vertical axis provides the variables of cost and benefit, thereby also indicating MC and MB, which are calculated by $\mathbf{MC_1 - MC_0}$ and $\mathbf{MB_1 - MB_0}$, respectively. The horizontal axis provides the variable of contractual completeness, which is a measure of the extent a contract provides the parties to economise on the transaction costs.[25]

We recognise that males would be closer to the point C in the above graph, owing to higher probability of education and experience in outdoor manual work.[26] At the same time, females are provided lesser opportunities than males, and there is lower probability of rural females, who are the primary beneficiaries of such unorganised employment opportunities, that they have passed the preliminary education, according to the NSS.[27] Hence, females would be nearer to the point of B in the above graph. However, this does not signify that males are

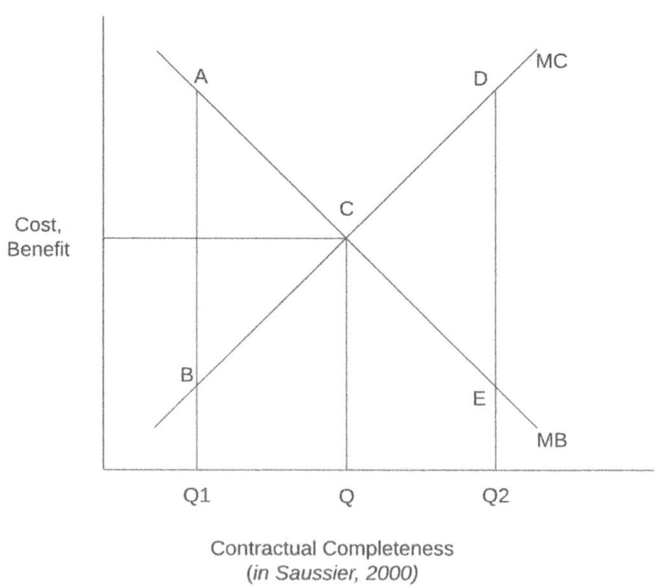

FIGURE 11.2 Graphical representation of MC, MB, and contractual completeness.

at a better position, precisely because very few unorganised labour employment schemes have the provision of a formal contract of employment.[28]

There is an indication that negotiating a standard form contract with each of the unorganised workers is an unachievable task, which would exponentially increase the transaction costs of the employer and the authorities. However, a statistical analysis can be undertaken to gauge the average wage level of the previous workers in the particular government schemes, which would enable a better fixation of the wages provided to unorganised workers. We recognise the aspect of efficiency versus equity here.

11.3.1.1 Comparing an Efficiency-Based Model with Equity Model

The efficiency approach to the question of gender wage disparity would be to function according to the market rates and the individual competency of the worker. The model would work when the average total cost (ATC) of the employer is the at the lowest point, and where the MC would be equal to the ATC.

MC = ATC; where ATC is at the lowest point

This would lead to a more pronounced disparity in the unorganised sector, as men have unequal access to better opportunities coupled with higher transaction costs for women,[29] hence making males an efficient labour force for the unorganised sector. Further, with males also being higher in the above graph nearer to point C, there is a probability of higher wages for males, with the employer not considering females as a competitor employee, as the female is nearer to point B.

Employment of males by the employer, either privately or through various schemes, would push up the wages in the labour market for males, incentivising more male labourers to seek employment. As a result, the quantum of the labour market may shift in absolute terms from $\boldsymbol{L_0}$ to $\boldsymbol{L_1}$, where $\boldsymbol{L_0}$ reflects the quantum of labour market before large-scale employment of males. This shift to $\boldsymbol{L_1}$ would increase the labour supply in the market, bringing real wages down in the short run. However, the long-run effect of this shift is that it would also provide bargaining power $\boldsymbol{B^{\star}M}$ to the male labour, which could then be combined to form a function of wages $\boldsymbol{W_0}$ (or more pertinently an increase in wages $\boldsymbol{\Delta W}$), as denoted in the mathematical formula below:

In the long run, (1)

$$\Delta W = L_{1.} B \star M;\ \text{where}\ \Delta W > 0.1(W_0)$$

This higher bargaining power at $\boldsymbol{B^{\star}}$ is the result of higher penetration in the labour and product markets, decrease in social costs for organisation of labour, and lower transaction costs. The assumption is that the $\boldsymbol{\Delta W}$ is at least greater than

10% of the current W_0. We also recognise the effect of ΔW on the ATC, which would subsequently increase due to W_1 being the new numerator:

With ΔW pushing W_0 to W_1, with $W_1 > W_0$,
$\text{ATC}_1 = W_1 / L_1$
where $\Delta W > \Delta L$

The above equation makes it clear that an increase in wages would be imminent with the current efficiency-based model. We also recognise that apart from wages for males (***W***) increasing, there is a difference in the contractual completeness between males and females, due to the operation of bargaining power ***B****, as given in Equation (1). The explanation for the difference between bargaining power of males (***B*M***) and bargaining power of females (***B*F***) lies in the aspect of contractual completeness of Saussier (2000). We must remember that after fall in wages due to excess labour force supply L_1, the male labour force has organised itself to increase its bargaining power, hence establishing an increase in wages $\Delta W = L_1 . B^\star M$. As a result, the bargaining power of females is lesser than that of males in the current labour market.

Therefore, $B^\star M > B^\star F$.

Hence, in the model elaborated in Equation (1), the variable of contractual completeness would be thus summarised:

$$CC_m > CC_f, \text{where } CC = f\left(W, B^\star, L_1\right)$$

Therefore, contractual completeness is a function of wages, bargaining power, and the new level of labour supply. We rely on Saussier's definition of a more complete contract in the present context, as a contract that gives a more precise definition of the labour market transaction and the consideration transacted. However, such a situation would not be Pareto efficient for the macroeconomy as a whole, due to the vast percentage of female labour left unemployed. The hypothesis originally laid down that an efficiency-based model would result in the best efficiency for the employer, highlighting the point of lowest ATC. This would be contrary to that particular hypothesis, as we can clearly observe an increase in ATC over the long run, which would not be at the point of Pareto efficiency.[30] This would also exacerbate the male–female gender wage gap in the unorganised sector, as the male labour market would have the higher wages W_1, whereas the female wages W^f would still be at the $W^f{}_0$ level. Hence, the efficiency model has to be rejected. This is due to the aspect that a perfect labour market is non-existent,[31] and hence in an imperfect-inefficient labour market, flawed efficiency would signify that the male labour force with higher bargaining power maintains its hold over distribution of costs in the market as indicated by Kaufman (2007). This is precisely the reason the efficiency model fails, primarily due to inherent inefficiency in distribution of bargaining power ***B****.

The equity model is also fraught with irregularities. The equity model would stipulate a nearly equal wage rate for both females and males, at the level where $W = W^f$. This would also render the labour market as reaching for a labour supply of or near to L_1 – which is the higher quantum of labour force supply – due to the increase in female unorganised workers. However, the principle of equity when applied to the labour market may give the effect of stagnant wages $\bar{W}$, as indicated by Mosomi (2019),[32] for both males and females who are comparatively better workers L_b. There would be an exodus of efficient workers (performing at the 90th percentile in the aspect of productivity) from the labour market due to stagnant wages, as described below:

Assuming $W = W^f$, leading to $\bar{W}$
$L_1 = L_0 - L_b, L_b < L_0$
Therefore, labour productivity L_p declines

The primary reason for this exodus is the pushing of wages downwards due to effect of the efficiency model. There is a crucial need to avoid the point of stagnant wages $\bar{W}$ and declining labour productivity. Therefore, the government must keep the welfare objective in mind and put forward full and complete information about the work and the contract that would influence the ability and willingness of the labourer to enter into the contract, irrespective of being male or female. There is a need to increase formalisation of the female unorganised labour, in order to increase contractual completeness CC_f and wages W^f. We recognise that a balanced approach is required for the females to reach pay parity with males. The use of law would be crucial, as the legislations such as NREGA and other schemes must provide for valid employment contracts to ensure full information to females.

11.3.2 Further Analysis of Wage Disparity between Unorganised and Organised Workers

Though this part is titled as elaborating upon the wage disparity on organised and unorganised workers, there is no hard bifurcation with the previous part, as it is intrinsically linked. As a result, the primary discussion regarding the theory and econometric model has been undertaken in the previous section, and the current part only appends the same. The argument of contractual completeness being different for males and females in the preceding section holds true in this analysis; however, the variables differ as we are now comparing organised and unorganised labour. We function on the assumption that organised labour would have better and more complete contracts as compared to unorganised labour:

$CC_{org} > CC_{unorg}$, where $CC = f(W, B^\star, L_1)$

Hence, *aggregate* $CC = \sum (W, B^\star, L_1)$

with CC_{org} denoting contractual completeness of organised workers and CC_{unorg} denoting the contractual completeness of unorganised workers. Unorganised workers have been defined under the Unorganised Workers' Social Security Act, 2008[33] as 'a home-based worker, self-employed worker or a wage worker in the unorganised sector and includes a worker in the organised sector who is not covered by any of the Acts mentioned in Schedule II of the Act'. Such Acts include (1) The Workmen's Compensation Act, 1923 (8 of 1923); (2) The Industrial Disputes Act, 1947 (14 of 1947); (3) The Employees' State Insurance Act, 1948 (34 of 1948); (4) The Employees' Provident Funds and Miscellaneous Provisions Act, 1952 (19 of 1952); (5) The Maternity Benefit Act, 1961 (53 of 1961); and (6) The Payment of Gratuity Act, 1972 (39 of 1972). We realise that the current legal framework of the 2008 Act only defines an unorganised worker, not putting in place any measures to move toward organised labour, or formalisation. The author believes that the foremost measure to be enacted is ensuring higher contractual completeness of unorganised labour ΔCC_{unorg} that would increase information ΔIN_{unorg} of the unorganised worker and lead to a cycle of higher wages and decreasing wage differentials between organised and unorganised labour.

A complete or nearly complete contract for unorganised workers would also safeguard them from seasonal changes in employment patterns and business cycles. Though welfare funds and social security schemes have been set up for unorganised labour, and the JAM trinity of Jan Dhan-Aadhar-Mobile has been instrumental in propelling a higher percentage of unorganised labour towards formal payment systems, the payment cycle itself remains erratic, due to the very nature of the unorganised work. Hence, the authors believe that the concept of equity through such schemes and funds is not adequate, and a balance between efficiency and equity is required to approach this issue, discussed in the conclusion.

11.4 Analysis and Conclusion

During a business cycle peak ΔB, the demand for labour increases from LD_0 to LD_1, and as a result, the wages also increase from W_0 to W_1. Rise in demand ΔLD and rise in wages ΔW result in an influx of labour supply, which rises to LS_0 to LS_1. This would also bring down the wages back from W_1 to W_0. However, the author believes that this fall from W_1 to W_0 would be lesser in quantum than the increase from W_0 to W_1.

Hence, the final wage rate for labour would settle as somewhere between W_0 and W_1, assuming it at W. This would mean that the labour wage rate has increased from W_0 to $W^\star$. The conclusion drawn is that the equity concept through schemes of the government is that the labour market may be clearing at a higher wage rate than lower, with declining labour productivity in the unorganised market due to labour productivity being a function of output and the market clearing wage rate.

In this backdrop, we also rely on the Blinder–Oaxaca Decomposition as evolved by Blinder (1973)[34] and Oaxaca (1973).[35] We take the model as adopted by Kumar and Pandey (2021)[36] given below:

$$\frac{W_f \; W_{if}}{W_{if}} = \frac{W_f}{W_{if}} - 1$$

where W_f is the wages of the formal worker and the W_{if} is the wages of the informal worker. The above equation signifies that the difference between W_f and W_{if} is expressed as a percentage of the W_{if}, which gives a clearer picture with regard to the fraction of wage differential. The author assumes that formal workers are at an advantage and the informal workers are at a disadvantage. Tables 11.2 and 11.3 provide an exposition of the variable Percentage Relative Gap (PRG) in terms

TABLE 11.2 Average real daily wage (in Rupees). Rate for formal and informal workers by sector and gender

	2004–2005			*2011–2012*		
	Formal workers	*Informal workers*	*PRG*	*Formal workers*	*Informal workers*	*PRG*
Male	547	180	67	729	294	60
Female	466	109	77	634	204	68
Rural	405	145	64	492	221	55
Urban	573	190	67	774	307	60
India	538	168	69	716	277	61

TABLE 11.3 Average real daily wage (in Rupees). Rate for formal and informal workers by occupation

	2004–2005			*2011–2012*		
	Formal workers	*Informal workers*	*PRG*	*Formal workers*	*Informal workers*	*PRG*
Administrative	785	468	40	1,282	512	60
Teaching, nursing, and midwifery Professionals	476	390	18	1,024	622	39
Professionals other than teaching, nursing, etc.	373	156	58	708	413	42
Clerical	259	148	43	565	343	39
Service	278	82	70	471	238	50
Sales	177	84	52	537	194	64
Agriculture and allied occupations	178	64	64	271	170	37
Production	226	91	60	480	222	54
Elementary	161	56	65	333	153	54

Source: National Sample Survey Organisation; Kumar and Pandey (2021).

of the absolute wage gap, which is employed by Kumar and Pandey (supra) as a measure of the wage differential in an identical manner as above, only the denominator is replaced by W_f. Hence, variable PRG measures the wage differential as a percentage of the wage of the formal (advantaged) worker. Though the NSS data points to falling PRG, thereby increasing pay parity among organised and unorganised workers:

$$L_1 = L_0 - L_b, L_b < L_0.$$

There is a need to move nearer to a point between R and S in Figure11.3. In order to ensure that there is a correct trend of falling PRG, there is a need to balance the equity and efficiency mechanism of the employment schemes. There is an opportunity cost for both choices, with higher emphasis on efficiency making growth inequitable, and greater bend towards equity might lead to loss in efficiency for producers. The discussion on gender wage gap leads to the question regarding the use of the efficiency or the equity model. It is noted through the economic model in Section 11.3.1. that the efficiency model would have the effect of exclusion of female workers, primarily due to contractual and transaction costs. However, implementing the equity model would result in social costs through an exodus of productive workers, due to enactment of stagnant wages to maintain equity. Therefore, a balance must be struck between equity and efficiency, leading to Pareto efficiency, as the equation above makes it clear that lopsided policy may lead to decline in labour productivity.

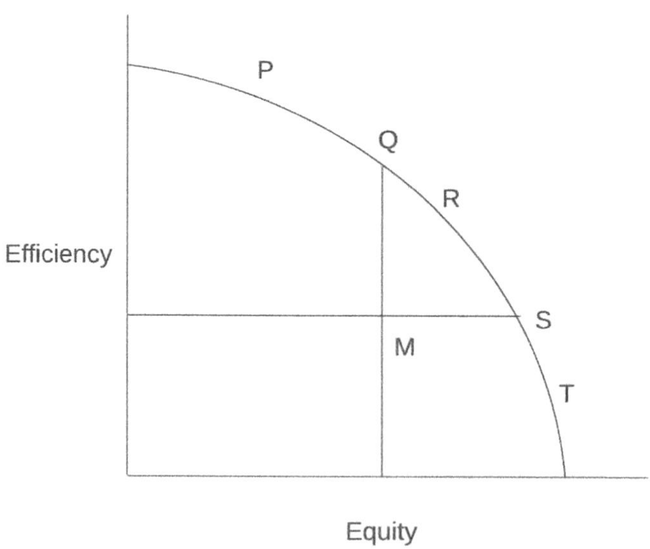

FIGURE 11.3 Equity–efficiency trade-off.

Notes

1 Cain, Glen G. (1976). "The challenge of segmented labor market theories to orthodox theory: A survey." *Journal of Economic Literature*, December, 1215–1257.
2 Wadhawa, K. K. (1975). *Minority safeguards in India* (Thomson, Delhi).
3 Berreman, G. D. (1979). *Caste and other inequities* (Folklore Institute, Delhi).
4 Bhaumik, S. K., Chakrabarty, M. (2008). "Does move to market have an impact on earnings gap across gender? Some evidence from India." *Applied Economics Literature* 15(8), 601–605.
5 Sengupta, A., Das, P. (2014). "Gender wage discrimination across social and religious groups in India estimates with unit level data." *Economic and Political Weekly* 49(21), 71–76.
6 Singhari, S., Madheswaran, S. (2017). "Wage structure and wage differentials in formal and informal sectors in India evidence from NSS data." *Indian Journal of Labour Economics* 60(3), 389–414.
7 Report by Google and Bain & Company – Powering the Economy with Her: Women Entrepreneurship in India, 2019.
8 Joshi and Kumra (2018). *Women and Wage Gaps: A Critical Analysis of the Indian Scenario*, Manpower Journal, 2018.
9 Boro, S., Mazumder, M. (2019). "Women and organized sector: A study on women staff in oil and natural gas corporation, Sivasagar District, Assam." *Adalya Journal* 8(11), 821–830.
10 Id. at 825.
11 Obadic, A. (2016). "Gender discrimination and pay gap on tourism labor market." *International Journal of Social, Behavioral, Educational, Economic, Business and Industrial Engineering* 10(3), 808–813.
12 Dubey, A., Abhinav, K., Hamilton, M., Kass, A. (2017). "Analyzing gender pay gap in freelancing marketplace." *SIGMIS* 1(1), 13–19.
13 Papola, T. S. (2013). Role of labour regulation and reforms in India: Country case study on labour market segmentation (Employment Sector Working Paper 147) International Labour Organisation (ILO).
14 Lindsay, R. (2020). Gender Pay Discrimination in Otolaryngology, The Laryngoscope, 1-7.
15 Srivastava, R. (2016). Structural change and non-standard forms of employment in India (Conditions of Work and Employment Series, ILO Working Paper 68). ILO.
16 Bishu, S., Alkadry, M. (2016). "A systematic review of the gender pay gap and factors that predict it." *Administration and Society* 49(1), 65–104.
17 Satpathy, I., Patnaik, B., Tripathy, N. (2017). "Review of literature on working and living conditions of workers in organized and unorganized sector." *International Research Journal of Human Resources and Social Sciences* 4(9), 463–473.
18 Srija, A., Shirke, S. V. (2014). An analysis of the informal labour market in India (Confederation of Indian Industry, CII Working Paper). https://ies.gov.in/pdfs/CII%20EM-october-2014.pdf
19 Sengupta, P., Puri, R. (2021). "Gender pay gap in India: A reality and the way forward – An empirical approach using quantile regression technique." *Studies in Microeconomics*. April 2021. doi:10.1177/2321022221995674
20 Blau, F. D., Kahn, L. M. (2006). "The US gender pay gap in the 1990s: Slowing convergence." *ILR Review* 60(1), 45–66.
21 Bergmann, B. R. (1974). "Occupational segregation, wages and profits when employers discriminate by race or sex." *Eastern Economic Journal* 1(2), 103–110.
22 National Sample Survey Organisation (NSSO), 68th Round, Government of India.
23 Blau, F. D., Kahn, L. M. (2017). „The gender wage gap: Extent, trends, and explanations." *Journal of Economic Literature* 55(3), 789–865.
24 "Transaction costs and contractual incompleteness: the case of Électricité de France Stéphane Saussier." *Journal of Economic Behavior & Organization* 42 (2000) 189–206.

25 Id. at 203.
26 Bhaumik, S. K., Chakrabarty, M. (2009). "Is education the panacea for economic deprivation of Muslims? Evidence from wage earners in India, 1987–2005." *Journal of Asian Economics* 20(2), 137–149.
27 National Sample Survey Organisation (NSSO), 68th Round, Government of India.
28 Khera, R., Nayak, N. (2009). "Women Workers and perceptions of the National rural employment Guarantee act." *Economic and Political Weekly* (2009): 49–57.
29 Hultin, M., Szulkin, R. (2003). "Mechanisms of inequality. Unequal access to organizational power and the gender wage gap." *European Sociological Review* 19(2), 143–159.
30 Beckman, S. R., et al. (2002). "Envy, malice and Pareto efficiency: An experimental examination." *Social Choice and Welfare* 19(2), 349–367.
31 Kaufman, B. E. (2007). "The impossibility of a perfectly competitive labour market." *Cambridge Journal of Economics* 31(5), Oxford University Press, 775–787, http://www.jstor.org/stable/23601651.
32 Mosomi, J. (2019). Distributional changes in the gender wage gap in the post-apartheid South African labour market. No. 2019/17. WIDER working paper, 2019.
33 Unorganised Workers' Social Security Act, 2008, Acts of Parliament (2008), India.
34 Blinder, A. S. (1973). "Wage discrimination: Reduced form and structural estimates." *Journal of Human Resources* 8(4), 436–455.
35 Oaxaca, R. L. (1973). "Male–female wage differentials in the urban labour market." *International Economic Review* 14, 693–709.
36 Kumar, M., Pandey, S. (2021). "Wage gap between formal and informal regular workers in India: Evidence from the National Sample Survey." *Global Journal of Emerging Market Economies* 13(1), 104–121. doi:10.1177/0974910121989458

References

Beckman, Steven R., et al. (2002). "Envy, malice and Pareto efficiency: An experimental examination." *Social Choice and Welfare* 19(2), 349–367.

Bergmann, B. R. (1974). "Occupational segregation, wages and profits when employers discriminate by race or sex." *Eastern Economic Journal* 1(2), 103–110.

Berreman, Gerald, D. (1979). *Caste and other inequities* (Folklore Institute, Delhi).

Bhaumik, S. K., & Chakrabarty, M. (2008). "Does move to market have an impact on earnings gap across gender? Some evidence from India." *Applied Economics Literature* 15(8), 601–605.

Bhaumik, S. K., & Chakrabarty, M. (2009). "Is education the panacea for economic deprivation of Muslims? Evidence from wage earners in India, 1987–2005." *Journal of Asian Economics* 20(2), 137–149.

Bishu S., & Alkadry, M. (2016). "A systematic review of the gender pay gap and factors that predict it." *Administration and Society* 49(1), 65–104.

Blau, F. D., & Kahn, L. M. (2006). "The US gender pay gap in the 1990s: Slowing convergence." *ILR Review* 60(1), 45–66.

Blau, F. D., & Kahn, L. M. (2017). "The gender wage gap: Extent, trends, and explanations." *Journal of Economic Literature* 55(3), 789–865.

Blinder, A. S. (1973). "Wage discrimination: Reduced form and structural estimates." *Journal of Human Resources* 8(4), 436–455.

Boro, S., & Mazumder, M. (2019). "Women and Organized Sector: A study on women staff in oil and natural gas corporation, Sivasagar District, Assam." *Adalya Journal* 8(11), 821–830.

Cain, G. G. (1976). "The challenge of segmented labor market theories to orthodox theory: A survey." *Journal of Economic Literature* December, 1215–1257.

Dubey, A., Abhinav, K., Hamilton, M., & Kass, A. (2017). "Analyzing gender pay gap in freelancing marketplace." *SIGMIS* 1(1), 13–19.

Joshi and Kumra (2018). *Women and Wage Gaps: A Critical Analysis of the Indian Scenario*, Manpower Journal, 2018.

Kaufman, B. E. (2007). "The impossibility of a perfectly competitive labour market." *Cambridge Journal of Economics* 31(5), Oxford University Press, 775–787, http://www.jstor.org/stable/23601651.

Khera, R., and Nayak, N. (2009). "Women Workers and perceptions of the National rural employment Guarantee act." *Economic and Political Weekly*: *44*(43), 49–57.

Kumar, M., & Pandey, S. (2021). "Wage gap between formal and informal regular workers in India: Evidence from the National Sample Survey." *Global Journal of Emerging Market Economies* 13(1):104–121. doi:10.1177/0974910121989458

Lindsay, R. (2020). "Gender pay discrimination in otolaryngology." *The Laryngoscope*, 1–7.

Mosomi, Jacqueline. Distributional changes in the gender wage gap in the post-apartheid South African labour market. No. 2019/17. WIDER working paper, 2019.

National Sample Survey Organisation (NSSO), 68th Round, Government of India.

Oaxaca, R. L. (1973). "Male–female wage differentials in the urban labour market." *International Economic Review* 14, 693–709.

Obadic, A. (2016). "Gender discrimination and pay gap on tourism labor market." *International Journal of Social, Behavioral, Educational, Economic, Business and Industrial Engineering* 10(3), 808–813.

Papola, T. S. (2013). Role oflabour regulation and reforms in India: Country case study on labour market segmentation (Employment Sector Working Paper 147) International Labour Organisation (ILO).

Report by Google and Bain & Company – Powering the Economy with Her: Women Entrepreneurship in India, 2019.

Satpathy, I., Patnaik, B., & Tripathy, N. (2017). "Review of Literature on Working and living Conditions of workers in organized and unorganized sector." *International Research Journal of Human Resources and Social Sciences* 4(9), 463–473.

Sengupta, A., & Das, P. (2014). "Gender wage discrimination across social and religious groups in India estimates with unit level data." *Economic and Political Weekly* 49(21), 71–76.

Sengupta, P., & Puri, R. (2021). "Gender pay gap in India: A reality and the way forward – An empirical approach using quantile regression technique." *Studies in Microeconomics*. April 2021. doi:10.1177/2321022221995674

Singhari, S., & Madheswaran, S. (2017). "Wage structure and wage differentials in formal and informal sectors in India evidence from NSS data." *Indian Journal of Labour Economics* 60(3), 389–414.

Srija, A., & Shirke, S. V. (2014). An analysis of the informal labour market in India (Confederation of Indian Industry, CII Working Paper). https://ies.gov.in/pdfs/CII%20EM-october-2014.pdf

Srivastava, R. (2016). Structural change and non-standard forms of employment in India (Conditions of Work and Employment Series, ILO Working Paper 68). ILO.

"Transaction costs and contractual incompleteness: the case of Électricité de France Stéphane Saussier." *Journal of Economic Behavior & Organization* 42 (2000), 189–206.

Unorganised Workers' Social Security Act, 2008, Acts of Parliament (2008), India.

Wadhawa, K. K., 1975, *Minority safeguards in India* (Thomson, Delhi).

INDEX

Note: **Bold** page numbers refer to tables; *italic* page numbers refer to figures and page numbers followed by "n" denote endnotes.

Abhinav, K. 174
abuse: economic 61; physical 61, 62; psychological 61, 62; sexual 61
Agricultural Census: 2010–2011 103, 105–106, **106**; 2015–2016 103
Akbar (Mughal King) 32
Alkadry, M. 175
All India Rural Financial Inclusion Survey (NAFIS) 2016–2017 101–103, *101*, *102*, **102**, 105, 107
Ambedkar, B.R.: theories of law 5
American Revolution 168
Anthropocene 11–13, 24n35
anthropogenic harm 3, 5, 11–13, 15, 20n7
Antigone (Sophocles) 151n5
Armed Forces (Special Powers) Act 67
Article 370 6, 39–44; abrogation of 51–52, *52*; erosion of 49–52, *50*, *51*, 53n13, 55n70
attributional bias 68
Atwood, M. 145
Aveek Sarkar v. State of West Bengal (AIR 2014 SC 1495) 120
Ayushman Bharat scheme 99

Baba Shri Chand 140n4
Bain & Company 173
Ballet, J. 81
Banesjee, A.: *Good Economics for Hard Times* 99
Bar Council regulations 166
Barde, J. 80
bargain theory 40, 42–45
Barker, T. 77
basic income support 98–111; direct 107–109; identification based on verifiable criteria 103–107; trade-offs 109–110, *110*; verifiable criteria 100–103
Baskin, J. 23n25
Bazin, D. 81
Becker, G.S. 60–61
behavioural economics 60, 64, 65, 67
Benedetto Croce 165
Benjamin, W. 23n34
Berreman, G.D. 172
Bible 58
Bishu, S. 175
Blinder, A.S. 183
Bloch, M. 165
Board of Film Certification 123
Bontems, P. 81
Boro, S. 173
Bourgeon, J. 81
Bovenberg, A.L. 84, 85
Bradley Commission on History in Schools 161
Brazil, foreign donations in democratic elections 36n8
Brougham, H. 1
Buchanan, J. 80
Bugge, T.D. 87

Cable Television Networks (Regulation) Act (1995): Section 3 125; Section 4 125; Section 5 125; Section 6 125
Canada 31, 36n8; corporate campaign contributions 37n10
carbon leakage 78
carbon tax 75, 77, 78, 82, 87
Carnegie Endowment for International Peace 36n8
Carr, E.H. 165, 166
Carrier, J. 133
CDR (carbon dioxide technology) 13
censorship 3, 113–126; of free speech 8; Indian Constitution, provisions of 122–125
Central Board of Film Certification 118, 126n2
Chandigarh 135, 136
Chandrakant Mansaram More v. State of Maharashtra, WP (CrL) No. 1577 of 2010 117
Char, E.H.: *What Is History?* 162
Cheal, D. 133
Chekhov, A. 143; *Home* 151n6; *A Visit to Friends* 151n6
Cinematograph Act (1952) 122; Section 3 123
climate change 3, 5, 11, 18, 19n4, 22n21, 23n25, 29, 74, 87; anthropogenic 13; denialism 12; impact on intergenerational inequality 14–15; litigation 12; mitigation 24n41; science 12
Coase Theorem 30
Code of Criminal Procedure (1973) 66
Collingwood, R.G. 165, 166
colonialism 167, 168
command-and-control approach 74, 75, 82, 83, 85
commercialization of women 62, 64
Committee of Ten's Subcommittee on history 161
commodification of women 68
Common Law 163
community violence 62–64
concern-for-externalities 5, 26, 31, 35
confidence-in-democracy 5, 26–29, 31, 32, 35
confirmation bias 67
constituent assembly of J&K (J&KCA) 42, 44, 55n53; dissolution, phase of 49–51, *50*, *51*
Constitution Act (1939) 45, 47, 48, 53n14
Constitutional Law 144
Constitution (Application to Jammu & Kashmir) Order, 15 November 1952 55n52
Constitution (Application to Jammu & Kashmir) Order 1950 53n60
Constitution (Application to Jammu & Kashmir) Order 1954 53n7, 55n54
Constitution of a Board 123
Constitution of J&K, 1957 48; Section 157 55n52
Consumer Price Index (CPI) 111n2, 111n10
contemporary socio-biology 61
Contemporary Standards Test' 118–119
Cook, G. 145
Cooley, T.M.: *A Treatise on the Constitutional Limitations* 123
corporate Neanderthalism 5
counterbalance market distortions 85–86
Covid-19 2, 7
CPI *see* Consumer Price Index (CPI)
Criminal Law (amendment) Act (2013) 66–67
Critical School 164
Cserne, P.: *Law and Economics as Interdisciplinary Exchange: Philosophical, Methodological and Historical Perspectives* 4
cultural innovation 145
cultural protectionism 114, 125
cultural spillover theory 61

Das, R.: *Interdisciplinary Approaches to Public Policy and Sustainability* 4
De, R. 169
default option 68
democratic elections, outside influence on 5–6, 26–37; confidence-in-democracy 27–29; externalities 29–33; money in politics 33–35, 36n4
denialism: climate change 12; non-compliance *versus* 13
Department of Women and Child Development, Ministry of Human Resource Development 59
Director General of Doordarshan v. Anand Patwardhan (2006) 8 SCC 433 120
discrimination 156; caste-based 166, 167; gender-based 166, 167, 174; labour market 172
Dole, C.: *The Time of Catastrophe: Multidisciplinary Approaches to the Age of Catastrophe* 4
Dostoevsky, F. 151n2
double-dividend hypothesis 84–85

Dowry Prohibition Act (1961) 65
dowry-related violence 60–61, 64, 65
Dubey, A. 174
Duflo, E.: *Good Economics for Hard Times* 99
Dwivedi, Y.K.: *Emerging Markets from a Multidisciplinary Perspective: Challenges, Opportunities and Research Agenda* 4

economics 5, 29, 30; behavioural 60, 64, 65, 67; law and 29, 30, 176–182
economic theory 60, 65, 67
efficacy of legislations 65–68
efficiency-based model 179–181
electricity, environmental levy on 76–77
Emerging Markets from a Multidisciplinary Perspective: Challenges, Opportunities and Research Agenda (Dwivedi) 4
Employees' Provident Funds and Miscellaneous Provisions Act (1952) 182
Employees' State Insurance Act (1948) 182
Employment – Unemployment Survey 2015–2016 111n8
England, Civil War 168
environmental authoritarianism 18
environmental degradation 6–7
environmental fiscal reform 74–93
environmental tax: inventives (*see* environmental tax incentives); penalties (*see* environmental tax penalties); reform instruments 75; regime 6
environmental tax incentives: adjoining policy objective 82–83; counterbalance market distortions 85–86; double-dividend hypothesis 84–85; not burden to fiscus 86; not overly prescriptive 83; social dilemmas 87; spur innovation 83–84; sustainable environmental benefit 86–87
environmental tax penalties 6; appropriate 78–79; cost of distribution and 78; damaging behaviour 81; inelastic goods/ consumption 81–82; international competitiveness and 77–78; object, achieving 80–81; object, subscribing 79; object to alter behaviour 79–80; poverty and 76–77; purpose not to enrich government 81; revenue extrapolative 76; source of revenue. 75
equity model 179–181
Esposito, R. 133–134
Europe: environmental tax 81; incentives on energy-efficient products 77
European Union 32, 168
externalities 29–33, 36n5; concern-for-externalities 5, 26, 31, 35; cross-border 30, 31; environmental 74, 75, 82; negative 30–32; positive 6, 32

faith-in-democracy 31, 32
fantasy fiction literature 145–147, 151
federalism 3, 12, 39, 53n9
female control theory 63
female labour force participation (FLFP) 172–173
feminism 3, 168
fiscal reform 74–88
flat-rate levy 78–79
FLFP *see* female labour force participation (FLFP)
Foreign Contribution Regulation Act 6
France: foreign donations in democratic elections 36n8
Franklin, B. 1, 9
freedom of speech and expression 24n38, 114–117, 122, 125
freedom of speech and press 123
"free-rider" phenomenon 76
free speech 7–8; censorship of 8; crisis 7–8; regime 7
French Revolution 168
Friedman, L. 164, 165
Fullerton, D. 85

Gaiman, N. 145
gender-based violence 60
gender disparity 173
gender equality 60, 174
gender pay disparity 9, 173
gender pay gap 174–175; loopholes 176–179, *177*, **177**, *178*; between unorganised and organised workers 181–183
gender wage disparity 9, 173, 177, 179
General Board Fund 136–137
geoenginnering techniques 13–15
Germany: foreign donations in democratic elections 36n8; renewable energy production, subsidy for 92n113
gift economy 132–133
Gilbert, G.W.: *The Grand Duke* 143; *Iolanthe* 143; *The Mikado* 143
Goetz, C. 80
Good Economics for Hard Times (Banerjee and Duflo) 99
goods and services tax (GST) 77, 79, 80, 83, 85
Google 173
governance of property 128–141

Government of India (GOI) Act: of 1935 40, 43, 45, 47, 48, 53n16; of 1950 48
The Grand Duke (Gilbert) 143
Granger, H. 148
GST *see* goods and services tax (GST)
Gujarat National Law University 158
Gurdwara Election Commission 136
Gurdwara Janam Asthan 132
Gurdwara Parbandhak Committee 138
Gurdwaras, history of 129–131
Guru Amar Das 132
Guru ka Langar 8, 128, 129, 131, 132
Gurumukhi 136
Guru Nanak 131, 132

Hailey, Sir M. 138
Hall, R.: *The Well of Loneliness* 119
Halpern, S.C. 165
Hamilton, M. 174
harm principle 117, 125
Harry Potter 146–151
Harry Potter and the Deathly Hallows 148
Harry Potter and the Half-Blood Prince 147
Harry Potter and the Order of the Phoenix 147
Harry Potter and the Philosopher's Stone 147
Haryana 135, 136
hegemonic heterosexuality 58–59
Heller, M. 137
Hicklin's test 118–120
Himachal Pradesh 135, 136
Hindu Widow Remarriage Act 167
historiography 165, 167, 168
history, relevance of studying 161–162
Hobb, R. 145
Hoeflich, M.H. 164
Home (Chekhov) 151n6
Horwitz, M. 164, 165
household violence 60–62
human degradation of the biosphere 19n3
human rights violations 12, 14

Ideas and Methods of Legal Research (Ishwara Bhatt) 4
Imperialism 58
income tax 77, 78, 86
Indecent Representation of Women (Prohibition) Act (1986) 68, 123–124; Section 3 123–124; Section 4 123–124
India 2; basic income support 98–111; commercialization of women in 64; confidence-in-democracy 28; Constitution of (*see* Indian Constitution); environmental fiscal reform in 74–93; environmental tax penalties 75–82; externalities 29; free speech regime 7; women's movement in 59; *see also individual entries*
Indian cinema, and obscenity 117–119
Indian Constitution 3, 115; Article 1 42; Article 19(1)(a) 114, 122; Article 19(2) 122, 125; Article 21 117; Article 35A 49; Article 39(b) 121; Article 367 49; Article 370(3) 55n52; Article 370 (*see* Article 370); Article 395 55n51; for censorship, provisions of 122–125; Section 2 53n10
Indian Councils Acts 157
Indian Evidence ACT 66
Indian Income Tax Act: Section 80JJA 85, 86
Indian Independence Act (1947) 43, 44, 46, 47, 55n49; Section 2 54n19
Indian Legal History Congress 158
Indian Penal Code, 1860 (IPC) 66, 122, 162, 168; Section 292 114, 115, 117; Section 292(1) 120; Section 304B 65; Section 354 67
Industrial Disputes Act (1947) 182
Indywood: The Indian Film Industry 118
inelastic goods/consumption 81–82
Information and Technology Act (2000) 122; Section 67 124
Innocence Project 151
innovation 4, 6, 24n41, 82; cultural 145; linguistic 145; spur 83–84
Instrument of Accession (IoA) 6, 41, 42, 44–46, 53n10, 54n26; execution of 47–48, *47*
Intellectual Property Law 144
interdisciplinary approach 2–4, 8, 9, 158, 160, 161, 169
Interdisciplinary Approaches to Public Policy and Sustainability (Mandal and Das) 4
intergenerational inequality, climate change impact on 14–15
international competitiveness 77–78
International Labour Organization 172
International Legal Centre: *Legal Education in a Changing World* 159–161
International Non-Use Agreement on Solar Geoengineering 16
International Stratigraphical Commission 11
International Union for Conservation of Nature 20n7
intimate partner violence 61–62, 64
An Invitation to the Law (Weeramantry) 162
IoA *see* Instrument of Accession (IoA)
Iolanthe (Gilbert) 143

IPC *see* Indian Penal Code, 1860 (IPC)
Ishiguro, K. 145
Ishwara Bhatt, P.: *Ideas and Methods of Legal Research* 4
Israel: foreign donations in democratic elections 36n8

Jain, M.P. 163
Jammu and Kashmir (J&K) 138; constituent assembly of (J&KCA) 42, 44, 49–51, *50*, *51*, 55n53; constitutional status (*see* Jammu and Kashmir, constitutional status of); as sovereign state 6
Jammu and Kashmir, constitutional status of 39–55; Article 370, abrogation of 51–52, *52*; Article 370, erosion of 49–51, *50*, *51*; bargain 42–43, 47–48, *47*; bargain, implementation of 43–44; Constituent Assembly 6; free speech crisis 7–8; IoA, execution of 47–48, *47*; J&KCA dissolution, phase of 49–51, *50*, *51*; lapse of paramountcy 46–47, *46*; law and history 40–42; legal orders 45–52; pre-independence phase 45–46, *46*; relationship by taking into account 1954 order and state constitution 48–49, *48*, *49*; set theory 45–52
Jan-Dhan Accounts 110
J&K *see* Jammu and Kashmir (J&K)
J&KCA *see* constituent assembly of J&K (J&KCA)
Japan: foreign donations in democratic elections 36–37n8
Jinnah, M.A. 43
Johnstone, N. 77
Jois, R. 163
Jones, Sir W. 58
Jordan, R. 145
Joyce, J.: *Ulysses* 152n18

K.A. Abbas v. Union of India (AIR 1971 SC481) 120
Karnataka: Rythu Bandhu scheme 100
Kartar Singh v. State of Punjab, AIR 1956 SC 541 116
Kashmir *see* Jammu and Kashmir (J&K)
Kasonen, K 77
Kass, A. 174
Kaufman, B.E. 180
Khushwant Singh 129–131, 140n3
Kirat Karo (earn with labour) 132
knowledge, and education 2
Krushak Assistance for Livelihood and Income Augmentation scheme 100
Kumar, M. 183, 184

Lady Chatterley's Lovers (Lawrence) 115
law and economics 176–182
Law and Economics as Interdisciplinary Exchange: Philosophical, Methodological and Historical Perspectives (Cserne and Małecka) 4
Lawrence, D.H.: *Lady Chatterley's Lovers* 115; *Rainbow* 119
legal aspects 120–122
legal education, purpose of 158–161
Legal Education in a Changing World 159–161
legal history, teaching of: necessity of 156–171; at NLSIU 166–169; outside India 163–165; relevance of 161–162
legal moralism 117
legal orders 45–52
legal paternalism 113–114
Le Guin, U. 145
Lindsay, R. 174
Lipstick Under My Burkha 8
LPG subsidy 100, 107
Lyotard 167

madhouse effect 12
Magna Carta 162, 168
Maharaja Ranjit Singh 129
Mahatma Gandhi National Rural Employment Guarantee Act (MGNREGA/MNERGA) 102, 106, 107
Mahindra 77, 89n29
Maine, H.S. 163
Maitland, F.W. 163, 165
"Make India" campaign 84
Małecka, M.: *Law and Economics as Interdisciplinary Exchange: Philosophical, Methodological and Historical Perspectives* 4
Malé Declaration on the Human Dimension of Global Climate Change 13–14
Mandal, N.: *Interdisciplinary Approaches to Public Policy and Sustainability* 4
Maneka Gandhi v. Union of India (AIR 1978 SC 597) 122
Manusmriti 58
market-based instruments 74–75, 83
market distortions, counterbalance 85–86
Martin, G.R.R. 145
Maternity Benefit Act (1961) 182
Mauss, M. 132

Mazumder, M. 173
Mcleod, S.A. 63
MDM *see* Mid-Day Meal (MDM) scheme
Media Law 144
Mehtab Singh 129
Menon, M. 159, 169
The Merchant of Venice (Shakespeare) 152n17
Metcalfe, G. 85
Mexico: foreign donations in democratic elections 36n8
MGNREGA/MNERGA *see* Mahatma Gandhi National Rural Employment Guarantee Act (MGNREGA/MNERGA)
Mid-Day Meal (MDM) scheme 100, 107
The Mikado (Gilbert) 143
Miller v. California (1973) 413 US1 119, 120
Ministry of Labour and Employment Labour Bureau 111n8
Mitchell, A. 20n7
money, in politics 33–35, 36n4
Monster Salary Index, 2019 172
monthly per capita expenditure (MPCE) *102*, **102**
Mooij, R.A. de 84, 85
moral depravity 113, 114, 116
moral economy 8, 129, 133, 134, 137, 139
morality 6, 68, 113, 115–117, 119, 122, 125, 126, 144
Mosomi, J. 181
'the most vulnerable constituency' test *see* Hicklin's test
MPCE *see* monthly per capita expenditure (MPCE)
Muggle Studies 149
Mukherjee, M. 169
multidimensional poverty 7, 100, 103, 105, 108
multidisciplinary approach 4
Musson, A. 163

Naam Japo (contemplate on God's name) 132
Nankana Sahib 130, 132
Narang, G.C. 138
National Bank for Agriculture and Rural Development (NABARD): All India Rural Financial Inclusion Survey (NAFIS) 2016–2017 100–103, *101*, *102*, **102**, 105, 107
National Commission for Women 59
National Democratic Alliance 100
National Education Policy (NEP) 2020 2
National Food Security Act 108
National Law School of India University (NLSIU) 157–159; teaching of legal history 166–169
National Law Universities (NLUs) 3, 157, 159, 160, 164, 169
National Rural Employment Guarantee Act (NREGA) 177
National Rural Employment Guarantee Scheme (NREGS) 99
National Sample Survey Organisation (NSSO) 98, 108; National Sample Survey (NSS) Employment–Unemployment Survey 176–178
National Savings Certificates 136
NBZ *see* negative bargaining zone (NBZ)
negative bargaining zone (NBZ) 43, 50, 52; establishment of *51*
Nehru, J. 41–43, 52, 54n39
neoclassical economics 133
Neo-Darwinism 61
NEP *see* National Education Policy (NEP) 2020
The Netherlands 31
NGOs *see* non-governmental organisations (NGOs)
Nicodème, G. 77
Nietzschean analysis 13
Nimrata (humble) 131
Nishkam (without desire) 131
Nishkapat (guiltless) 131
NLSIU *see* National Law School of India University (NLSIU)
NLUs *see* National Law Universities (NLUs)
non-governmental organisations (NGOs) 6
NREGA *see* National Rural Employment Guarantee Act (NREGA)
NREGS *see* National Rural Employment Guarantee Scheme (NREGS)
NSS 70th Round 103, 108
NSSO *see* National Sample Survey Organisation (NSSO)

Oates, W. 75, 80
Oaxaca, R.L. 183
Obscene Publications Act (1959) 119
obscenity: defintion of 113; and freedom of speech and expression 114–117; Indian cinema and 117–119; legal aspects of 120–122
Odisha: Krushak Assistance for Livelihood and Income Augmentation scheme 108
OECD *see* Organisation for Economic Co-operation and Development (OECD)

Oil and Natural Gas Corporation 173
online labour marketplaces (aka freelancing marketplaces) 174
oppression of women 58, 59, 61, 68
Organisation for Economic Co-operation and Development (OECD) 78, 80, 83
organised sector, gender pay gap 181–183
Owens, J. 80
The Oxford Handbook of Legal History 165
Oxford Principles 17–18, 24–25n45

Pakistan 31, 43, 46, 54n20, 173
Pandey, S. 183, 184
Paris Climate Agreement 5, 21n11
Patnaik, B. 175
patriarchy 59
Patterson, C.D. 79
Payment of Gratuity Act (1972) 182
PDS *see* Public Distribution System (PDS)
Pearson, M. 82
People v. Cahill 809 N.E. 2d 561 (N.Y. 2003) 143, 151n7
Pigovian taxes 75
pluralistic discourse 3
PMAY *see* Pradhan Mantri Awas Yojana (PMAY)
PM-KISAN *see* Pradhan Mantri Kisan Samman Nidhi (PM-KISAN)
PM-KISAN Yojana 100, 111n7
political contributions 32
political science 160, 169
pollution 7, 30–32, 75, 79–81, 83–85
pop culture 144, 152n10
popular culture 143–151
Porter, M. 83
possession 63, 104, 114, 116, 129, 130, 135
Potter, A.S. 148
Pound, R. 5
poverty 7, 14, 15, 59, 62, 86, 99–101, 103, 105, 107, 108, 111n2, 111n10, 111n14, 166, 167; and environmental tax penalties 76–77; multidimensional 7, 100, 103, 105, 108
Pradhan Mantri Awas Yojana (PMAY) 100, 107
Pradhan Mantri Kisan Samman Nidhi (PM-KISAN) 98–99
Pratchett, T. 145
Prem Nath Kaul v State of Jammu & Kashmir (1959) Supp (2) SCR 270 6, 40, 41, 48, 54n21, 54n28, 55n53, 55n62, 55n65
Press (Objectionable Matter) Act (1951) 124–125
Press Council of India Act (1978): Section 13 124; Section 13(2)(a) 124; Section 13(2)(c) 124; Section 14(1) 124
private spaces: Dowry Prohibition Act (1961) 65; Protection of Women from Domestic Violence Act (PWDVA) (2005) 66; violence in 58–71
Protection of Women from Domestic Violence Act (PWDVA) (2005) 66
Public Distribution System (PDS) 99–100, 107, 108
public finance theory 80
public spaces: Criminal Law (amendment) Act (2013) 66–67; Indecent Representation of Women (Prohibition) Act (1986) 68; Sexual Harassment of Women at Workplace Act (2013) 67–68; violence in 58–71
Punjab 135, 136
Punjab Legislative Council 130, 138
Puri, R. 176, 177
PWDVA see Protection of Women from Domestic Violence Act (PWDVA), 2005

Quasi-Basic Income Transfer 99, 110
Quasi-Universal Basic Rural Income (QUBRI) 111n1; Impossible Trinity of 109–110, *110*

Raack, D.W. 163
Raack, S.B. 164
racial discrimination 30
Rainbow (Lawrence) 119
Raj Kapoor and others v. State and Others (1980 AIR 258, 1980 SCR (1)1081) *(Delhi Administration)* 120–121
Ramnath, K. 169
Ranchordás, S.: *Time, Law, and Change: An Interdisciplinary Study* 4
Rangarajan committee 101, 111n2, 111n10
Ranjit D. Udeshi v. State of Maharashtra (AIR 1965 SC 881) 115–117, 120
rape 62–63
Regina v. Hicklin (L.R., 3 Q.B. 360 (1868) 119
Rehman Shagoo and Ors. v. State of Jammu and Kashmir 1958 CriLJ 885 54n27
Reorganisation Act (1966) 135
Report of 5th Census of Minor Irrigation Schemes 104
resource theory 61
retributive justice 156–157
revenue extrapolative 76
Rig Veda 58

Roth v. United States, 354 U.S. 476 (1957) 119
Rowling, J.K. 145–151
Roznai, Y.: *Time, Law, and Change: An Interdisciplinary Study* 4
Russia: foreign donations in democratic elections 36n8
Rythu Bandhu scheme 100

Sacred Sikh Scriptures 138–139
Sampat Prakash v The State of Jammu and Kashmir and Anr. (1969) 2 SCR 365 55n71
Sanderson, B. 145
Sarbat da Bhala 131
Sarva Shiksha Abhiyaan (SSA) 100, 107
SAS *see* Situation Assessment Survey (SAS) 2013
Satpathy, I. 175
Saussier, S. 177, 178, 180
science fiction 11, 143, 145, 152n10
SECC *see* Socio-Economic Caste Census (SECC) 2011
Sehajdhari Sikhs 138
Sengupta, A. 176, 177
set theory 45–52, *45–52*
seva (service) 128, 129, 131–133, 137, 139, 140n12
sexual harassment 63–64, 67, 68, 116
Sexual Harassment of Women at Workplace Act (2013) 67–68
sexual violence against women 117, 162, 168
SGE 13, 23n25
SGPC *see* Shiromani Gurdwara Parbandhak Committee (SGPC)
Shagoo, R. 47
Shakespeare, W. 151n2; *The Merchant of Venice* 152n17
Sheikh Abdullah 41, 43, 52, 54n39, 54n40
Shils, E. 158
Shiromani Akali Dal 138
Shiromani Gurdwara Parbandhak Committee (SGPC) 130, 134–139, 141n42
Shiromani Gurdwara Parbandhak Committee v. Shri Som Nath Dass & Ors AIR 2000 SC 1421 141n36
Sikh Gurdwaras Act (1925) 129, 130, 133–139; emerging difficulties 137–139; Part III, Chapter IX 136; Part III, Chapter VI 136; salient features of 134–137; Section 7 135; Section 85(1) 136; Section 106(1) 136; Section 106(2) 136; Section 119 137
Sikh Gurudwara Act 8
Sikhism 131–133, 140n12
Singh Sabha movement 130
Situation Assessment Survey (SAS) 2013 103, 108
Sixth Great Extinction 11
Skillingon, T. 23n34
Smith, S. 82
social exchange theory 61, 63
social identity theory 63
Societies Registration Act (1860) 135
Socio-Economic Caste Census (SECC) 2011 99, 103–106
sociology 157, 160, 169
solar engineering technology, non-use of 15–17
solar geoengineering (SRG) 12, 13, 16, 17
solar radiation management (SRM) 13, 17–19; weaponization 18–19
Sophocles 143; *Antigone* 151n5
South Africa: confidence-in-democracy 29
speculative fiction 145
spur innovation 83–84
Sreenivasa Murthy, H.V. 163
SRG *see* solar geoengineering (SRG)
Sri Guru Granth Sahib 131, 134, 141n3
SRM *see* solar radiation management (SRM)
SSA *see* Sarva Shiksha Abhiyaan (SSA)
State Bank of India v Santosh Gupta & Others (2017) 2 SCC 538 53n10
stick and carrot approach 75

Takhts 141n32; Akal 130; Sikh 136
Tata 77, 89n29
taxation: on environmental impacts, instrumentality of 3
tax incentives *see* environmental tax incentives
tax recycling 76
Thompson, E .P. 133
Thomson Reuters 64
Thornhill, R. 62
Thunberg, G. 5
Time, Law, and Change: An Interdisciplinary Study (Ranchordás and Roznai) 4
The Time of Catastrophe: Multidisciplinary Approaches to the Age of Catastrophe (Dole) 4
Tolkein, J.R.R. 145
Touahri, D. 81
tourism industry 174
trade-offs 2, 98, 100, 109–110, *110*, 173; equity–efficiency 175, 176, *184*
A Treatise on the Constitutional Limitations (Cooley) 123

Tripathy, N. 175
Trump, D. 12, 21n11, 21n12

UBI *see* universal basic income (UBI)
Ujjawala scheme 99
Ulysses (Joyce) 152n18
UN *see* United Nations (UN)
UNCITRAL Model Law on Electronic Commerce of 30 January 1997 124
UN Declaration on Violence against women: Article 1 60; Article 2 60
UN General Assembly 64
United Nations (UN) 32; on climate change 19n4
United Nations Security Council 41
United States (U.S.): Articles of Confederation 21n11; confidence-in-democracy 28; Constitution 1, 12; externalities 29–31; gender pay inequity 174; non-compliance *versus* denialism 13; Preamble to the US Constitution 21n11; race discrimination 30; right-wing countermovement 12; teaching of history to law students 158, 164
United States v. Various Articles of Obscene Merchandise (705 F.2d 41 (1983)) 126
universal basic income (UBI) 3, 99, 110
Universal Declaration of Human Rights 168
unorganised sector, gender pay gap gender pay gap
Unorganised Workers' Social Security Act (2008): Schedule II 182
urea subsidy 100, 107
U.S. *see* United States (U.S.)

value-added tax (VAT) 77, 79, 85, 129
Vand Chako (share with others) 132
verifiable criteria measures 103–107
violence: community 62–64; comparative analysis 68–69; definition of 60; dowry-related 60–61, 64, 65; gender-based 60; household 60–62; intimate partner 61–62, 64; in public and private spaces 58–71; sexual 162, 168; on women 3
violence against women 6, 59, 60, 64, 69, 168
A Visit to Friends (Chekhov) 151n6
vulgarity 116, 122, 125

Wadhawa, K.K. 172
wealth effects 31, 32, 36n7
Weasley, R. 147, 148
Weeramantry, C.G.: *An Invitation to the Law* 162
The Well of Loneliness (Hall) 119
What Is History? (Char) 162
White, J.B. 144, 148
Wilson, W. 161
Wisconsin School 164
women empowerment 172–184; analysis of 182–184, **183**, *184*; literature review 173–176; research gap, identification of 175–176; research questions, formation of 173–176; wage disparity 176–183, *177*, **177**, *178*
Workmen's Compensation Act (1923) 182

zero price effect 63
zone of possible agreement (ZOPA) 43, 50

For Product Safety Concerns and Information please contact our EU
representative GPSR@taylorandfrancis.com
Taylor & Francis Verlag GmbH, Kaufingerstraße 24, 80331 München, Germany

www.ingramcontent.com/pod-product-compliance
Ingram Content Group UK Ltd.
Pitfield, Milton Keynes, MK11 3LW, UK
UKHW020140200926
475702UK00005B/840

* 9 7 8 0 3 6 7 6 7 8 5 3 1 *